BUCK EWING

BUCK EWING

A Baseball Biography

Roy Kerr

McFarland & Company, Inc., Publishers
Jefferson, North Carolina, and London

LIBRARY OF CONGRESS CATALOGUING-IN-PUBLICATION DATA

Kerr, Roy, 1947–
    Buck Ewing : a baseball biography / Roy Kerr.
      p.   cm.
    Includes bibliographical references and index.

    ISBN 978-0-7864-6948-2
    softcover : acid free paper ♾

    1. Ewing, Buck.   2. Baseball players — United States —
Biography.   3. Cleveland Spiders (Baseball team) — History.
I. Title.
GV865.E93K47 2012
796.357092 — dc23
[B]   2012018922

BRITISH LIBRARY CATALOGUING DATA ARE AVAILABLE

On the cover —*foreground*: Studio portrait of Buck Ewing, 1888
(National Baseball Hall of Fame Library, Cooperstown, New York);
background: "The Winning Run," *Harper's Weekly*, August 22, 1885
(Wood River Gallery). Front cover design by Rob Russell

Manufactured in the United States of America

*McFarland & Company, Inc., Publishers
  Box 611, Jefferson, North Carolina 28640
  www.mcfarlandpub.com*

For my home team:
Annie and Ed

Acknowledgments

Many people helped make this book possible. Ed Borsoi, Leon Lyday and Margaret Lyday reviewed and critiqued the text with care and insight. Director Randall MacDonald and specialist Nora Galbraith at Florida Southern College's Roux Library, and the staff at the Lending Library of the Society for American Baseball Research (SABR), were of invaluable assistance in my microfilm searches. SABR moved its offices from Ohio to Arizona during the course of my research, and I am grateful to Executive Director Mark Appleman for making sure that my microfilm requests were expedited during the organization's busy transition.

Images and photographs for the project were provided by Mark Rucker of Transcendental Graphics, the Library of Congress, the New York Public Library, Don Prout of www.cincinnativiews.net, Wright State University, and the National Baseball Hall of Fame Library. I am indebted to the dedicated librarians at the New York State Library at Albany and to Chris Smith at the Cincinnati Library for their kind assistance.

Jean Wallis, retired researcher at the Highland County Historical Society, Donnie Jones, of Hillsboro, Ohio, and Rory Ryan of the *Highland County Press* all were of great assistance in discovering the truth about Buck Ewing's birthplace.

I am especially grateful to baseball historian Bill Jenkinson for reviewing the manuscript, for allowing me to access his exceptional home run logs, for his assistance in verifying Buck Ewing's remarkable six steals in a game on May 29, 1888, and for the multitude of other ways that he supported and encouraged my research.

Table of Contents

Preface

While attending a conference on nineteenth-century baseball at the Baseball Hall of Fame in 2010, I had the good fortune to be introduced to David Nemec, perhaps the foremost expert on the early years of professional baseball. In the course of our brief conversation, I mentioned to him that I was working on a biography of Buck Ewing, the great Giants catcher. Nemec's careful, one-sentence response, "That will be difficult," proved to be prophetic.

Forgotten today, William "Buck" Ewing was once one of the most popular and well-known players in baseball, and his contemporaries — managers, owners, sportswriters, on-field opponents and teammates — all considered him the greatest catcher and all-around player of his era. While Ewing's statistical record is accessible to any researcher, defining him as a player or as a man is not as simple as adding up his hits, runs and errors.

Although the record books list him as a catcher, Ewing played less than half his career at that position, either due to injuries or because his managers found him too valuable a player to risk injuring him there. When he did catch, he was the acknowledged best at his position. He was the first receiver to catch from the crouch, the first to use a snap forearm throw to catch runners napping — at second base as well as first — and the first National League player to use a catcher's mitt. For many years he was believed to hold the record for steals in a game as a catcher — three. Actually, he stole four in a game while catching several times, and while taking a break from his receiving duties during a contest against Washington in 1888, he played third base and stole six bases. He is the only catcher to lead his team in stolen bases (53) during a season.

Ewing spent the other half of his career playing every other position on the field. He is one of two men who have played at least 25 games as a catcher, first, second and third baseman, shortstop and outfielder — and who also pitched. He also led the league in fielding at two different positions — third base and catcher.

Offensively, Ewing defined himself as a place hitter who was skilled at executing the hit-and-run play. As a captain and manager he strongly discouraged his players from swinging hard while at the plate. Nevertheless, he once led the league in home runs, becoming the first man to reach double digits in that category, and he hit some of the longest four-baggers of his era. He could hit, hit for power, run, throw and field any position well.

Ewing's personality was as multi-faceted as were his playing skills. Existing biographical sketches of him — derived in all probability from the many obituaries published upon his untimely death in 1906 — portray him as an affable and modest individual. The truth in this regard, however, is much more complex. Early in his career he was branded with the nickname "Bread and Butter Buck," for trying to negotiate a contract independently, thus violating National League regulations. At the height of his career, his exploits on the diamond were the subject of dime novels, his image appeared on the cover of national magazines and in cigar and beer advertisements, and serious proposals to place his likeness on a postage stamp were entertained in the press. During the same period, however, he was condemned for allegedly betraying the Players' League by consorting with National League representatives in 1890, accused of deliberately losing games to insure Boston's pennant win over Chicago in 1891, and routinely criticized for not playing when injured, or even for faking injuries.

The most interesting and least-known aspect of Ewing's personality was his penchant for "kicking," that is, vociferously objecting to an umpire's decisions. He single-handedly raised the practice of umpire-baiting to an art form, earning for himself the nickname "Prince of Knockers" in the process. Ewing's protests, devoid of the vulgarity, profanity and physical intimidation that were the hallmarks of "kickers" like his contemporaries, Patsy Tebeau, Cap Anson and John McGraw, seem harmless today. There was, however, a clear purpose in their use — getting the umpire to change his decision. Ewing was so successful in this regard that newspaper accounts often humorously listed him as a game's official umpire.

The difficulty in preparing a biography of Buck Ewing that was predicted by David Nemec during our brief Cooperstown conversation was indeed a fact. Such difficulty, however, derived not from a lack of information on Ewing's life and career, but rather, because his great versatility on the ball field was matched by a rich and complex personality off the diamond. In life as in baseball, Buck Ewing proved to be one of a kind.

Chapter 1

The Cincinnati Kid: 1859–1879

"I became a ball player by practice and natural gift." — Buck Ewing,
Philadelphia Inquirer, October 11, 1889

In the final decades of the eighteenth century, the fledgling United States, having secured its independence, undertook an ambitious new endeavor — the expansion of its territorial limits beyond the boundaries of the original 13 colonies. The first such project involved an enormous expanse of land bounded on the north by Canada, on the south by the Ohio River, on the east by Pennsylvania, and on the west by the Mississippi River, an area that by 1787 was being referred to as the Northwest Territory. In ensuing years historians would rename it the Old Northwest.

Within this broad stretch of unsettled land lay a smaller yet substantial parcel known as "the Ohio Country," whose boundaries roughly approximated those of the modern state bearing the same name. Settlement of the Ohio Country, begun even before the Constitution was ratified, was further encouraged by the passage of the Federal Land Act of 1820, which allowed settlers of modest means to purchase 80-acre plots at $1.25 per acre: "Land, inexpensive and fertile, was the magnet which drew most people to Ohio in the early years."[1] By 1850, 43 years after achieving statehood, Ohio's population exceeded one million, and it was the nation's leading producer of corn and wheat.

Virginian Thomas Ewing was one of thousands who found Ohio's cheap land, rich soil and temperate climate an irresistible attraction. Soon after the War of 1812, he settled in Gallia County, in the state's southeastern corner. By 1850, Thomas owned farm lands worth $1,600, and his wife had given birth to five children.[2] A decade later, Ewing's second-eldest son, Samuel, born in 1823, had traded in his farmer's plow for a teamster's wagon, married

3

an Ohio native, Martha Esterbrook, settled in Highland County and fathered three children: Edward, Josephine, and William.[3]

Edward eventually worked for the railroad in Cincinnati, while Josephine married and moved out of state. After a brief stint as a teamster himself, William, known as Billy or Buck, became a professional baseball player, one whose skills were of such caliber that he eventually was elected to the Baseball Hall of Fame.

Ascertaining William "Buck" Ewing's actual birth place and birth date has proved frustrating for baseball historians, primarily because Ohio did not require birth certificates until 1880. Researcher Paul Herbert's 1987 inquiry to the Baseball Hall of Fame summarized the problem—published sources cited three different Ohio locations and three different 1859 dates for the event.[4] Buck's own statements on these issues further confused them. His self-disclosed 1900 U.S. Census data lists his birth date as March, 1860, and during his playing career he affirmed that he was born in Cincinnati.[5] Thanks to the efforts of a Historical Society researcher in Highland County, Ohio, we know today that the future Hall of Famer was born in late 1859 in Hoagland, then and now little more than crossroads located a few miles outside the town of Hillsboro, in Highland County, Ohio, about 50 miles east of Cincinnati.[6]

Shortly after William's birth, the Ewing family moved to the Cincinnati area, having been drawn there as much by the need for protection from marauding bands of Confederate troops as for the economic opportunities to be found in Ohio's largest city. The Ewings settled in working-class Pendleton, a neighborhood bordering the Ohio River, in Cincinnati's East End. There, three more children were born in the 1860s—John, Charles, and Emma.

Cincinnati's strategic location on the Ohio River quickly solidified its position as the region's major commercial and cultural center, and its growing cosmopolitanism earned it the grandiloquent epithets of "Queen City" and the "Athens of the West." Economic prosperity was spurred by early development of meat-processing and meat-packing industries. By 1860, nearly a half-million hogs were processed annually in its plants, a statistic that earned Cincinnati a less-glamorous nickname: "Porkopolis."

Despite the veneer of culture and gentility experienced by its well-to-do citizens, the Cincinnati of the era was a rough-and-tumble town, especially for its working class:

> Housing was poor, health care unheard of, sanitation was primitive. Even the more affluent had to maneuver the same filthy "pig infested" streets the poor traversed.... The stench of thousands of porkers driven through the streets to the processing plants penetrated the air.... The plants themselves would appear to modern folks as a nightmare of squeals, blood, offal, and noxious substances.[7]

Within this gritty environment, Billy Ewing matured quickly, learning self-reliance, Huck Finn–style. His experiences taught him to secure his own future before giving way to heroic or humanitarian impulses. In his later baseball career, as we shall see, such lessons and attitudes helped insure his financial security, but at times earned him the criticism or censure of fans, the press, team owners, and fellow players.

Like most working-class children of the era, Billy's formal education did not advance beyond elementary school due to the need for him to help support his eight-member family. By his early teens he was working as a teamster for one of the city's biggest industries — the distillery business. Heavy consumption of spirits was the custom in the Buckeye State:

> One might say that Pioneer Ohio had its own kind of "high society." Residents consumed spirits at work sites, militia musters, social events, and even at religious camp meetings. Many stores kept an open keg of spirits, and a dipper, for use of its customers. Whiskey not only encouraged social interaction, it was also believed to help ward off chills and fevers, and it temporarily dulled chronic aches and pains, as well as loneliness and isolation.[8]

From his early teens until he joined the Rochester Hop Bitters baseball club in mid-summer, 1880, Billy Ewing worked six days a week for Cincinnati's Maddox and Hobart Distillery, loading 42-gallon whiskey barrels onto a four-mule-team wagon, transporting the merchandise to local saloons and stores, and unloading the barrels on site. The job was strenuous and potentially dangerous, but it helped develop Billy's rock-hard shoulders, forearms and powerful wrists, physical attributes that would enable him in later years to do what no other catcher of the era could do — use a snap forearm motion to throw a man out trying to steal a base, all the while remaining in the crouch position.

Although his job at Maddox and Hobart, located just a few blocks from his home, was backbreaking, unrelenting labor, Billy still hoped for a better future. For an aspiring ball player in Ewing's era, there was no better place to dream about a baseball career than Cincinnati, for at the time it was both the epicenter of the baseball world and the cradle of the professional game.

By the 1830s, popular children's ball-and-stick games in America had been adopted as a featured activity in upper-class men's social clubs. Baseball in this era was still little more than an amusing pretext for healthful exercise and male camaraderie. In 1845, Alexander Joy Cartwright, of New York's Knickerbocker club, drew up a set of baseball rules that became so popular they were soon adopted everywhere. By 1858, the year of the establishment of the first national amateur baseball organization — The National Association of Base Ball Players — interest in the game had spread beyond the genteel upper-class clubs, and rules consistency and advancing player skill levels were leading to increased competition. As the game's popularity grew, "The demand for skilled players led prominent citizens to import them, and what started out as a purely civic pastime developed into a professional one."[9]

Cincinnati's Red Stockings amateur baseball club was established by a group of local lawyers in 1866. By 1868, the team's roster included four paid players. Among them was Harry Wright of New York, a professional cricket player of British heritage who years earlier had given up the English sport for baseball. In 1869, team owners, led by an attorney with a prescient name, Aaron B. Champion, decided to field a completely professional nine, and chose Harry Wright as the team's player-manager. It was a felicitous choice. In addition to being a superior athlete, Wright, who was trained as a jeweler, possessed uncommon organizational and administrative skills, coupled with an acute attention to detail acquired during his apprenticeship in the jewelry trade.

Prior to the 1869 season, Wright scoured the country in search of the best baseball talent, and soon assembled the first openly acknowledged all-professional team. Only one member, first baseman Charley Gould, was a Cincinnati native. Baseball's era of professionalism had arrived.

Cincinnati's Red Stockings barnstormed around the country in 1869, taking on teams from all quarters and never losing a game. Their winning ways continued into the following year, until they were defeated, 8–7, in an 11-inning game by the Atlantics of Brooklyn, in June, 1870. The Reds' success and national notoriety prompted other cities to follow suit and form teams, and in 1871, the first professional baseball league, the National Association of Professional Base Ball Players, was formed (*baseball* in the era was spelled as two words).

Ironically, Cincinnati, the cradle of professional baseball, was not a participant in the new league. Clubs in Boston, Chicago and Washington offered the Queen City's players handsome salary increases to play for their new teams, and the Red Stockings disbanded. Publicity from the club's two-year barnstorming odyssey was sufficient, however, to establish the dream of a professional baseball career in the minds of many young men, including Billy Ewing. A quarter-century later, he related the history of his early years in the game in a letter to a New York newspaper:

> I first began to play ball when I was a boy and used to run away from school to play fungos. The first regular club I played with was in Pendleton, Ohio.... At one time I was the only stockholder, secretary, captain, manager and catcher. We had 75 cents in the treasury and owned one ball and bat. I was then about 14 years old.... I used to work all week driving four big mules of a distillery wagon and play ball on Sunday.[10]

In the same correspondence, Ewing disclosed how he acquired his famous nickname:

Now, how did I get the name of Buck? I'll tell you that with pleasure, and hope it will stop the hundreds of letters which come to me asking where and how I got the name. My family name is Billy.... When I was a youngster, about 6 or 7 years old, I used to play marbles in Pendleton with a big boy who was called "Buck" Drury. There was a big shoemaker's shop where we used to play, and the men used to come out every day about lunch time and bet on the game. They didn't know our names, but called him Big Buck, and when I wasn't around they would ask for "Little Buck." That's all there is in it.[11]

The humble sandlot ball field where Buck Ewing first played, the Pendleton Grounds, had a brief national exposure in 1891, when a new park, called the East End Grounds, was constructed there to house "Kelly's Killers," an American Association team led by Mike "King" Kelly. Once a great ballplayer and the most recognized star in the game, Kelly was by this time beginning his slow slide to oblivion when he agreed to serve as player-manager for the woeful Killers. The team was 32 games behind first-place Boston by mid–August, when the Association transferred the franchise to Milwaukee, where it played the final 36 games of the season. The grandstand and bleachers of the abandoned East End Grounds were subsequently damaged by flood and fire, and its remains finally demolished in 1900.

Late in his life, his long career over, a sportswriter dubbed Ewing "the Duke of Pendleton,"[12] as a nostalgic tribute to his sandlot beginnings. Ironically, the new nickname's real meaning and context could only have been grasped by those few who were familiar with the star's early years in Cincinnati's East End. Aspiring young Queen City ball players can still throw and hit today on the grounds (now named Schmidt Park) where Buck Ewing began his career nearly 140 years ago.

Ewing's 1889 newspaper correspondence detailing his start in baseball continued, "In 1879 I went to the Mohawk Browns, of the West End, then the best semi-professional club in Cincinnati. I received my first money from them for playing ball. I got $10 a game. Among the well-known players to-day [1889] who were then with me was John Reilly, of the Cincinnatis [*sic*], and old Joe Sommer, recently released by the Baltimores.[13]

Apprenticed to a Cincinnati lithography company at the age of 12, John Good Reilly subsequently enjoyed long, successful careers both as a graphic artist and a ball player. With the exception of the 1882 season spent with the then-independent Metropolitans of New York, Reilly played on home town Cincinnati American Association or National League teams for his entire career. Standing 6' 3" and weighing 178 pounds, the aptly nicknamed "Long John" was a free-swinging first baseman who hit over .300 in five of his ten seasons, and his 13 home runs in 1888 lead the Association. Reilly had scant tolerance for those who were not as conscientious as he with regard to training and on-field effort, an attitude that occasioned numerous feuds with his teammates. Nevertheless, he was an enthusiastic supporter of young talent, and it was his recommendation of Billy Ewing to the Mohawk Browns that gave Buck his first opportunity in a career that would lead to the Hall of Fame.

The Mohawk Browns were so-named because the majority of the team's original players lived in the vicinity of the Mohawk Bridge, located at the opposite end of the city from Buck Ewing's working-class neighborhood.[14] The Browns for a time sought to retain some of the customs of the earlier amateur era of ball play, including that of insisting on high social standing for club membership: "In addition to the base ball team the club was of a social kind, composing many members who were of the contributing order. It had a regular set of officers, the president being invested with executive power to be used at his own discretion."[15]

In order to keep pace with rival clubs, however, the Browns soon found it necessary to ease their social requirement in order to attract better players. "Long John" Reiley, who, like Ewing, hailed from the East End, was one of the first of these additions to the team. When it came time to recruit a second baseman to take the place of a player who had become weak in that position, Reiley was consulted with regard to a replacement:

Studio portrait of a young Buck Ewing, early 1880s (courtesy National Baseball Hall of Fame Library, Cooperstown, New York).

In recalling the players he knew, he happened felicitously to bring up Ewing. He had met "Buck" on the old Pendleton club grounds ... a year or two before, and was struck with his ease and graceful manner of playing. Jumping up, he announced that he had the very man, who would not only fill the weak spot, but greatly strengthen the club. "Who is he?" demanded several of the club members. "A fellow named Ewing, who lives up in Fulton," replied John. "Why, we never heard of him," was the answer.[16]

Thanks to Reiley's persistence, however, the Mohawks' president was persuaded to make the trip across town to scout Ewing during a Sunday morning game, and the impression was so favorable that Ewing was approached afterward and offered his carfare and $9 per game [Ewing, as we recall, said the team offered him $10] to join the Browns:

"When can you join us?" was asked.

"Do you play this afternoon?"

"Yes, at 3 o'clock."

"I'll be there."

And he was there, and played a game at second that opened the eyes of the big gathering present, jumping at once into popular favor. While with this club he developed his catching ability, and he alternated behind the bat and at second base.[17]

Semi-professional baseball came of age in Cincinnati from 1871 to 1875. After the dissolution of the original Red Stockings and the city's inability to finance a team for the new National Association, which began in 1871, Queen City baseball fans had two options: content themselves with reading about the exploits of other cities' Association teams or support local semi-pro nines. They chose the latter option, following the weekly contests of local teams such as the Stars, the Mohawk Browns, the Shamrocks, the Ravens, and the Americus nine.

When the National League debuted in 1876, eager Cincinnatians raised enough money to obtain a franchise, and the city once again had a fully professional team. Charley Gould, the only local from the original Red Stockings, was named player-manager for the new Reds, who, since their principal stockholder owned a meat-packing plant, were often, as previously mentioned, ungraciously referred to as the "Porkopolitans."

Semi-pro teams, nevertheless, continued to thrive, thanks to a symbiotic relationship between them and the Queen City's new league team. National League rules prohibited its teams from playing on Sunday and selling liquor at games. The enterprising Red Stockings, however, rented their grounds to semi-pro teams on Sundays and allowed them to sell alcohol to their fans. For a few years, therefore, until the League expelled the Reds for such practices, crowds of up to 5,000 sipped beer at the Reds' Avenue Grounds and watched semi-pro games between teams like the Stars and the Browns on the Sabbath. At the close of the 1880 season, however, National League President William Hulbert expelled the Reds from the league for allowing such activity to take place on the team's grounds.

Although, as we have seen in Ewing's 1889 letter to the *Philadelphia Inquirer* (originally published in the *New York Sun*), he described his earliest baseball position as that of catcher at the Pendleton Avenue Grounds, he must also have spent a lot of time there in the infield, for he was hired by the Browns primarily as a second baseman. In 1879 he played 14 games at second, two behind the plate, and during the course of one contest played both positions. In his six appearances with the team the following year, he played first base twice and covered third base four times. During his Browns tenure he did, however, catch twice on "picked nine" (all-star) teams, once against the Cincinnati Stars and once in an exhibition against the National League Reds. Thus, although the Browns used him sparingly as a "change" (substitute) catcher, the team clearly felt he was more valuable to them as an infielder.

The 1879 and 1880 Browns battled the aforementioned Cincinnati semi-pro teams as well as nines from Kentucky (the Covington Stars, the Louisville Eclipse, the Lexingtons), Indiana (the Lawrenceburgs), and other parts of Ohio (the Live Oaks of Hamilton, the Mutuals of Columbus). All semi-pro teams in this era were fluid enterprises, and regularly disbanded or reorganized. Players switched teams and occasionally left their home squads temporarily to play on picked nines against special adversaries. Games were played only on weekends and holidays, and schedules were haphazard, often determined by following the amateur baseball custom of years gone by by offering another team a formal, written, elaborately-stipulated challenge:

> The Mohawk Brown Stockings have authorized us [the *Cincinnati Enquirer*] to inform the Star Club that they will play them a series of four games, provided the Stars will play them (the Browns) on the latter's grounds the first game, the other games to alternate. Should each club win two of the four games, the club which shall have scored the most runs shall have choice of grounds on which to play a fifth game.[18]

Buck Ewing debuted with the Mohawk Browns on May 4, 1879. He fielded flawlessly at second base and went 1-for-4 in a 10–1 win against Covington. His defensive performance in his first game earned a notice in the next day's *Enquirer*: "Smith played first and Ewing played second. Each played their position perfectly."[19] His defensive prowess failed him in the Browns' next outing against Americus, as he committed four of the team's seven-error total in a 15–5 win. Press reports, however, treated him kindly: "Ewing, although having [a] few errors, deserves credit for the pluck he shows in attempting to take difficult chances."[20]

He redeemed himself the following week in a 10–2 win against the Shamrocks, banging out two hits, scoring two runs, and playing errorless ball. In reviewing and assessing such performances, one must recall that Ewing and all other fielders of the era played their positions barehanded. Catchers employed (on both hands) tight-fitting, open-backed gloves that resembled today's handball gloves. Some first basemen were also adopting such gloves, but regular use of fielding mitts by other players was still a decade away.

Cincinnati's Doug Allison is reputed to have been the first catcher to protect his hands behind the plate, probably with a pair of "common kid gloves,"[21] during his team's cross-country tour in 1869. In 1875, Fall River's player/manager, Frank "Mac" McGunnigle, developed the first innovation in catching gloves during a game against Harvard's team: "Mac's hands were very sore, but it was necessary that he should catch. He sent out for a pair of bricklayer's gloves, thick, strong things of hard leather.... He found that while they protected the palms, there was not liberty enough for the fingers to throw. An idea struck him. He whipped out a jackknife ... and cut off the fingers of the right hand glove."[22]

Harvard's catcher, James Tyng, who later invented the catcher's mask, set about to improve McGunnigle's gloves by lining the palms of a pair of bricklayer's gloves with thin sheets of lead. After Tyng's glove proved unwieldy, it was modified by Louis Guinasso of Lowell's New England League team. Guinasso wore a pair of thickly lined walking gloves (with the fingers cut out) underneath McGunnigle's fingerless bricklayer's gloves.

Sporting goods companies quickly got into the act, opening the back side of the glove below the knuckles by removing some of the leather, and providing more padding for the left-hand glove than the right. Soon many catchers were ordering left-hand gloves padded to their own specifications. The most famous of these innovators was St. Louis Browns catcher Doc Bushong. Bushong took great care to protect his hands, since he planned to (and eventually did) practice dentistry after his baseball career. He wore the largest glove he could find, and added pads until it looked like a pillow.

Sporting Life credits Buck Ewing with finally bringing the catcher's glove to its present size. Following Bushong's lead, Buck

> continued to add stuffing to the glove and covering it with patches of new leather. The growth of the glove was closely watched by the fans, who marveled at its expansion. Any rip in it was instantly mended by Buck himself with any kind of leather, so it was sure one of the most conspicuous things on the ball field, with its patches of all kinds of hide. It really became one of the attractions of the game, and scores of fans, influenced by newspaper comments, went to the game merely to get a look at Buck's glove. Naturally manufacturers took the hint and began making the big glove, and have not quit making it to this day.[23]

In one of two reported Browns games in June, 1879, Ewing continued his strong hitting, going 3-for-7, including a double, in a 28–0 rout of the Live Oaks of Hamilton. He caught his first game for the team on July 6, making one error on a wild throw, but collecting three hits, including a double. It was his performance behind the plate, however, that attracted the attention of the press. "Meyer's hand being too sore to catch, Ewing went behind the bat and Carey to second. The playing of both was fine, this being Ewing's first attempt to catch Williams. His many friends were pleased to see him do well."[24] This brief commentary is the first press notice in Ewing's long and storied career that highlighted his prowess behind the plate. Like the Browns catcher he replaced, Ewing himself would frequently be sidelined with hand injuries until his adoption of the catcher's mitt late in his career.

Back at second base the following Sunday, Buck went 2-for-5 and scored three runs, but went hitless in the team's next two contests, which were split with the Stars. In September Ewing's bat was hot: he went 5-for-6, including a triple, a double, and two singles in a win against the Stars, and 3-for-5 with two runs scored against the same team the following week. The triple/double combination in a game soon became a hallmark of Ewing's offense.

Ewing got his first taste of major league competition in early October, when the semi-pro Browns were defeated, 21–0, by a team composed of members of the Buffalo and Cincinnati National League squads, which was barnstorming its way to the west coast for a series of games in California. The "Buffcinatis," as the team was humorously referred to in the press, contained some of the premier players of the era, including pitcher Jim "Pud" Galvin, a future Hall of Fame member who would tally 365 career wins; Cal McVey, who had played on the original Red Stockings 1869 team; John Rowe, who in 1882 would bat 308 times in 75 games without once striking out; and John Clapp, a catcher with a strong, accurate throwing arm who hit over .300 during six consecutive seasons (1876–81). Four years later, Clapp would manage Ewing in New York in the first year of the Manhattan club's franchise.

Ewing made a poor impression that day in the field in the game against the Cincinnati and Buffalo stars, committing four of the Browns' horrendous total of 28 errors in the contest. Clearly, the semi-pro "stars" were as yet no match for their professional counterparts.

In 1880, Ewing played a game on a picked nine squad that took on the Cincinnati National League team in the latter's last spring training contest before the start of the season:

> The Cincinnati team to-day will play, weather permitting, a strong local organization, the American team, composed of the following players: Mitchell, pitcher; Ewing, catcher; J. Reilly, first base; Bower, second base; Wallace, third base; Merney, short stop, W. Riley (of last year's Clevelands) left field; Deagle, middle [center] field, and Jennings, right field. Will White and [John] Clapp will [pitch and] catch for the regular team. The American's team is not to be underrated. Game will be called at three o'clock, and only twenty-five cents admission charged.[25]

Rain postponed the contest on the original date, but it was finally played the following Wednesday, April 29. Despite the confidence expressed in the local squad by the *Cincinnati Enquirer*, the picked nine fell to the League team, 9–0, and Buck Ewing, catching left-hander Bobby Mitchell, had an erratic afternoon defensively, committing three errors on "wild throws" and allowing three passed balls. He managed one hit in four attempts against Cincinnati's ace, Will White, who had won 43 contests for the Reds the previous season.

In the coming weeks, Ewing made up for his embarrassing showing against the city's League team by his fine offensive performance and steady field work. Alternating between first and third base during his final month with the Browns, he rapped out 11 hits in five games, including three doubles and three home runs. Such numbers raised eyebrows in the Queen City and in other quarters.

While published accounts of Ewing's brief eight-month stay with the Browns are neither complete nor definitive, they nevertheless provide early proof of his talent. In 25 games with the Mohawks and on picked nines, he collected 37 hits for an average of .330, and with the exception of two poor defensive efforts, demonstrated that he could hold his own at four different positions. Although Ewing spent time behind the plate, his value to the team was primarily as a hitter and an "all-around" or utility player. Given his performance with the Browns, it was no surprise that in June, 1880, Rochester Hop Bitters Manager Horace Phillips invited him to join the team as a full-fledged professional player.

Ewing's recollection of this event is succinct: "Horace Phillips happened to see me about that time, and in June 1880 I signed to play with the Rochesters. I received about $100 a month."[26] Ewing's friend and East End neighbor, Long John Reilly, offered an account of the signing that provided more details, including his own involvement in the process:

> A year later, while in Rochester, N.Y., with Joe Gerhardt, Reilly was met at the hotel one evening by the manager [Horace Phillips] of the local club, which was in need of a catcher. It was for the purpose of getting one that he called, and asked the visiting club where he could get one. After a moment's thought, Gerhardt looked up and said: "Why wouldn't that young fellow Ewing do?" "Just the man I was thinking about," replied Reilly. The result was that Buck was telegraphed that night and caught the season out.[27]

Joe Gerhardt, a light-hitting, good-fielding second baseman, played for Cincinnati in 1878 and 1879, and was Ewing's teammate on the New York Giants from 1885 to 1887.

In early spring, 1880, rumors surfaced suggesting that Ewing and two other East-End semi-pro players might be picked up by the Reds: "when catching for the Mohawk Browns in 1880 it was proposed by the directors of the League team [the Reds] to engage him [Ewing], Reilly and Joe Sommer."[28] The proposition, however, was promptly dismissed: "Nobody [in Cincinnati] will pay to see a lot of Millcreek Bottom amateurs play ball."[29] When the National League season started, however, Reilly was the Reds' first baseman and Sommer was a team substitute. Ewing, who, as we have seen, had performed poorly in his only game against the Reds that spring, was not offered a contract by his hometown team.

The Rochester nine was well-known in Cincinnati. Game accounts of their contests were regular features in Cincinnati newspapers, two members of the original 1869 Reds, Doug Allison and Andrew Leonard, were early team members, and the squad had played (and lost) an exhibition game against the Reds in the Queen City in October, 1879, a contest that Ewing himself might have attended. Thus, when the familiar Hop Bitters made Ewing an offer, he jumped at the opportunity. The 20-year-old had no idea what awaited him. The next two months would test his mettle both as a player and a man, for the 1880 Hop Bitters were an oddly-named, hastily and haphazardly assembled team playing in a floundering league that was about to disappear.

The second National Association (not to be confused with the earlier league with the same name) was originally organized in 1877 as the International Association; two of its original seven teams were from Ontario, Canada. The "International" component of its name was dropped the following year when the two Canadian clubs folded. The organization resembled a semi-professional league, since fewer than 20 games of its teams' schedules were played against other Association squads (Rochester; Pittsburgh; Manchester, New Hampshire; Lynn, Massachusetts; Columbus, Ohio). In between such weekly contests, however, teams earned extra money by playing a host of National League and Independent nines. Never financially sound, the Association dissolved before the end of the 1880 season. This combined schedule of exhibition and league games was common in the era, and it allowed upshot regional leagues to pay their players salaries that were close to the range offered by the National League. The League itself benefited from scheduling contests against organizations like the National Association on its off-days, giving its teams an opportunity to scout potential new talent.

In 1878, Rochester's original entry in the International Association, the Flour Citys, disbanded "after a rough season that included several charges of game-fixing."[30] When the 1879 Albany entry to the Association — now renamed the National Association — folded two weeks into the season, a new Rochester financial backer, Asa Soule, signed most of the ex-Albany players and renamed the club the Hop Bitters. Soule's company produced the patent medicine, "Hop Bitters," an exotic elixir containing hops, dandelion and mandrake roots, buchu (an herbal diuretic), and a liberal amount of alcohol. "It was hawked variously as a cough remedy and a reliever of sleeplessness, nervousness and urinary troubles."[31]

Patent (proprietary) medicines were extremely popular and profitable in the nineteenth century. A scarcity of doctors and the high cost of their services, limited knowledge of diseases and their causes, and a completely unregulated business climate fostered the industry's growth. Patent medicine companies pioneered many modern advertising techniques, including free samples, outdoor signs, testimonials and newspaper ads. No baseball team prior to the Hop Bitters, however, had been named after a commercial product (imagine, for example, a present day nine named the Coca Colas), although our modern-day stadiums named for large companies approximate the practice.

Asa Soule sponsored a successful barnstorming version of the Hop Bitters after the 1879 season, but he delayed offering financial backing to the 1880 team, and as a result it did not join the National Association (now down to four teams: Baltimore, Albany, Washington and Rochester) until mid–June. Horace Phillips, who had managed Troy's 1879 National League entry, was brought in to skipper the club. The selection was unfortunate, for Phillips, an erratic, impulsive promoter, was already displaying the type of behavior that a decade later would cause him to be declared legally insane and institutionalized. While traveling with his wife and brother in August, 1889, Phillips suddenly began behaving strangely, making extraordinary statements to all who would listen. He declared himself worth millions as the sole owner of all the baseball clubs in the country, insisting also that he had bought a number of hotels and theaters in major cities. A doctor called to intervene declared that Phillips was a hopeless case and that his reason was "entirely gone."[32]

Near the end of June, 1880, the erratic manager was still signing players for the 1880 Hop Bitters, including Buck Ewing and Bobby Mitchell from the Mohawk Browns. Phillips further added to his roster by convincing four Baltimore players, including future Hall of Famer Dennis Brouthers, to jump their Baltimore contracts and join the Rochesters. Brouthers was at this time a relative unknown, and he was struggling to overcome the trauma of an on-field accident in which he was involved in 1877. Playing for Poughkeepsie that year, Brouthers collided with Harlem Clippers catcher John Quigley while trying to score. The blow killed Quigley. Devastated, Brouthers initially vowed never to play again, and sat out the 1878 season before returning to the diamond. He acquired his famous nickname, "Big Dan," in the ensuing dozen years, after leading the league in slugging seven times, in batting average three times, and in hits and runs twice.

By convincing Brouthers and other Baltimore players to jump their contracts and sign with Rochester, Horace Phillips guaranteed the dissolution of the Association. The Baltimore club folded after losing its players to Rochester, and a week later Albany followed suit. At this point the Association ceased to exist. Desperate to remain in business, the two remaining teams, the Nationals and the Hop Bitters, scheduled a series of 15 games against each other, and then sought out other teams as exhibition opponents. Manager Phillips abandoned the team in late July, taking with him the club's $1,400 in assets. Asa Soule then withdrew his support for the team, and young Buck

Ewing and the remaining Hop Bitters were left adrift in New York State without a manager, an owner, a league, or a steady paycheck.

Buck Ewing's debut with the Rochesters took place against Baltimore on June 25. Playing errorless ball at shortstop, he went 1-for-4 at the plate. The following day he caught his first game for the team, and although he went hitless, his defense drew praise: "Ewing's catching was a manifest improvement upon that of Kearns."[33] Thus, for the second time in which he debuted behind the plate for a team, Ewing's skill at the position drew plaudits from the press. Disturbing reports about the league's organizational weakness, however, were beginning to surface. "Things are not progressing very regularly in the National [National Association] camp, the schedule having become mixed [i.e., irregular]."[34]

Through late June and early July, Ewing continued playing well *behind* the plate, but struggled while *at* the plate, with his batting average hovering around .200. Even in the weak National Association, the pitching he was facing was significantly better than what he had faced with the Browns.

Although in 1880 pitchers were still required to throw underhanded from a distance of 45 feet, these were not the genteel days of the old New York Knickerbockers, in which the hurler's job was simply to set in motion the real game between the "striker" (hitter) and the fielders. By the late 1860s, Brooklyn pitchers Jim Creighton and Arthur "Candy" Cummings had added the rising fastball and the curve to the pitcher's repertoire. In the early 1870s, Boston's Al Spalding added a deceptive change-up to that mix. After pitching rules were modified in 1873 to allow a wrist-snap upon release of the ball, the pitcher's motion approximated that of a modern-day fast-pitch softball hurler. Although sidearm throwing was still technically illegal, by the time Buck Ewing signed on with Rochester, most pitchers, like Michael "Smiling Mickey" Welch, were already violating the regulation with impunity. The National League recognized the inevitable and legalized the sidearm motion in 1883. The following year it waived all delivery restrictions and the age of overhand pitching began.

According to the rules of the era, batters were able to request low or high balls from the pitcher. This practice, which would seem to be greatly advantageous to the hitter, was deceptive, since the respective strike zones for such requests were either from the *top* of the shoulders to the waist, or from the waist to the *bottom* of the knees. Either one of these choices approximates the size of today's small strike zone. Walks were a rarity, since a free pass to first base required eight balls in 1879. That number gradually declined to four in 1884. Boston's Charley Jones led the league in bases on balls in 1879 with a paltry total of 29.

Until 1901, home plate was a 12-inch-by-12-inch square. While its small size may appear to have favored the hitter, the width of the strike zone as estimated by the umpire was not based on the plate's tiny width, but rather on the length of the hitter's bat, a measure that legally could extend to 42 inches.

Buck Ewing's switch from catcher to shortstop in mid–July during a two-game series with Albany proved disastrous. He committed three errors there in the first contest and seven (of a team total of 14) at the position the following day. This poor personal performance was soon followed by the worst possible news with regard to the league: "This week ends the last vestige of the [National] Association clubs' existence, inasmuch as the reorganized Albany team has disbanded, and the Rochesters have left their own city, to temporarily play in Albany and pick up the crumbs from the tables of the League clubs passing through the Capitol City."[35]

John Reilly's account of Buck Ewing's Rochester experience simply states that Ewing "caught the season out"[36] there, and Ewing's own version of events makes no mention of that summer's turmoil. It is not difficult, however, to imagine how young Buck might have felt by midsummer. His euphoria over signing his first professional contract must have quickly dissolved into a state of disappointment, uncertainty, and apprehension. He was 20 years old, far away from home for the first time, possessed limited financial resources, and was out of a steady job. His options were limited — either to return home to the semi-pro Mohawk Browns and to his six-day work week as a distillery teamster, or barnstorm with the remains of the Hop Bitter team until season's end, hoping to be noticed and signed by another club. He chose the latter option, and never looked back.

The newly-independent Rochesters played a three-game series of games in Springfield, Massachusetts, in late July, against the other orphaned squad, the Washington Nationals, winning two and losing one. They then surprised Buffalo's National League team (and themselves) by beating their better-known rivals, 7–6, in an exhibition game that undoubtedly was the highlight of their summer. Ewing caught regularly and well, but his hitting woes continued, and he took the collar no less than a half-dozen times.

In mid–August, the barnstorming Hop Bitters organized another series against the Nationals at Brooklyn's Union Grounds. Located just north of today's Bedford-Stuyvesant neighborhood, the Union Grounds was the country's first enclosed park when opened in 1862, and as such, ushered in the era in which fans had to pay for entry to the ball field in order to see games. During the Grounds' two-decade existence, it was home to legendary Brooklyn clubs like the Eckfords, the Mutuals and the Atlantics.

It is not clear who was handling publicity for the Washington and Rochester squads. However, based on a wildly exaggerated notice for the series that was placed in *Brooklyn Eagle* that suggested that the two orphaned teams were battling for a national championship, that individual deserved a marketing award:

> There is to be a week of professional playing this week, and the contesting clubs
> are the National and the Rochester clubs now contesting for the National
> Championship ... the match being the first of a series of best
> two of three for a purse of $300, so the bills state."[37]

After deductions for field rental, advertising, room and board, and some compensation for the losing team, such a purse might have yielded each man on the winning squad 15 dollars for a week's work.

The Union Grounds series got off to an inauspicious start when the disorganized and leaderless Hop Bitters failed to show up at the appointed hour and location for the first game. The series began the following day, with Buck, mistakenly identified as "Ewing, of Philadelphia,"[38] catching George "Stump" Wiedman and delivering two hits in a ten-inning loss.

In the return match the next day, Ewing caught Hugh "One-Arm" Daily, whose physical impairment, his missing left hand, attracted the interest of the fans; "the noted one armed pitcher of Baltimore was substituted for Weidman, greatly adding to the interest of the contest, the novelty of a one armed player pitching, batting, and fielding, and doing all of these things well, proving to be one of the attractive features of the match."[39] The Hop Bitters lost again, 6–5, but Ewing's throwing and receiving again garnered press attention: "Morrisey ... was ... finely thrown out at second by Ewing, who caught finely throughout the match,"[40]

"One Arm" Daily later pitched for seven big league clubs between 1882 and 1887. "Stump" Wiedman spent nine years in the major leagues, and briefly teamed with Buck Ewing again as a substitute hurler for New York in 1887–1888.

Ewing sat out the final game of the Brooklyn series with Washington, but he shared the Rochester bench that day with a local substitute, Lip Pike, who, though unknown to most fans today, was one of the greatest players of the early age of baseball:

> The match was made specially interesting to the spectators, from the fact that in
> consequence of Myerle's lame back and Daly's [Daily's] sore arm, two substitutes had to be provided in the Rochester team, and the two players selected
> were Pike, formerly of the old Atlantic club, and Nelson of the Eckfords, both,
> of course, having played on a great number of professional teams since they
> graduated from Brooklyn.[41]

It is unclear if both Myerle and Daily actually were unfit to play, or if this substitution was a clever ploy by the visiting Rochesters to curry favor with the local Brooklyn crowd in preparation for the announcement of a second series of games to be played there.

Lipman "Lip" Pike, of Dutch heritage, was born in Manhattan in 1845, and raised in Brooklyn. In a career that started in the mid–1860s and spanned nearly 20 years, Pike, regarded as baseball's first Jewish player and manager, played for a dozen professional teams. Pike was blessed with great speed, a powerful, if erratic, throwing arm, and enormous power. Nevertheless, his prickly personality, aggravated perhaps by the ubiquitous anti–Semitic climate of the age, caused him much trouble with teammates throughout his career. No one, however, denied his abilities as a slugger, which early on earned him the nickname "The Iron Batter." He led the National Association three times and the National League once in home runs. While playing for Cincinnati in 1877,

> Lipman Pike recorded what might have been the longest drive produced up to the moment in baseball annals. Batting leadoff to start the game against Boston's Tommy Bond (a three-time, 40 game winner), Lip did the seemingly impossible. Beyond the right field fence was a brick kiln. It was situated about 100 feet past the outer stadium barrier, and had rarely been approached by a batted ball. Yet, on this historic occasion, Lip actually cleared it on the fly![42]

Besides being an outstanding hitter, the "Iron Batter" was a great showman who was always ready to demonstrate his skills before an audience:

> Pike once raced a standardbred horse for $200—and won. The incredible race, which covered one hundred yards, featured the horse, named Charlie, starting off twenty-five yards behind Pike. Once the standardbred reached Pike, then the ballplayer took off. Pike and Charlie galloped neck-and-neck for most of the race until the speedy hardballer began to pull away from the horse. Charlie seemingly realizing his embarrassing role in the annals of equine history, suddenly began to gallop furiously, but to no avail. Pike won the race by four yards.[43]

During Pike's tenure with the Reds (1877 and part of 1878), young Buck Ewing must have had numerous opportunities to see "The Iron Batter" play in Cincinnati. Two decades later, while managing for Cincinnati, Ewing commented on hitting techniques for reporters. Recalling Pike's wrist-hitting style (which was also Ewing's own), he categorized it as the best approach at the plate: "A quick snappy movement is often better than a swing. 'Lip' Pike, one of the best hitters who ever lived, had this quick wrist movement and, although he apparently made little effort, he made some of the longest hits on record."[44] Despite the trials of his precarious professional situation in August, 1880, it must have been a thrilling experience for young Buck Ewing to share the bench with early diamond idol Lipman Pike.

On August 16, 1880, Ewing played his final game for the Hop Bitters, catching both Stump Wiedman and One-Arm Daily, and registering a hit in an 8–0 loss to Washington. The *Brooklyn Eagle* reported that after the game,

Catcher Buck Ewing, Troy Trojans, circa 1880. Buck caught for three years before chest protectors were available and for eight years prior to the introduction of the catcher's mitt (courtesy National Baseball Hall of Fame Library, Cooperstown, New York).

"Ewing, the fine catcher of the team, left for the West ... to join the Troys, who want a change catcher. They have undoubtedly selected a first-class man for the position. Brouthers also left for the same destination."[45]

The *Eagle's* report was not entirely accurate, for, much as in the case of Ewing's signing with the Hop Bitters, there are multiple versions of what actually occurred. Ewing's own summary is typically laconic: "During the last month of the season Bob Ferguson (Troy's manager) came after me and signed me to play with the Troys."[46] Long John Reilly's account suggests that Ewing wasn't signed by Troy until long after the end of the season. "The following winter Bob Ferguson, hearing his [Buck's] playing lauded by a manager who was about to sign him, quietly slipped off and engaged him for the Troy club."[47]

A late–August number of the *New York Clipper* provided the most comprehensive coverage: "A nine including Larkin, pitcher, Ewing, catcher, Brouthers, Briody and Sharpe on the bases, Ahearn, short-stop, with Lavin, Harbridge, and Higham in the outfield will play amateur games under the auspices of the Troy club during the absence of the latter professional team."[48]

There is a bit of truth in all of these stories. Ewing and Brouthers did leave the Hop Bitters, but they did not join the Troys on their western tour. The franchise was in financial trouble and could not have paid to send the untested pair west for a few games. Troy's crusty manager, Bob Ferguson, an old warhorse from the days of the original National Association, had probably heard of Ewing, but would not have signed him to a contract without a tryout. Seven of the nine players mentioned in the *Clipper* article *were* given brief tryouts by Troy in actual games in September, 1880, after the team returned from its western tour. Only one of the seven, Buck Ewing, was signed by Troy for the 1881 season, an event occurring, in all probability, sometime in the winter of 1880–1881, as suggested by Long John Reilly.

In less than a year and a half, playing in fewer than 75 games for the Mohawk Browns and the Rochester Hop Bitters, Buck Ewing, catching and playing every infield position, had made the transition from an East-End Cincinnati amateur player to the National League. With the exception of one year spent with the Players' League Giants in 1890, he would remain in the Senior Circuit as a player, captain, and manager, for the next 20 seasons.

Chapter 2

Trojans and Gothams:
1880–1884

"In any position in the field except possibly that of pitcher, few can come up to him [Ewing] in point of effect and usefulness ... there are many men who excel in one position or another, but few who can play any position up to the highest mark."—*New York Clipper*, August 20, 1882

The National League's decision to grant franchises to Troy, New York, in 1879, and Worcester, Massachusetts, in 1880, was an act of desperation by an organization that was in deep financial trouble. The league's stubborn insistence on a 50-cent admission fee precluded the growth of a fan base among the working class, since that sum represented a significant portion of an average worker's daily wage. Its prohibition of Sunday ball and liquor sales at games discouraged attendance by many immigrant groups, particularly the Irish and Germans, who did not share the league's teetotaler and Sabbatarian views.

Prior to admitting Troy and Worcester, the league had expelled — and subsequently refused to reinstate — teams from the country's largest potential fan markets, Philadelphia and New York, for failing to complete their schedules due to financial woes. Louisville's team was expelled due to a game-fixing scandal. The Hartford, Saint Louis, Indianapolis and Milwaukee franchises all folded due to insolvency. Cincinnati, which was dismissed for the same reason, and then promptly reinstated when new backers took control of the club, was expelled yet again at the end of the 1880 season for allowing teams like Buck Ewing's Mohawk Browns to rent its grounds on Sundays and sell beer during their games there.

Such policies had reduced the league to six teams in 1877 and 1878, and forced it to waive its 75,000 population minimum for city franchises and offer them to smaller towns like Worcester and Troy. These new teams did not help solve the League's economic dilemma, for each, like many franchises that had preceded them, lasted just a few years.

Troy was a booming industrial town with a distinguished baseball pedigree. Long before railroad lines crisscrossed New York State, the city's strategic location on the Hudson River facilitated its development as a major distribution center for goods shipped north and south on river schooners. Troy turned to iron and steel production in the 1820s, when it began importing Pennsylvania coal from the nearby Erie Canal terminus at Cohoes. It owes its nickname, "The Collar City," to the development of a light industry that came into existence during the same period. Detachable shirt collars and cuffs were invented in Troy, and they quickly became popular across the country. Collar and cuff production remained Troy's commercial mainstay well into the twentieth century.

By 1860, a Troy amateur team, the Victories, had secured membership in the National Association of Base-Ball Players. In 1866, the Lansingburg Unions — named after a small village adjacent to Troy that would later be annexed by the city — shocked the baseball world by sailing down the Hudson and defeating New York City's powerful nine, the Mutuals. Highly embarrassed, the Gotham press ridiculed the team as hayseeds and christened them as the "Haymakers," a nickname they adopted with gusto.

In 1869, the Haymakers battled Cincinnati's touring professional team to a tie. It was a controversial outcome that was the only blemish on an otherwise perfect season for the Queen City team. In 1871, Troy joined the nation's first professional league, the National Association of Professional Base-Ball Players, playing their first home game against Boston on May 5, and attracting 2,500 spectators in a 9–5 loss. They finished sixth in the nine-team league, led by none other than Lipman Pike, who played in 29 of the team's 31 contests, banged out 49 hits, scored 43 runs, and tied for the league lead in home runs with four.

The fine attendance figures of the team's early home games, however, diminished during their second season, and the team folded for financial reasons in late June 1872. In 1879, the Collar City was ready to try its luck again in the professional arena, fielding a team in the four-year-old National League. Both the league and the city hoped that Troy's baseball heritage, its proximity to Albany, the state capitol (eight miles away), and the region's strong industrial base would help the team turn a profit. Such high expectations were not met.

Led initially by the seemingly ubiquitous Horace Phillips, the 1879 Troy National League team, known formally as the Troy Citys, and informally as the Trojans or the Troys, finished their first season in last place with a 19–56 record, 35 games behind league-leading Providence. Phillips was replaced in August by player/manager Bob Ferguson, who would skipper the team until its dissolution at the end of the 1882 season.

Phillips and Ferguson represented two different approaches to the art of managing, which, like every other aspect of nineteenth-century baseball, underwent a significant evolution during the professional game's first quarter-century. Ferguson was a player/manager, while Phillips' role was similar to that of a modern team's business manager. For practical reasons, team owners' initial preference was for a player/manager. However, baseball's first professional player/manager, Harry Wright of the 1869 Cincinnati team, set a standard that could never be equaled. Wright played center field for the Red Stockings during their perfect-record first season, and he coached, recruited and disciplined players, and served as the field general. In addition, he arranged all travel and lodging for the constantly barnstorming nine, kept the financial books, issued salary checks, and even designed the team's uniforms.

Succeeding player/managers tended to be better on-field leaders than businessmen, prompting some franchises to experiment with skippers who had never played professional ball, but who were better at balancing the books. Among the most successful of these were Frank Bancroft, who managed several teams in the 1880s, Jim Mutrie, who led the Giants to two pennants and world championships in 1888 and 1889, and Boston's Frank Selee, who piloted the Beaneaters through the 1890s. Although these and other non-player/managers customarily were savvy baseball men, they usually relegated on-field decision-making to a team captain.

Not surprisingly, conflicts often arose between these managers and their captains with regard to who controlled the team. Such a conflict in Boston between Frank Selee and slick-fielding team captain Billy Nash in 1895 prompted manager Selee to trade Nash to Philadelphia for future Hall of Famer Billy Hamilton. In like fashion, Giants manager Pat Powers' decision to wrest full control of on-field operations from team captain Buck Ewing in 1892 initiated a struggle that was not fully resolved until Powers was fired by team officials and Ewing was traded to the Cleveland Spiders for George Davis by incoming skipper John Ward. In the mid–1890s, Cincinnati became one of the first teams to adopt the modern practice of formally dividing business and field operations by naming Frank Bancroft as business manager of the Reds and appointing Buck Ewing as the on-field manager/captain.

Although slender, balding Bob Ferguson did not look the part of a tough, uncompromising team skipper, appearances in his case were deceptive. When he assumed the managerial role at Troy in 1880, he was a seasoned 34 year old who had played organized ball since the age of 18 — including years of service with New York's Mutuals and his home-town Brooklyn Atlantics during the 1860s. Bob player/managed two clubs in the National Association during its five-year existence in the 1870s, and for two years served concurrently as the organization's President, thus becoming "the only player in baseball history to simultaneously serve as player, manager, umpire (which he did on occasion) and league executive."[1]

An extremely versatile player, Ferguson caught, pitched, and played third base, second base and shortstop during his long career. The game's first switch-hitter, he compiled a lifetime batting average of .265. His switch-hitting was situational, and not always based on whether the opposing pitcher was left-handed or right-handed. Ferguson's fine fielding, and in particular, his innate ability to track down pop fly balls, earned him the curious and colorful nickname, "Death to Flying Things." Ferguson regularly used subterfuge to gain advantage on the diamond. In the era before the infield fly rule was established, he was a master of the trapped-ball play — that is, with men on base, he pretended to catch a pop up, but then dropped it at the last second and threw to a base to force a runner. He also executed the first successful hidden-ball trick in National League history when he caught Chicago's Cap Anson napping off third base on May 25, 1876.[2]

Ferguson was the first manager to experiment with shifting infielders and outfielders when specific hitters came to the plate. He "was not above abusing umpires,"[3] even though he himself often served in that capacity. Once, Nat Hicks of the New York Mutuals questioned a call that Ferguson made while umpiring an 1873 game. Ferguson settled the issue by breaking Hicks' arm with a bat. Since he was serving as League president at the time, no charges were filed against him.[4]

Despite his years of managerial experience and on-field skills, Ferguson's dictatorial leadership style, bad temper, and routine impatience with his players when they made mistakes occasioned many near-insurrections on his teams. When he died suddenly of apoplexy at age of 49 in 1894, *Sporting Life*'s obituary, while describing him as a man of "sterling integrity," also noted that "he was impulsive, rather quick-tempered, and often talked too sharply to his men when irritated."[5]

Buck Ewing was 20 years old when he came under Ferguson's authority late in the 1880 season. Although Ewing was by nature more personable and even-tempered than the prickly Ferguson, it is clear that the rookie adopted many of his later playing and managing strategies from "Old Fergy." Both men were catchers who also thrived as multi-position players. Behind the plate in the 1860s, Ferguson was one of the earliest backstops to move in closer behind the hitter — an extremely daring move given the fact that in that era the catcher wore neither a mask nor a chest protector. A generation later, Ewing, wearing both, was one of the first to move in even closer "under the bat."

Like his Brooklyn-born mentor, Ewing became a regular "kicker" (one who complained about umpire calls) and employed many on-field tricks, such as leaving his mask in the path of an approaching runner, in order to gain an advantage. Like Ferguson, Ewing was an innovator as captain and as a manager, and was one of the first skippers to use hand signals to re-position players in the field. Later in his career, Ewing was a stern disciplinarian like his mentor, yet unlike Ferguson, he tempered his criticism with praise and encouragement:

> Buck is severe on his men, and does not hesitate to "lace" them on the field. Indeed he does quite as much scolding in public as he does in private. He always manages, however, to smooth over his rebukes afterward, and if a player is doing good work, Buck is not scant in his praises. Ewing's greatest forte is smoothing over quarrels and differences among the men.[6]

Manager Ferguson faced a daunting task in reorganizing the Troy Trojans after the team's dismal first season in the National League. He achieved modest success in this regard by replacing the entire pitching staff and all but three of the fielders. Many of his acquisitions were players he had seen perform in the moribund International/National Association while he was player/managing the Springfield squad in 1879.

Ferguson's new pitching ace, Mickey Welch, was acquired from Holyoke. He started 65 of the team's 83 games in 1880, winning 34 of Troy's 41 victories and posting a 2.54 ERA. The slender, 5'8", 160-pound Welch relied on a change-up and an assortment of curves rather than the fastball. It was a strategy that eventually would earn him 307 wins and a plaque in the Hall of Fame. Ironically, Bob Ferguson, while with the Springfield nine, had vociferously complained to umpires about Welch's delivery, arguing that "Smiling Mickey" raised his throwing arm above the hip (illegally, according to the rules of the day, but usually ignored by the umpires) when delivering the ball. Ferguson's complaints landed on deaf ears. "Defeated, yet impressed, Ferguson signed Welch for the National League Club [Troy] at the first opportunity."[7]

Despite the fact that during his years with Troy the local press invariably identified him as "Welsh" or "Walsh," Mickey Welch never suffered from an identity crisis. His easy-going disposition and the fact that he squinted while in the pitcher's box when facing a batter, led to his "Smiling Mickey" nickname, although photographs of the era invariably portray him with a serious expression on his face. Like Manager Ferguson, Welch honed his baseball skills in his native Brooklyn. Although Christy Mathewson is generally credited with the invention of the screwball — his famous "fadeaway" — Welch used a similar pitch 20 years earlier: "I had a fadeaway, although I didn't call it anything. It was just a slow curve that broke down and in on a right handed batter, and I got good results with it."[8] The spitball, popularized in the early twentieth century by Jack Chesbro, was apparently part of Welch's repertoire also, since reports of the period note that he "expectorates on either hand"[9] when preparing to pitch.

Ferguson replaced light-hitting Herm Dorscher (.220 in 1879) at third base with another Holyoke player who would, like Mickey Welch, eventually be named to the Hall of Fame. At 6'3", Roger Connor, the pride of Waterbury, Connecticut, manned the hot corner for the Troys in 1880, playing in every game (83), and leading the team in hits (113), triples (8), home runs (3), RBI (47), batting average (.332) and slugging percentage (.459).

As an adolescent, Connor developed his powerful physique working 12-hour shifts in a copper foundry and playing semi-pro ball for his hometown Waterbury Monitors. Originally a right-handed hitter, he began hitting from the opposite side of the plate after an unsuccessful two-week tryout with the New Bedford Whalers of the International Association in 1878. Released by the Whalers for failing to hit, he began swinging from the left side, and slowly blossomed into one of the greatest power hitters in the game. Although he did not reach double figures in home runs until his eighth year in the major leagues, Connor finished his career as the nineteenth century's home run king (138) and triples leader (233), ranking second in hits, walks and total bases, and fourth in doubles. Despite his size, Connor was an excellent base stealer, averaging 20 thefts a year, and is credited with inventing the "pop-up" slide as a defensive measure after dislocating his shoulder sliding to a base in 1882. Occasionally, when facing left-handed pitchers or when field or weather conditions warranted (short left-field fences or wind factors), Connor would amaze his fans, teammates and opponents by returning to his right-handed stance and knocking the ball out of the park. After being stationed around the diamond for several years, he would finally settle in at first base, where he became an accomplished fielder, leading the league defensively at his position four times.

Off the diamond, Connor was a well-respected boxer who sang for his friends in a sweet tenor voice and accompanied himself ably on the piano. The quintessential Victorian athlete — soft-spoken and quiet — he was stoic in defeat and modest in victory. In an 18-year career, he was never ejected from a game, earning the title of "Gentleman of the Diamond" from his fans. Connor enjoyed a second career as owner and player/manager of two teams in the Connecticut League for many years, and he was still stealing bases and hitting four-baggers in semi-pro leagues when in his early fifties. While his major league accomplishments were forgotten for a half-century, Connor finally received the plaque he deserved in Cooperstown in 1976.

Late in the season, Ferguson also acquired pitcher Tim Keefe from Albany after a surreptitious encounter with the young ace in an unlikely location. "The Troy directors arranged a meeting with Keefe, the Albany's pitcher, at a very appropriate place, the Albany cemetery — and there in the night time made the advances which in the city and during the day they were ashamed to offer."[10] Although Keefe's start with Troy was delayed by illness, he pitched in 12 games at the end of the season, breaking even at six wins and six losses, but posting an 0.86 ERA, the best ever in the history of the National League. Fireballer Keefe would come into his own after sidearm pitching was legalized in 1883, winning a career total of 342 games and a place in the Hall of Fame.

Despite his aggressive pitching style, Keefe had a sensitive, emotional nature, and was easily affected in the pitcher's box by events on the diamond. In August 1886, one of his fastballs hit Boston second baseman Jack Burdock in the temple, knocking him unconscious. While Burdock recovered fully, Keefe suffered a nervous breakdown as a result of the incident. In the decade he spent with the Giants, Keefe benefited significantly from the calming and encouraging assurances of his usual battery mate, Buck Ewing, and in his retirement he recognized his catcher for such assistance: "He was a great man for his pitcher, for he knew how to steady him."[11] During his New York years, Keefe was co-owner of a sporting goods store in Manhattan. After his pitching career ended, he had a brief stint as a major league umpire, after which he retired and lived comfortably off his real estate investments in his native Cambridge, Massachusetts.

Thanks to the acquisition of Welch, Connor, Keefe, and other competent but less prominent players, Bob Ferguson moved the Troys up to fourth place by season's end, bolstered by a ten-game win streak in mid–August.

On September 10, the *Troy Daily Times* reported that "Ewing and Brouthers made their first appearances on the Troy nine yesterday — and the impression they created so far as playing is concerned is favorable."[12] Buck Ewing spent the last two weeks of his first National League season batting ninth for Troy and alternating behind the plate and in right field defensively. Not accustomed to the superior League pitching, he struggled mightily at the plate, but on two occasions managed to bring in the winning run for the Troys. Against Worcester on September 18, his single in the ninth inning assured his team a 4–3 victory. In a 3–1 win at Providence on September 25, "The Troys won in the second inning when a safe hit by Ewing sent home two runs."[13] After the League season ended, Troy played an exhibition game in Manhattan against the independent New York Metropolitans, with Buck putting in a steady game at third base and contributing a hit in a 4–2 win. It was the young Cincinnatian's first game in the Big Apple.

Historically, the contest is more notable for its location than for its final score. Two weeks earlier, the *New York Times* had reported that the Metropolitans had played their first game in their new park, the first enclosed baseball field in Manhattan. "The polo grounds [*sic*] of this city were opened to the public yesterday for the first time as a base-ball arena. Between 2,000 and 3,000 people were there — by far the largest assemblage that has gathered on a ball field in this vicinity in three years."[14]

The original Polo Grounds, located between Fifth and Sixth Avenue, and 110th and 112th Street, at the north end of Central Park, was the first of several Manhattan fields to carry that name during the ensuing 77 years. The original venue was Buck Ewing's home field for six years in the mid–1880s, while he played for New York's National League team. City street construction forced the team to move 45 blocks north to a second location, which was dubbed "the New Polo Grounds," during the 1889 season.

Despite the fact that Buck hit just .178 in his two weeks with Troy in 1880, Bob Ferguson had seen enough of his defensive versatility to offer him a contract for the 1881 season, at a salary of $1,000. It is less understandable why Ferguson did not also offer to re-sign Dan Brouthers, the future Hall of Famer who accompanied Buck Ewing to Troy upon the dissolution of the Rochester Hop Bitters. Big Dan saw action in just three games with the Trojans during his September 1880 tryout, hitting a paltry .167. Nevertheless, in the 39 games he played for Troy in 1879, after having been signed in mid-season by then–Troy manager Horace Phillips, he led the team in hitting at .274 and finished third in the League in home runs with four.

Brouthers may have burned his bridges behind him with Bob Ferguson, for whom he played six weeks at Troy in 1879, by choosing not to return to the Trojans in the spring of 1880, opting instead to join Baltimore of the National Association, and then, as we have seen, jumping his Baltimore contract at the behest of his former Troy manager, Horace Phillips, to join the ill-fated Rochesters. Although Ferguson, either by choice or in error, declined the opportunity to mentor one future Hall of Famer — Dan Brouthers — he still holds the honor of signing and managing the greatest rookie class in the history of baseball — Welch, Keefe, Connor and Ewing — all future members of the Hall of Fame.

Dan Brouthers' personal decision not to return to the National League team he played for during the previous (1879) season would soon not be an option for any League player. Desperate for a way to control costs and reverse the trend of financial losses that had plagued nearly every team, National League administrators took a significant step in reducing their most expensive budget item — player salaries — at the conclusion of the 1879 season. The solution was passage of a new rule stipulating that when a player signed a contract, he was automatically "reserved" for the following year by the team with whom

Troy National League team, circa 1881, including future Hall of Famers Mickey Welch, first row, left; Roger Connor, second row, far right; Buck Ewing, third row, far right. Center, second row: Troy manager Bob Ferguson. Not shown: future Hall of Fame pitcher Tim Keefe (courtesy TranscendentalGraphics/theruckerarchive.com).

he signed. All players were thus bound to the same team until such time as the team chose to release them.

The League initially used an underhanded ploy to hide this rule from the players. From 1880 to 1886, no specific mention of the policy appeared in individual contracts. Nevertheless, all players were required to adhere to the League's constitution, where the reserve clause was specified. For the first three years in which the regulation was in effect, only five players from each team were reserved. That number gradually rose to 12 in 1886, and 14 (that is, virtually the whole team) in 1887.

The Reserve Clause soon became the most hated rule in baseball, and was a major factor leading to the establishment of the American Association in 1882 and the Players' League in 1890. Buck Ewing tested this rule after the 1882 season, and was lambasted by the press and the league for doing so. In 1890, he was actively involved in the formation of the Players' League, which likewise opposed the Reserve Clause, but, as we shall see, he was also controversially linked to this league's demise. For better or worse, press, franchise, fan, and teammate responses to Ewing's actions in these affairs significantly affected his popularity and stature as a major league star for the remainder of his career.

The 1881 and 1882 seasons were Buck Ewing's apprenticeship years in the National League, but as his own skills continued to improve against the league's superior competition, his Troy team was in a slow process of financial disintegration. By the time Ewing had fully adjusted to the league's rigorous playing standards, the Troy franchise was out of business.

Manager Ferguson's only major change in the team roster in 1881 was the acquisition of Cleveland Blues third baseman Frank Hankinson. Hankinson's arrival allowed Roger Connor to move to first base. Workhorse Mickey Welch got some needed help from the 1880 latecomer, Tim Keefe. Pitching in tandem in 1881, the duo collected all of Troy's 39 wins, registering a combined ERA of 2.96. At season's end, the Trojans had more than doubled their previous year's victory total and moved out of the cellar and into fifth place.

Bob Ferguson originally planned to alternate Buck Ewing with journeyman catcher Bill Holbert behind the plate, but after shortstop Ed Caskins sprained his knee at midseason, Ewing spent more time at that position than as a receiver for the remainder of the year. Offensively, he started off well, stroking a home run in an exhibition contest against Ferguson's former team, the Brooklyn Atlantics, and banging out four hits, including two triples, in the season's first league series against Troy's weak New England opponent, the Worcester Ruby Legs. Hitting became more of a challenge as soon as Ewing began to face better pitchers, like Chicago's Larry Corcoran, Providence's John Ward and Hoss Radbourn, and Buffalo's Jim Galvin. While Ewing's average would continue to rise annually from its 1881 low of .250, it would take him another three years to break the .300 barrier.

Ewing did steady work as a bare-handed shortstop — infielders would not regularly use gloves for another decade — but it was his play behind the plate, and particularly his throwing, that was gaining attention. After a 4–2 loss to Boston, for example, the *Troy Daily Times* noted that "The throws of Ewing from the home plate to second base were simply marvelous, putting out by that means four men."[15] Besides cutting down potential base stealers, Ewing himself was busy stealing bags, and was praised for his "admirable running."[16]

By mid–July, Troy had climbed to fourth place, but soon afterward they began a downward slide from which they did not recover. The team's greatest problem was winning on the road, where their loss total nearly doubled that of their wins. Home attendance, meanwhile, was in the hundreds rather than the thousands, an average that was not helped by local press reports, which regularly ridiculed the team as "Ferguson's Sluggards"[17] and prefaced its game summaries with headlines such as "The Monotony Continues — The Troys Trounced Again."[18] By August the owners owed the players back pay, and when the season ended the franchise was $3,000 in debt.

Although Troy won just four fewer games in 1882 than in the previous season, the team finished in seventh place. With no money to recruit established players, Ferguson was forced to promote three minor leaguers to fill his roster. Louisville native Fred Pfeffer took over at shortstop. He hit just .228, but led the league in fielding his position. New Yorker John "Chief" Roseman landed the right field spot. Pitchers Keefe and Welch, who combined for 771 innings in 1881, pitched 114 fewer frames in 1882, with the slack taken up by rookie hurler Jim Egan.

Despite Buck Ewing's fine performance behind the plate the previous year, Bob Ferguson used him even less frequently in 1882 as a backup for catcher Bob Holbert. Now aware of the young Cincinnatian's versatility, Troy's manager opted for employing him as a utility man as well as an occasional "change" catcher in order to keep him healthy and in the lineup daily. Accordingly, Ewing spent the first month of the season alternating between the outfield and second base, infrequently relieving Bob Holbert behind the plate. In late May he was moved to third base to replace the released Frank Hankinson, and was reported to be "perfectly at home there."[19] He remained at the hot corner for the balance of the season, and the press soon declared that "Ewing's third base play is unequaled."[20]

Six weeks into the season, Ewing had collected 35 hits, "excelling the record of any other member of the Troy team."[21] While in Buffalo for a three-game series, however, he suffered a reversal that kept him out of the lineup for three weeks. "Ewing accidentally cut his hand in a severe manner Sunday, and is now receiving treatment at his home in Cincinnati."[22] He was not the only wounded Trojan. Roger Connor, on his way to a breakout season offensively, had a sore throwing arm. Both Mickey Welch and Bob Ferguson had sprained ankles, and receiver Bill Holbert suffered a severe gash on his cheek after a batted ball broke his catcher's mask. When the team returned from its disastrous road trip, the *Troy Daily Times* lamented, "A hospital for Troy's disabled players would be in order. Keefe, Harbridge and Roseman are the only three who have not been maimed this season."[23]

Recovered from his hand wound, Buck Ewing hit regularly and well during the last months of the season, and he was moved from ninth to first in the batting order. His daring, heads-up running, which became a feature of his offensive play in later years, was also in evidence. In a late July win against Boston, for example, Ewing singled and advanced Mickey Welch to second. Then

Connor's [fly] out to [center fielder] Hotaling advanced Welch a bag, and he scored on a passed ball by [catcher] Deasley. While the latter was determining what to do with the ball, Ewing ran to third. Deasley then threw the ball to [third baseman] Sutton [in an attempt to catch Ewing there], leaving the plate uncovered. While Sutton was telephoning the umpire that he had touched Ewing [,] the latter galloped to the unguarded plate amid the laughter of the spectators.[24]

Neither Ewing's base-running heroics nor Roger Connor's hot hitting in the last months of the season could prevent Troy from finishing seventh in the league standings. While the *Troy Daily Times'* September 11 headline, "Troy Going to Pieces,"[25] was meant to refer to the club's losing ways, it was also an accurate portrayal of the teams financial status. Midway through the season, "Troy ... had to be rescued by funds from other League clubs,"[26] to keep from quitting before the end of the season.

Sensing the franchise's imminent demise, representatives from other league and American Association teams began courting Troy's players, offering them higher salaries and other perks.

One of the baits thrown out by the American association [*sic*] whereby to catch league players for next season, is to promise them release from the obligation to purchase their own uniforms and to rescind the rule whereby fifty cents a day is deducted from a player's salary while the team is away from home. Promises are also made to deposit certain sums of money in the bank for the benefit of said players in advance of the season.[27]

The Philadelphia Athletics had even offered Ewing's teammate, Roger Connor, a house and a lump sum in cash to sign with them.

In mid–September an anonymous Troy team administrator undermined any hope that the players might remain loyal to the franchise by asserting that "We will have a different nine next year. [Manager] Ferguson will probably not be here, and there will be other changes, but we cannot engage our players [by League rule] until after October 1."[28] A week later, the league gave Troy the choice of resigning or being expelled from the organization. In order to save face, team owners accepted the former alternative. Events began to move quickly. On September 26, Troy's directors voted to make a formal application for admission to the American Association. Although the following day the *Troy Daily Times* reported that Ewing, Roger Connor, Mickey Welch, Tim Keefe and several other Trojans players had declared that "they will play in Troy if the club wants them, even at a lower figure than they would get else-where,"[29] the truth of this report is questionable. Ewing and the other young Troy stars, after all, had been forewarned of Troy's owners' intent to make significant roster changes on any future squad (should there be one), and the players likewise would be guaranteed significant salary increases as soon as they signed with other teams. Buck Ewing himself, for example, reportedly had received an offer of $2,800 to sign with Detroit's National League team. Another report affirmed that he had signed with Chicago.

Having been witness to and a victim of the dissolution of his first professional team, the Rochester Hop Bitters, only a month after he signed on with the squad, Buck Ewing had no intention of committing to an uncertain future in Troy. It had been widely reported in September that the New York Metropolitans and the Philadelphia Quakers had been admitted to the National League after the expulsion of Troy and Worcester. When it became apparent that no Association offer to Troy was forthcoming, Buck Ewing signed with the Metropolitans shortly after October 1.

In doing so, Ewing's logical assumption was that since the Troy team no longer existed, he was free to negotiate personally with other franchises. He was unaware that even though Troy had disbanded, under league regulations he had no individual right to sell his services to the highest bidder. Although bankrupt and expelled from the League, Troy had reserved Ewing for 1883, and thus still "owned" his contract, which would need to be purchased from them by another team before Ewing could negotiate salary and sign a contract with another franchise.

Additionally, by the end of the 1882 season, the League and the Association had come to the realization that their internecine bidding wars for playing talent were proving financially disastrous for both organizations. In February 1883, representatives from each major league circuit and one from the Northwestern League, a minor league organization, met in New York to hammer out a truce that would be mutually beneficial to all. The result was a historic pact, known today as the National Agreement, by which the reserve clause was extended to include 11 players on each club, dates for circulation of reserve lists, signings, and contract lengths were standardized, and all signatories promised to respect each other's player contracts. The new regulations, "for all practical purposes, ended bidding for players between clubs and between leagues."[30]

Once again Buck Ewing found himself on a team that no longer existed, but this time his misfortune occurred at the precise historic moment in which the two previously warring major professional leagues had formally agreed to collaborate in order to regulate and control player rights in baseball. The press subsequently suggested that baseball's need to establish revised timetables for contract signings was due to Ewing's "illegal" signing with the (still independent) Metropolitans.

The new National Agreement stipulated that all players on a team's roster were considered members of their team until November 1 (one month later than the previous deadline). Reserve lists for all teams were required to be submitted to the Secretaries of the League and Association on September 20, and then circulated for informational purposes to all clubs by October 10, after which contracts could begin to be tendered (ten days later than the previous deadline). Teams thus had written documentation on all reserved players in each league before signing their own players or any new candidates. Hereafter, teams could not feign lack of knowledge of existing contracts when signing already-contracted players. Finally, it was agreed that any player signing two contracts would be expelled.

Even though Buck Ewing was not the only player to try to circumvent standing league policy in the wake of Troy's demise, he took the brunt of the criticism for the action. "This [new agreement] is aimed at such men as 'Bread and Butter' 'Buck' Ewing, and that gang, who were condemned in unmeasured terms by all the members, nearly all of whom had experiences to relate of Ewing's perfidious conduct. If he gets more than 1,000 [dollars] next year he'll be in luck."[31]

While Ewing's reputation was tarnished by this episode, and the "Bread and Butter" nickname would stick with him until the end of his career, his pocketbook was not damaged. John B. Day and Jim Mutrie soon surprised the baseball world by enrolling the Metropolitans in the American Association for 1883, and then creating a new, second Manhattan professional squad that joined the National League. Buck was assigned to the new league team at a salary of $3,100.[32]

Historically, Manhattan was rich in baseball teams but scarce in ball fields — so scarce that as early as the mid–1840s, the city's famed Knickerbockers nine elected to play their contests in Hoboken, New Jersey, at the wistfully named Elysian Fields, a short ferry ride from Manhattan. After the enclosed Union Grounds opened for baseball contests in the early 1860s, Manhattan squads began to abandon the New Jersey site in favor of the revenue-generating fields across the East River in Brooklyn.

The financial success of the Union Grounds prompted the opening of a second enclosed field, the Capitoline Grounds, in Brooklyn's Bedford neighborhood, in 1863. A few years later, this field was the site of one of the most famous baseball games in history. On June 14, 1870, Harry Wright's touring Cincinnati Red Stockings, who had not lost a game since their founding the previous year (an 81-game streak), battled the Brooklyn Atlantics, who were managed by Bob Ferguson, in an eleven-inning contest played before an estimated 20,000 fans. The Brooklyn nine downed the previously undefeated Red Stockings, 8–7, in what was regarded at the time as the greatest game ever played. Ferguson won the game for the local team by advancing from first to third on a single in the 11th frame, and then making it safely to home when the throw from the outfield was bobbled.

Manhattan's best team in the 1860s was The Mutuals, who were named after the New York Fire Department's Mutual Hook-and-Ladder Company. A charter member of the National Association, the "Mutes," as they were nicknamed, fielded a nine each year of the organization's five-year existence, and in 1874 finished second in the league to the powerful Boston Red Stockings. The Mutuals joined the National League in its premier season, 1876, but were expelled for not completing their last western tour due to financial difficulties. The Mutes played all their Association and League home games in Brooklyn at the Union or Capitoline Grounds.

Professional baseball began to be played in Manhattan thanks to the efforts of two men from Massachusetts, Jim Mutrie and John B. Day. Mutrie had the dream; Day had the money. One of the most colorful figures in baseball history, Mutrie was of Scottish descent. He had the "gift of gab" of an Irishman, the sense of drama of a prima donna, and the marketing flair of a modern advertising executive. Early on, his propensity to stretch the truth earned him the sarcastic nickname, "Truthful Jeems." Tall, dark and handsome, and sporting a stylish handlebar moustache, Mutrie was an all-around athlete who played cricket before picking up baseball, and in addition was an ardent bicyclist and long-distance walker. The latter sport was known as "pedestrianism" at that time, and in his old age, Mutrie affirmed that he regularly defeated rivals in 100-mile walks.[33]

Mutrie managed and played numerous positions for a variety of New England baseball teams, and in his last season as a full-time player, held down the shortstop position for New Bedford in 1879. There, for a brief two-week period, he shared the left side of the infield with Roger Connor while the Waterbury native was unsuccessfully trying out for a spot on the team.

Moving to New York in 1880, Mutrie did factory work and played on picked nines while trying to sell the idea of opening a ballpark in Manhattan to anyone who would listen. "I wore out shoe leather walking up and down this town trying to get backers. They all laughed at me and wanted to appoint an insanity commission."[34]

John B. Day, a native of Colchester, Massachusetts, was a wealthy tobacco merchant with Tammany Hall connections who pitched on amateur teams in his free time. While on the diamond in the spring of 1880, he met Mutrie, who convinced him to underwrite a lease option he had negotiated for a field at the Manhattan Polo Grounds, a four-city-block expanse of land at 110th Street and Fifth Avenue, just north of Central Park. The land's owner, James Gordon Bennet, Jr., also owned the *New York Herald*, and was an avid promoter of all types of sporting events. He discovered polo while on a trip to England in 1875, brought the game to the United States, and established the Manhattan Polo Grounds as his playing field.

With John Day on board as his principal backer, Mutrie quickly used his extensive baseball connections to organize an independent professional team, the Metropolitans (Day and Mutrie preferred the singular, "the Metropolitan," as the team's name), with Mutrie serving as manager and occasionally playing first base. Many of the players Mutrie recruited were members of the now-defunct Rochester Hop Bitters squad for whom Buck Ewing and Dan Brouthers had played.

The Mets played most of their abbreviated 1880 schedule at the Union Grounds in Brooklyn while the Polo Grounds was being converted to a baseball venue. In addition to competing against National League teams on the latter's days off, the team played all comers, including independents, college nines and other amateur squads. As previously noted, on September 15 the Metropolitans played their first game at the Polo Grounds, defeating the independent Washington Nationals, 6–2. Hugh "One-Arm" Daily, Buck Ewing's battery mate at Rochester, was the Mets' winning pitcher.

In less than a year, Mutrie and Day had accomplished the seemingly impossible task of bringing professional baseball to Manhattan, and as Mutrie had predicted, the venture was a great financial success. Amateur and independent teams leased the Polo Grounds when the Mets were on the road, and often played morning games there prior to Mets home games, which were scheduled for mid-afternoon. In the Mets' first full season (1881), their take-on-all-comers philosophy allowed them to play 188 games.[35] Thus, when the opportunity presented itself, Day and Mutrie had both the financial and physical resources to introduce National League and American Association play to the island of Manhattan.

Owners of new teams in both the National League and in the American Association had belatedly realized that while the Reserve Clause did prevent contract jumping and kept player salaries low, the rule likewise prevented start-up franchises from acquiring quality veteran talent from established top teams. It was not surprising, therefore, that Mutrie and Day found the pickings slim when it came time to staff their New York National League entry, the "New-Yorks" (the original hyphenated spelling will be repeated here only in quoted material from the era). The pair negotiated the transfer of four starters from the 1882 Troys: Buck Ewing, Roger Connor, Mickey Welch and Pete Gillespie, and then drafted three men who had played for the Trojans earlier in their short history: infielders Frank Hankinson and Ed Caskin, and outfielder Mike Dorgan. These acquisitions provided field coverage for all positions except second base and center field. The team also needed a "change" (backup) catcher and a second pitcher.

To fill these vacancies, Mutrie and Day succeeded in acquiring two veterans who were considered "back numbers" (beyond their prime): journeyman catcher John Clapp, who was also to manage the team, and pitcher John Ward, whose right arm was presumed dead after averaging 29 wins a year in five seasons with Providence.

The burly Clapp (5'7", 194 pounds) was the prototype of the stocky Roy Campanella–model catchers of the twentieth century. A fine backstop who had registered four .300-plus seasons at the plate, Clapp had plenty of experience, having played previously for seven Association or league teams, including player/manager service with five of them. Clapp had spent the previous year with the Metropolitans, allowing Mutrie and Day to simply transfer him to their National League club.

With his pitching career fading due to overwork, John Ward taught himself to throw and hit left-handed in his early years in New York until his right arm recovered sufficiently to play the field, thereby extending his career another decade as a shortstop. This transition enabled him to become the only player in history to win 100 games as a pitcher and collect 2,000 hits. Although he was only 23, Ward had been left off the Providence reserve list for 1883.

> The club probably knew it would do them no good to reserve him, and made the best of a bad situation by vacating Ward's slot for another player. First of all, Ward had already suggested ... that he had already "laid by" enough money to quit baseball and return to school.... Secondly, he was in great demand ... and he could always "jump" to the American Association if Providence or any other League team didn't meet his price.[36]

Baseball's first Renaissance man, Ward ultimately earned a law degree from Columbia University in the off-season, and was the architect of the ill-fated 1890 Players' League rebellion.

Although Buck Ewing's first two professional teams folded a short time after his arrival, he had the singular good fortune of playing during his early years under the guidance and tutelage of two veteran catchers, Bob Ferguson and John Clapp. Since Ewing's only previous service as a backstop was limited to infrequent work at that position with the semi-pro Mohawk Buckeyes, the mentorship of these experienced men proved invaluable to the young, rising star. Indeed, two characteristics of their play behind the bat would become hallmarks of Ewing's catching career.

Catching in the 1860s with no mask or chest protector, Ferguson was one of the earliest in his trade to begin to inch closer to the batter to gain an advantage. Ewing, wearing a mask — and eventually a chest protector — was one of the first to move in even closer to the batter after the rules were changed to require that a called third strike be caught by the catcher to record an out. Clapp, who was one of the early backstops to use hand signals for pitches, found an apt pupil in Ewing, who adopted the same practice, and later, as a manager, used hand signals to position his fielders. Ewing's emergence as a premier catcher in the mid–1880s owes much to the instruction he received from veterans Ferguson and Clapp.

Although their Association and League squads were under contract for 1883, John Day and Jim Mutrie faced another pressing dilemma — they had a full roster on both teams, but only one field on which to play. Their awkward solution was to divide the Polo Grounds in half, creating a southeast field, to be used by the New York Nationals, and a southwest field, for use by the Metropolitans. A canvas fence separated the playing areas, an arrangement that at times created havoc at the ballpark: "balls rolling under the fence remained in play, causing the bizarre scene of an outfielder emerging into the opposing field in pursuit of the ball."[37] Fortunately for both teams, the occasions on which they played at home at the same time were relatively few.

Since the mid–1870s, pitchers had been violating with relative impunity the requirement that their throws be released from below the hip. The National League recognized the inevitable in 1883 by allowing sidearm pitching. The fact that batting averages remained steady the year that the new rule was introduced strongly suggests that so many pitchers had already been violating the existing underhand requirement that most hitters had already adjusted to the change. The following year, 1884, all restrictions on the throwing motion were dropped, and the era of overhand pitching began. This innovation proved to be much more challenging to hitters, especially because the front end of the pitcher's box was located just 50 feet from home plate. As a result of the change, batting averages tumbled an average of nearly 20 points.

The new pitching angles made possible by the rulings allowed the ball to be thrown at greater velocity and produced greater spin on breaking balls, resulting in a more pronounced curving motion. Curves thrown with a sidearm motion caused the ball to break across a horizontal plane; those thrown with an overhand motion broke down in a vertical plane.

Thus within the brief span of two seasons, a pitcher's potential arsenal was augmented considerably, and a new crop of sidearm hurlers, such as Tim Keefe and John Clarkson, and overhand stylists like Kid Nichols and Amos Rusie, soon came to prominence. All four made it to the Hall of Fame. Underhand pitching, however, did not completely disappear. Jim Galvin began his career long before the new rules, but pitched another decade after their implementation, using the traditional submarine- style delivery to compile 365 wins. Although he occasionally experimented with the sidearm style, Hoss Radbourn also threw submarine-style, which created less stress on his arm. The resulting durability allowed him to register 59 wins in 1884.

Since New York manager John Clapp was nearing the end of his career as a player and planned to appear sparingly in games (he played in just 20 contests), he chose another player as field captain. Clapp must have liked what

he saw in young Ewing, for instead of selecting veteran John Ward for the role, he entrusted it to Ewing.

Resplendent in their white and magenta uniforms (hence their frequent nickname — the Maroons), Manhattan's new team entertained Boston at the Polo Grounds on May 1, 1883, in their first National League game. More than 15,000 fans paid their 50-cent admission to be present — among them former President Ulysses S. Grant, now slowly dying of throat cancer. Home teams were as yet not required to bat last — nor would they be until 1950. Boston won the coin toss and chose to take the field first — thus giving the Gothams the opportunity to bat first in their new home grounds.

With the exception of Dasher Troy and John Ward, the home nine might have been attending a Troy Trojans team reunion: Captain and catcher Buck Ewing led off, followed by first baseman Roger Connor and Ward, playing center field. Carbondale, Pennsylvania's lanky Pete Gillespie started in left field and hit cleanup. Right fielder Mike Dorgan hit fifth and pitcher Mickey Welch, a decent hitter, batted sixth. The remaining weak-hitting infielders, Ed Caskin at second base, Dasher Troy at shortstop, and third baseman Frank Hankinson filled the seventh, eighth and ninth slots in the lineup.

Leading off, Buck Ewing made the first New York out in the Polo Grounds by ingloriously striking out, but he later contributed a hit and caught a steady game in the Gothams' 7–5 victory. To the surprise of all, the team swept the three-game series from the Hub City nine. The euphoria was short-lived, as Gotham's team was promptly swept by Providence, behind the pitching of Hoss Radbourn, who had taken over for the Grays in the box upon the departure of John Ward. Radbourn won all three games against New York on the way to a 48-win season. It was not the first time, nor would it be the last, that Radbourn's underhand delivery would enable him to collect three wins in three successive games.

Plagued by injuries and poor fielding, New York fell to seventh place in June, but managed to salvage sixth place at season's end by preying on the woeful cellar-dwelling Philadelphia Quakers, winning 12 of their 14 encounters. Providence, which had placed second to Chicago the previous three seasons, jockeyed with the Cleveland Blues for first place during the first half of the 98-game season. It was Boston, however, that took the pennant, winning 31 of their last 38 games on the strength of Jim Whitney's right arm. The

Opposite: The 1883 New York Nationals. Known informally as the Magentas (for their purple socks) or the Gothams, the team included player-manager John Clapp, second row, center, and future Hall of Famers Buck Ewing, third row, far left; John Ward, third row, far right; Roger Connor, second row, far right; and Mickey Welch, first row, left (courtesy National Baseball Hall of Fame Library, Cooperstown, New York).

Conklin, New York, native registered 37 victories and led the League with 345 strikeouts.

Several bright spots in New York's 1883 season helped dispel the gloom of a sixth-place finish. Mickey Welch pitched 21 games more (55) than his 1882 total, nearly doubled his wins (25), nearly tripled his strike outs (144), and lowered his ERA almost a point (2.73). After switching from third to first base, Roger Connor played in every game and solidified his reputation as an established slugger by leading the team in batting average (.357), walks (25), hits (146), doubles (28) and triples (15). It would still be several years before his home run prowess would become evident.

By every measure, 1883 was Buck Ewing's breakout season. Hitting over .300 for the first time (.303), he led the league with ten home runs, the greatest one-year total of his career, and the first time any National Leaguer had registered double digits in this category. He was one of the league's hottest hitters until sore hands from his catching duties slowed him down midway through the season.

The catcher's mitt had not yet been introduced in 1883, and backstops attempted to protect their hands by wearing a pair of skin-tight, fingerless gloves that were lightly padded on both sides between the knuckles and the fingers' first digits. Until the heavily-padded mitt made its appearance a few years later, the greater speed generated by the now-legal sidearm and overhand pitching motions wrought havoc on catchers' hands, as player/manager John Clapp discovered in an early July game. "Clapp had the middle finger of his left hand broken while playing under the bat. The bone was driven through the flesh and blood flowed freely from the wound."[38]

Early in the season Ewing was a hitting machine, with many hits coming in bunches. Between May 30 and June 4, he had a four-hit game and a trio of three-hit games. His three-hit effort against Detroit on May 30 included a home run and a triple. He went 4-for-4 against Chicago on June 2, including a home run; a week later he again collected four hits, including three triples. He collected four hits against Philadelphia on July 3, and in the first game of a doubleheader the following day against Boston, two of his three hits were home runs. In an era in which two four-baggers would be considered a good total for a season, two in a game evoked high praise from the fans. In the eighth inning, having homered in the third inning, "Ewing made another home run, sending in O'Neil and giving the home team a lead of three runs. At this point the spectators stood up in their seats, took off their hats, and cheered Ewing until they could be heard blocks away."[39]

Defensively, Ewing showed his great versatility in 1883 by playing six positions: third base, second base, shortstop, center and right fields, and catcher. While his work at shortstop was shaky, elsewhere his performance was steady, and he drew special praise playing second: "Ewing covered second base and convinced the spectators that he can hold his own against any of the crack second basemen."[40]

It was as a catcher, however, that he garnered most attention in his first year in New York. "Ewing's catching was, as usual, admirable, though it was far from easy to catch the wild deliveries of both pitchers."[41] The bulk of such praise was reserved for his throwing ability, for he not only cut down runners trying to advance, but also discouraged many from even making an attempt.

Although base stealing was not officially recognized statistically until the 1886 season, the steal was a vital weapon in nearly every team's arsenal. Two months into the 1883 season, *Sporting Life* reported that "Ewing, in the games he has caught for the New York team, has not had a single player steal second base on him this year."[42] A news account of a June contest with Buffalo ended with the comment that "some pretty catches and the throwing to the bases by Ewing were the features of the game."[43] Reporting on a 6–3 loss to Cleveland, the *New York Times* noted that "The Cleveland men ... were prevented from increasing their score by some clever throws by Ewing."[44]

When Ewing was eventually sidelined due to a hand injury, his offensive and defensive value to the team was confirmed and his loss lamented. "Ewing's hand was sore and he laid off for several games last week. With the absence of this heavy batter and strong catcher, New-York was handicapped to some extent, and this, in a measure, accounts for the numerous defeats received at the hands of the Buffalo players."[45]

Since most players on the New York squad were older than Ewing — some, like Hankinson and Gillespie, were already in their mid-thirties — it is doubtful that young Ewing could have been a strong disciplinarian during his first captaincy. Nevertheless, he was already demonstrating knowledge of the game and a strategic flair in this new role — unusual traits for a 23-year-old.

Use of relief pitchers was rare in the era, and they had to be chosen from one of the other eight members of the team on the field except in the case of severe injury. In a close game against Detroit, Ewing's decision to switch pitchers in order to preserve a lead was lauded by the fans and the press. "Captain Ewing wisely called Ward in from centre field to face to batters of the visiting club, and the followers of the team were happy. They applauded Ewing for his good judgment."[46]

Most games in the pre-electricity era were scheduled to begin at 3:30 P.M. In those of long duration, particularly in the spring and fall and during inclement weather, darkness often prevented the completion of the contest. Savvy captains and managers of teams who were losing such games often used deliberate delaying tactics to prevent the game from continuing, thus preventing a loss. In a close contest with Chicago in early June that had experienced a rain delay, Ewing successfully directed his men to deliberately delay beyond the 30-minute rain-delay allowance (presumably granted by the umpire), thereby causing the game to be called and arousing the ire of the White Stockings' manager/captain, Cap Anson.

> The game on the Polo Grounds between the New-Yorks and the Chicago club yesterday was called in the beginning of the fifth inning on account of rain. At this point the score stood 3–2 in favor of the Chicago players, and they tried every scheme to play the five innings, which would constitute a game. The New-York players, however, were equal to the emergency, and to the delight of the spectators and the disgust of Capt. Anson, delayed the game until the time allowance in case of rain had expired.[47]

One further Ewing attribute was revealed during the 1883 season. It is a trait never previously noted in the brief biographical portraits published on his life and career, but one that was an essential element of his ballplayer persona. Ewing was an inveterate "kicker," which in the baseball parlance of the era meant that he constantly questioned and critiqued the performance of the umpire. It did not take him long in 1883 to display such behavior. In the second game of the season he was fined ten dollars by Umpire Decker for disputing a decision. Although often criticized in the press, "kicking" became a persistent component of Ewing's baseball strategy. Moreover, as we shall see, it was a tactic that often achieved its aim.

In his first year with the New York club, Ewing had established himself as a steady hitter and long-ball threat, a versatile all-around athlete who could play multiple positions at a major-league level of competence, an outstanding catcher with a strong and accurate arm, and an able field captain who was not above using subterfuge and intimidation to achieve his goals. Turning 24 at the end of the season, he must have had occasion to look back with amazement at the combination of talent, circumstance and serendipity that had brought him from the sandlots of Pendleton to the gaslights of Broadway in just four years.

In early October, Buck accepted an offer to play winter ball in New Orleans on a picked nine composed of some of the greatest league stars, including Mike Kelly, Fred Pfeffer and George Gore from Chicago, Jim Whitney from Boston, and Hoss Radbourn of Providence. Ewing's inclusion among such players meant that he had been accepted in an elite fraternity. The Cincinnati Kid had arrived.

The 1880s were a period of profound, turbulent change in baseball, and 1884 was no exception. The National League and the American Association enjoyed a year of peace after the signing of the National Agreement before a rival league rose up that year to test their baseball monopoly.

The Union Association was the brainchild of Henry Lucas, a genial St. Louis railroad millionaire and amateur player. Lucas had a passion for baseball and believed the reserve rule was unfair. He convinced a group of investors to found the new league, placing teams in six cities that already had either National League or American Association teams, a seventh nine in Washington, D.C., and an eighth in the unlikely location of Altoona, Pennsylvania. Lucas owned the St. Louis entry, signed the best players whom he could convince to jump from the National League or the American Association to staff it, and built lavish grounds for the squad on his estate outside St. Louis. His team, nicknamed the Maroons, finished the season with a 94–19 record, and was so superior to its competition that it succeeded in killing any interest in Union Association games by mid-summer.

The Union Association folded after its inaugural season. Lucas, who later went bankrupt after another unsuccessful baseball venture, spent his last years earning $75 a month while working for the St. Louis Department of Streets. Despite the failure of the Union Association, player discontent over the reserve clause would continue to simmer for another five years, and then come to a boil in 1890 with the founding of the Players' League.

In late November 1883, while Ewing was in New Orleans playing with the National League picked nine, a report surfaced in the *New York Times* indicating that he was giving serious consideration to an offer to join Henry Lucas' Union Association Maroons. Under the headline, "A Baseball Catcher in Great Demand," the item asserted that

> Buck Ewing, the high priced catcher of the New-York League base-ball team, is negotiating with the new [Union Association] St. Louis Club. Letters from here were seen to-day, and as the terms which he named are acceptable, he will in all probability be engaged immediately by T.P. Sullivan [Ireland-born outfielder Ted Sullivan, manager of the Union Association St. Louis Maroons], the new St. Louis Club's agent, who is now playing with Ewing in the South. This will be news to the managers of the New-York Club, who have placed Ewing on their reserved list.[48]

Further details and corroboration were not forthcoming, and Ewing returned to New York to play in 1884. Perhaps Ewing was just being polite to his barnstorming teammate Sullivan, agreeing to hear him out on what the St. Louis Maroons could offer. Or perhaps "Bread and Butter Buck" was just living up to his nickname, and planned to use any Union Association offer as a bargaining chip in salary negotiations with the Gothams' owners. Ewing's penchant for exploring independently all possible options for his future would earn him the enmity of some players and news journals during the brief Players' League rebellion of 1890.

The legalization of overhand pitching in 1884 further shifted the advantage from the hitter to the pitcher in the National League, and, as previously mentioned, batting averages plunged on almost every team as a consequence. As a sop to the hitter, the number of balls required for a walk was reduced from seven to six. The three-year period of 1884–1886 became the most dangerous era for a batter in the game's history. During these years overhand pitchers were throwing to helmet-less hitters from a pitcher's box whose front line was just 50 feet from home plate.

When New York slid into the second division in 1883, attendance at the Polo Grounds dropped dramatically and remained at low levels for the rest of the season. Consequently, John Day and Jim Mutrie took drastic action in 1884 to try to improve their National League team and win back fans. John Clapp was relieved of his duties as manager in May and sent back to the Metropolitans. His place was filled by James L. Price, a Major in the New York Militia with no baseball experience. He appears to have served as a figurehead, since Jim Mutrie, while still managing the Metropolitans, had become increasingly involved in the affairs of the New York National League team. Manager Price proved to be a poor choice, and after twice having been discovered stealing from the team's cash receipts, he was fired late in the season and control of the team's business affairs was handed over to John Ward.

Ward also replaced Buck Ewing as team captain in 1884. Day and Mutrie apparently concluded that since the former Providence ace had more experience, he could better enforce team policies, especially among veteran players. The debonair Ward also moved effortlessly among New York's social and cultural elite, and could be expected to attract new fans from this milieu to the ball park. The cordial but intense rivalry between Ward and Ewing that arose as a result of this change continued for more than a decade.

Some of Day and Mutrie's other changes seemed less reasonable. Once again the owners had to contend with the fact that, due to the Reserve Clause, they had no ability to attract quality veteran players. To spell Mickey Welch and the fading pitching arm of John Ward, they hired Manhattan-born rookie Ed Begley, who would go 12–18 before being shipped off to the Mets. Mutrie signed 27-year-old Alex McKinnon, who had been expelled from the league for contract jumping and later reinstated, as a replacement for Roger Connor at first base. McKinnon would hit .272 and register the league's lowest fielding average at the position after making 53 errors. The left-handed Connor was shifted about in the infield and outfield, and his batting average dropped 40 points. Utility man Danny Richardson, the third new face on the team, hit .253 in 1884, while alternating between shortstop and the outfield on a substitute basis. Popular with Polo Grounds fans, Richardson would eventually find a home at second base and help lead the team to its first pennant.

In May, former Troy team members briefly reunited with Bob Ferguson when the old veteran "was engaged to cover second base"[49] for New York. Two weeks later Ferguson left to become manager/captain of the American Association Pittsburg [*sic*] Alleghenies without having played an inning for the Gothams. His tenure in Pittsburg was brief. In September he made his debut at the Polo Grounds as a National League umpire in a game in which the home team defeated Detroit, 11–3.

Transportation issues in 1884 at times hindered the Gothams' play, and occasionally even left them without the means to take the field. After playing a listless game at Providence in late May, a news account of the contest explained that "the Providence boys had ridden in the [railroad] cars from 3 o'clock yesterday afternoon until 5 this morning, and were too tired to exert themselves. The New-Yorks were on the same train, and also lacking sleep, were not in a condition to play brilliantly."[50]

The Gothams' final stop on the way home from a long Western trip in late June and early July was in Philadelphia. The team arrived on time, but their uniforms did not. Roger Connor had packed one in his personal luggage, and Danny Richardson borrowed a white uniform from the Philadelphia club. The rest of the team was reduced to borrowing "a set of uniforms from the Cincinnati Unions," whose color was described as "crushed mud."[51]

Given the new overhand throwing rules in 1884, some hitters found it more difficult to dodge errant, potentially dangerous pitches. "While at bat in the sixth inning [Mickey] Welch was hit on the head with a pitched ball with such force as to render him senseless. He fell like a log and for some time it was thought that he was seriously injured. After a few spasmodic kicks, he regained consciousness, and was assisted to his feet, but was unable to pitch and Begley [*sic*] took his place."[52]

Buck Ewing's year began with some personal bad luck. A month after his return from the winter baseball season in New Orleans to his East End home in Cincinnati, located near the banks of the Ohio River, the *Cleveland Herald* reported that "Buck Ewing was a flood sufferer, his home in Cincinnati being covered to the eaves."[53]

During the course of the 1884 season Ewing was forced to "lay off" on numerous occasions due to sore hands. His injuries were the direct result of the increased pitching speed after the legalization of the overhand motion, and the lack of protection provided by the flimsy gloves used before the introduction of the catcher's mitt. His batting average tumbled to .275, the last time it would fall below .300 for a decade. Ewing's other offensive statistics, however, equaled those of the previous year, and in one category — triples — his total rose from 13 to 20, enough to lead the league.

When not catching, Ewing played shortstop, third base, left and right field, and made his New York debut as a pitcher. During the pre-season, a

Buck Ewing and New York team mascot Willie Breslin circa 1884. Human mascots were considered good luck charms by many early players, and Ewing was almost always involved personally in their recruitment during his career (courtesy National Baseball Hall of Fame Library, Cooperstown, New York).

successful pitching outing had evoked high praise: "Ewing ... twirled the ball ... in a manner that clearly showed him to be fully competent to take charge of any of the nine positions."[54] He lost the only official game he pitched in 1884 to Chicago by a score of 3–2, working eight innings, striking out three, walking four, and allowing only one earned run. Reports of his effort were favorable. "Ewing pitched for the New-Yorks, and with the exception of giving men bases on called balls, he proved very successful."[55]

Ewing's work behind the plate and the power of his strong arm to intimidate would-be base stealers continued to garner praise. "Ewing caught and filled the position behind the bat in a manner that is seldom witnessed. He had no occasion to throw to the bases, as none of the Boston men attempted to steal them, but his work as a backstop and a batter was frequently applauded."[56]

Two years before the stolen base was recognized officially as a statistic, fans and the press were also realizing in 1884 that in addition to being a fine hitter and fielder, Ewing was both a speedy and a crafty base runner. In the sixth inning of an August contest with Buffalo, for example, Ewing and John Ward pulled off a picture-perfect delayed double steal. Ewing was on third base and Ward on first.

> When the latter cooly walked toward second, [catcher] Rowe threw the ball to [second baseman] Richardson, and Ewing started for home plate. In trying to catch him, Richardson threw the ball too high and the catcher of the New-York club scored. This clever piece of base running was applauded.[57]

The run that Ewing scored proved to be the difference in the 3–2 win for New York.

In a June game against Buffalo, Ewing stole three successive bases, including home. "He was sent to first on called balls, stole around to third and then had the rare nerve to tackle home plate with [catcher] Myers close up. The very daring attempt carried him through, and he scored amid the laughter and the cheers of the spectators."[58]

In spite of Ewing's troubling injuries and lower batting average, the season was not without its lighter moments for him and the Polo Grounds fans. As sly as he was on the field, for example, it was still possible to (literally) "get his goat."

> Buck Ewing, who is a great admirer of dogs, was promised a handsome Newfoundland while in Worcester. It was to be sent express, and Buck told all Harlem about his fine dog. The crate arrived last week, and instead of finding a dog, it contained a long-legged, skinny goat, which was taken upon the field and presented to Ewing during the progress of the game by a very funny-looking little boy who greatly resembled a spider. The goat has since been presented to Manager Price's young son, who utilizes him as drawing power for a little cart.[59]

In winter, 1884, Buck Ewing turned 25. Having started the 1880s as a Sunday-only semi-pro player, he would ring in 1885 as the toast of Manhattan and one of the National League's highest-paid stars. The best, however, was yet to come.

Chapter 3

One of a Kind

"The great and only Buck..." — O. P. Caylor, *Sporting News,* August 13, 1892

Standing five feet, ten-and-a-half inches in height, Buck Ewing was considered a tall player for his era. In his prime he carried 180 pounds on a medium frame. Playing winter ball regularly helped keep his weight steady, but after his marriage in 1889 he remained in Cincinnati at the end of the regular season and usually gained 10 to 15 pounds, which he worked diligently to shed every spring through daily steam baths and running. In his last full season, 1896, he was just seven pounds over his original playing weight.[1]

A rare action photo of Ewing jumping high in the air for a ball reveals that his legs and trunk were slender, with the bulk of his weight distributed through his shoulders. It was a body designed for speed and agility, and not for the punishment he would endure behind the plate. Persistent, nagging injuries would hound him for his entire career.

Fair-skinned, with sandy hair, Ewing's protruding ears were the only exception to his otherwise regular features. Although he cultivated the bushy moustache popular during the 1880s, he refrained from twisting its ends into a handlebar shape — the sophisticated signature of the Victorian age. While players in most of the stylized portrait photographs of the period affected serious poses, Ewing's photographs frequently depict him with the faint wisp of a smile, hinting at his good nature.

As his fame increased in the 1880s, Ewing's personality, baseball skills, and knowledge of the game, as well as his foibles, became the subject of many sports commentaries. *Sporting Life* described him as "a game player ... who never quits until the last out."[2] His personality changed completely when the game was over.

Away from the ball field Ewing is as unassuming and modest as he is the reverse when in the best of the battle. He is a quiet man. He is not a student like [John] Ward or [Jim] O'Rourke [ballplayers who earned law degrees in the off-season]. He reads the newspapers religiously but somewhat superficially, his attention being chiefly arrested by sporting news. "Buck" is a great sport and an ardent admirer of the manly art [boxing] ... and is considered to be quite handy with the gloves himself. He is fond of games of chance and a great theater goer. While not a total abstainer, he only indulges moderately. There are few ball-players who are steadier or who take better care of themselves than William Ewing.[3]

Ewing's favorite game of chance was poker, at which he excelled. "He could gather more on a pair of deuces than the man who invented the game."[4] Some fellow ball players once conspired to show him up at his specialty, only to find themselves tricked by "Bread and Butter" Buck.

One Saturday evening at Philadelphia's Continental Hotel, Ewing's poker-playing friends hired Herrmann the Magician, a vaudevillian and "playing-card wizard," to sit in on a game and beat Ewing. At the start of the evening, Ewing made an unusual request: "he insisted on money being played. He said he was superstitious on Saturday nights ... and wouldn't stand for [poker] chips."[5]

As the game progressed, the other players gradually withdrew, leaving Ewing and the magician to fight it out between themselves. Ewing lost steadily, and finally quit. As he rose to leave, Herrmann revealed his identity, saying, "This whole thing was a joke on you. I dealt the cards to suit myself.... I always knew what you held and simply took your money as I pleased."[6] As he counted out the $50 he had won from Ewing and handed it back to him, Ewing indignantly refused to accept the money and left the room. The other players were delighted to have tricked the great catcher and looked forward to kidding him about being duped.

It was the players and the magician, however, who had been taken in by Ewing. Having gotten word beforehand of the plot and the magician's identity, he put on a fine performance while turning the situation in his favor by substituting counterfeit bills for the real ones during the game. "That's why he wouldn't play with chips. He had got hold of some of the queer stuff [counterfeit bills] and after winning Herrmann's good money, held it out and passed over the phonies [bills] when Herrmann began to gather [win]."[7]

At the height of his popularity in the late 1880s, *Sporting News* succinctly summarized the difference between the great catcher's on-field persona and his true nature: "Buck in uniform, from a distance, looks like a very rough individual, but he is just the opposite, being one of the most obliging men you could find in a day's work."[8] All bets were off, however, if you ever tried to put one over on him in a poker game.

Throughout his career, "Bread and Butter" Buck was described as a man who was careful with his money. "As Buck is not a spendthrift, he is generally credited with having a good sized nest egg in the bank."[9] Nevertheless, he also could exhibit considerable largess in his spending habits. After his Reds team swept a series from Cleveland in 1895, for example, every member of the Cincinnati nine was "wearing a new, stylish derby hat. True to his promise that if the team would win three straight from Cleveland, he would give each player a new hat, Ewing marshaled his players and marched them to a Fourth Street establishment. Including himself, there were 18 in his party, and it took $90 to settle his hat bill."[10]

Comments — including his own — about his hitting, fielding, running, and his run-ins with umpires were frequent in newspapers and sports journals during his prime. While hitting, for example, it was noted that Ewing's "position at the plate is easy. In waiting for the ball he swings his bat up and down and hits out at the ball mostly from the wrists.... His great forte is hitting to right field."[11] He considered footwork and timing in meeting the ball to be more important than the power of the swing:

> Footwork has as much to do with successful batting as it has in pugilism. A player who steps away from the plate as he swings at the ball can be put down as an easy victim for an "out curve," and it is a pitcher with a very poor head who does not serve up out curves in profusion to such a batter.... A great mistake made by many players, both professional and amateur, is to imagine that they are obliged to swing fiercely at the ball to make it travel fast and far. There was never a bigger mistake. The whole secret of successful batting is in timing the ball so as to meet it squarely with force.... If you are an instant late or an instant too soon you will lose the driving power to your blow. It all lies in the step a batter takes in going forward to meet the ball.... By just meeting the ball ... a player can master the art of placing the ball with much greater ease than by a terrific blind swing. The latter way is bound to throw a man off his balance and to get his eye off the ball. Pitchers are always on to the free swingers or "swipers" and will change their pace on such batters, dishing up slow "lobs" and swift ones in the most perplexing profusion.[12]

The length of the bat that Ewing used to produce his offensive numbers is of historic significance. In 1869, maximum bat length was set at 42 inches. Baseball historians have assumed — perhaps with right reason — that while this rule remains on the books today, "it is pretty much moot, as no major leaguer is known ever to have used a bat that long."[13] However, an 1885 game account reveals not only that Ewing was using a bat that was 3½ feet long, but also that he was doing so to good effect:

> There were very few in the vast assemblage that didn't either clap their hands, stomp their feet, or in some way demonstrate their kindly interest in the Cincinnati boy [Ewing] the first time he shouldered his big forty-two inch second-

growth ash and started for the rubber [home plate].... Three balls and one strike were called, and then Buck sent the blood coursing through the veins of his admirers.... He brought his bat around with a terrific swish and the next instant the regulation Spalding [baseball] was speeding through the air with a through ticket to centre field. It carried on the fly to the embankment, not a foot from the bottom of the fence. It was a great hit, and Buck made two bases on it.[14]

Photographs of Ewing holding his bat suggest that he was able to use such a long piece of lumber successfully because its barrel was much smaller in width than the typical bat of the period.

Although — as we shall see — Ewing hit many memorable long-distance home runs, he was also a fine bunter. At a time when bunting was often criticized, he respected those who could successfully produce what the press dismissed as "baby hits:" "Buck Ewing says that men who can bunt the ball should be appreciated, as few of the many players can do it as it should be done.[15]

He attributed much of his hitting success to his ability to read the "signals" in a pitcher's delivery and to steal signs from the catcher:

There are only four or five pitchers in the league who can fool us [the Cincinnati Reds] on the sort of ball they are going to pitch.... The experience of many years is calculated to make a good mind reader of a man. The signs of nearly all the pitchers are no mystery to me. I can tell you just what sort of ball most of them intend to pitch me. The signals of the catcher are an aid to a batsman. Cy Young hasn't a ball I can't solve. This art of batting is all a matter of getting your natural pose and a clear swing at the ball.[16]

Boston Globe sportswriter Tim Murnane, himself a veteran of National Association and National League play, affirmed that Ewing was adept at hitting almost any pitch, and hitting it hard: "'Buck can kill a straight or curve ball; the latter he can meet and place out to right field as good as any man I ever saw."[17] John B. Foster, sportswriter for the *New York Evening Telegram* and later editor of *Spalding's Official Baseball Guide*, suggested that a curve ball in the right spot was the only remedy for keeping him off the bases: "He simply murdered the ball.... [His] weakness was a low curve around the knee. He would always go after it, and the pitcher who could keep the ball far enough out would send Ewing back to the bench."[18]

While endorsing the use of the sacrifice in a "tight pinch near the end of the game, when one run is absolutely necessary,"[19] late in his career, Ewing claimed that his offensive play of choice was the hit-and-run.

I am not opposed to sacrifice hitting ... but I believe it is being carried to an excess, and that more chances to score runs are being thrown away by its use than are ever scored following it.... I believe in training players to hit to right field. Then play the hit and run game. Have the batter hit just as the runner starts to steal second. The second baseman will leave his position to cover second, and often times the hit will go safe. It is rare that a double [play] can be made off it. I'll admit that the sacrifice is the surest way of advancing the runner, but it almost always [is] an out and does not afford the percentage for a batting rally that the hit and run game does. I believe in sacrifices when a run is imperative or when you have a good lead and want to clinch your place, but I don't believe in sacrificing in the earlier stages of the game when there is a chance to win the game by legitimate playing.[20]

Such observations, made in 1896, contrast with Ewing's own remarkable sacrifice record with Cleveland in 1893. That season he once sacrificed three times in a game,[21] and ended the year with a total of 35, a record that drew praise from *Sporting Life*: "Ewing played for his team, his purpose being always to advance the base runners."[22]

Besides hitting the long ball, moving runners along with the hit-and-run play, or dropping down an occasional sacrifice bunt, Ewing at times employed unusual strategies at the plate. These included striking out deliberately on a passed ball, and purposely being called out for refusing to run to first base. In a tie game against Chicago at the Polo Grounds, for example, Ewing was at bat in the eighth inning with two strikes against him, when

a ball pitched by Clarkson came skimming along the ground. Ewing struck at it and started for first base. The ball passed Sutcliffe, the catcher, and the base runner continued on his journey to second base. Another passed ball followed and Ewing added third base [to his steal tally]. Gillespie then hit a short ball to left field out of Dalrymple's reach, and Ewing scored the winning run amid great applause.[23]

In an 1886 game whose completion was threatened by rain, and with New York ahead, 4–1, Ewing was called out for not running out a ground ball. The newspaper account of the subsequent victory explained that "He [Ewing] did this purposely, as it was raining, and he wanted to finish the fifth inning."[24] Summarizing Ewing's overall offensive prowess, C. F. Mathison, New York correspondent for *Sporting Life*, issued a challenge to the baseball world: "If there is anybody in America that can beat Buck Ewing hitting the ball with or without men on bases, the latter preferred, let him be trotted out."[25]

The hallmarks of Buck Ewing's catching were his radically new stance behind the batter — the crouch — and his strong, accurate snap-throw to the bases. Beginning in 1880, Ewing's first year in the National League, a new rule requiring that third-strike foul tips be caught on the fly forced catchers to move closer to the batter. Exactly how close is a matter of speculation, since the stance a typical catcher took — a stoop — did not allow him to come too close, for fear of interfering with the hitter's swing. Catching close-in increased the chance of injury, and at the time, the only protection a catcher had was an unpadded mask and skintight gloves on both hands. In 1883, Detroit's Charlie Bennett introduced a chest protector made of cork, and the following year, inflatable protectors debuted.

Baseball historian William Curran affirms that Buck Ewing was the first catcher to position himself behind the plate in a crouch.[26] Curran's assertion is confirmed by a Ewing contemporary, Billy Sunday, the Chicago White Stockings outfielder-turned-evangelist.[27] In addition to allowing better positioning for catching third-strike foul tips, crouching close to the batter enabled the catcher to provide an exceptional target for the pitcher. It also allowed him to "frame" the pitch in an attempt to influence the umpire — that is, pull a ball that was not a strike into the strike zone.

The primary disadvantage of the crouch was the same as that of catching close in — greater susceptibility to injury. After Ewing was struck on the finger by a foul tip in an 1884 game, for example, the *New York Times* complained that he was "playing too close to the bat."[28] At first glance, catching from the crouch would also seem to be disadvantageous when attempting to throw out advancing base runners, since a catcher normally had to rise from the crouch to a "stoop" position in order to throw the ball. Unlike his contemporaries, however, Buck Ewing possessed the ability to throw to bases with a snap throw while remaining in the crouch. A decade would pass before another backstop, Marty Bergen of Boston, was able to imitate Ewing in this manner.

When Ewing signed with Troy in 1881, manager Bob Ferguson initially was not fully aware of the power of his back-up catcher's throwing arm. Ewing recalled that Ferguson discovered it during a game at Worcester while playing second base when he himself was catching.

> It was while playing with the Troys that I made my first great impression on Bob Ferguson, then manager and second baseman of the club, as a hard thrower. It was in 1881 and we went down to Worcester to open the season. It was cold and windy, and I had to throw against the wind. It would cut the ball's progress so that it always came down low and nailed Bob in the shins. About the fifth inning Bob came in and said in the most serious manner in the world — "William, throw them high, out in centre field. I want to go home alive."[29]

Pitcher Tim Keefe was in a unique position to comment on Ewing's throws to second base. After he came over to the New York National League team from the Metropolitans, Ewing became his regular battery mate. When George E. Stackhouse, sports editor of the *New York Tribune*, asked Keefe if he was afraid of being hit by Ewing's "lightning throw" to second base while in Ewing's direct line of fire, Keefe replied,

I was nervous for a time but soon got over it. When I saw that a man was going to start to steal second, I always delivered the ball as quickly as possible and then stood perfectly still. That remaining like a statue was the only thing that saved my life. Ewing could grab that ball and send it down to second without looking. He had placed in his mind just where the ball must go to do the most good before he received it and the instant it touched his mitt it was off. Ewing used a slight curve in throwing to the bases, and the curve was just enough to allow the ball to whistle past my right ear and land a few inches in front of second base.[30]

Of Ewing's throwing prowess, fellow catcher Connie Mack observed[31] that some receivers of the period could catch runners napping at first base, but Ewing could catch them napping at second base. Ewing once accomplished both of these feats in the space of two games during a series with Boston. On July 23, 1888, he gunned down inattentive shortstop Sam Wise at first base. The following day he caught pitcher Kid Madden napping off second. Ewing repeated the latter feat once in unusual fashion, to the embarrassment of the White Stockings' Cap Anson. In 1887, Anson traded his star center fielder, George Gore, to New York, and while Gore was content to play in the Big Apple, he wanted to take revenge on Anson for the trade. Accordingly, during a game at the Polo Grounds, after Anson had doubled and was taking his lead off second, Gore, on a signal from Ewing, began sneaking in behind Anson from center field.

Then, all of a sudden, with the signals working in absolute harmony, Gore was seen to race directly to the second base, and Ewing, having started his throw the moment Gore raced toward the bag, the big Chicago captain was trapped. Ewing's throw was a perfect one, and, as the astonished Anson plunged toward the base, Gore was waiting for him with the ball.... Of course Gore was the happiest man in the ball park, for he had squared accounts with his old leader.[32]

Late in his career while managing the Reds, Ewing recalled another play at second base that he had perfected years earlier.

The modern catchers are all right when it comes to backstop work, but they are slow to take advantage of the points. It is hard to drill catchers into making a play that I used to sneak in pretty often with great success. Nine times out of ten when an outfielder throws to the plate after a base hit the runner keeps on to second [base]. I've tried to educate our catchers to size up the situation and if they figure that the play will be close at home to run and meet the ball and catch the runner at second base. Many is the player I've fooled with that trick, but how often do you see it now? Fans know how rare the old play has become.[33]

Fifteen years later, former Chicago third baseman Tom Burns cited a specific example of Ewing's use of this play:

It was Ewing who first ran onto the diamond to get a thrown ball from the outfield when [Mike] Kelly was sliding home, and whipped it back to second, clearing the base of runners. Ewing had figured that Kelly had eight chances out of ten in scoring because of his terrific twisting slide, and he took a chance of retiring the runner at second. The play has come down to our generation and is often used when the man coming home cannot be retired.[34]

Ewing's arm was so effective that examples abound of teams not even attempting to steal when he worked behind the plate: "the visitors, instead of taking every chance, stuck close to their bases and were afraid to leave them, so unerring was Ewing's arm"[35]; "Ewing's catching was greatly admired. So accurate was his throwing that not one of the local [Boston] men attempted to steal a base"[36]; "Ewing's unerring aim and swift throwing have a tendency to make them [the Washington club] hug their bases as closely as one would a cheerful stove on a blizzard night."[37]

An account of a game against Boston at the Polo Grounds in 1887 reveals well the extent of Ewing's ability as a catcher to intimidate the opposition. Early in the game, Jim O'Rourke had been doing the receiving while Ewing covered third base. Boston runners were taking liberties with O'Rourke, and in the eighth inning, with the most famous base stealer in the country, Mike Kelly, due to bat, Ewing went behind the plate:

> As Ewing put on the breast pad ... the spectators cheered heartily, while the delegation from Boston was correspondingly sad. The only Kelly [a Kelly nickname] made a base hit, but, knowing Ewing's ability as a thrower, he did not attempt to steal to second. As a result, a ball batted to [second baseman] Richardson by [Boston infielder Billy] Nash gave the New Yorks a double play and Boston was easily retired.[38]

Half in awe, half in consternation, Cap Anson noted another Ewing demonstration of magnificent throwing ability. The Chicago manager affirmed that Ewing used to toss the ball in front of the plate to give a runner a chance to start, and then throw him out without any trouble.[39] John McGraw confirmed Anson's statement: "Ewing had so much confidence in his throwing that I have seen him deliberately roll the ball away from him[self] just to tempt the base runner into a steal."[40] Few observers of the era would argue with *Boston Globe* reporter Tim Murnane's assertion that Ewing had "no superior when throwing to bases."[41]

In addition to introducing the crouch and the snap throw to major league baseball, Ewing is credited with introducing the catcher's mitt to the National League in 1888. Catchers like St. Louis's Doc Bushong had been experimenting with adding padding to the traditional left-hand glove since the early 1880s, and journeyman backstop Harry Decker patented a padded mitt that went into production in 1889.

Ewing's introduction of his own version of the padded mitt caused a sensation in New York. His first appearance with the glove,

> which looked for all the world like a big boxing glove crushed out flat by a road roller, caused a shout of laughter from the assemblage, but when the game was over Buck declared that his hand was not swollen a particle, and that thereafter nothing could tempt him to relinquish his new guard to his big left hand. All through that season Buck wore the glove, and soon it was recognized as indispensable in the paraphernalia of the big back stop.[42]

The timing of this development was not surprising, given "the sheer number of debilitating hand injuries resulting from overhand deliveries by pitchers.... It was one thing to encourage a catcher to shake off a blow to the head or chest, but a catcher with an injured hand was liable to hurt his team by his inability to throw to the bases or otherwise fulfill the other duties of his position."[43] Necessity, in this case, really was the mother of invention.

Accepting the padded mitt for use, however, was not a simple proposition for receivers, since doing so required them to accept a completely new method of catching. In the old style, the receiver used the partially-protected fingers of both hands to make the catch. In the new style, receivers had to learn to catch the ball in the palm of one hand, which was protected by the thickly-padded mitt. This change of technique was quickly adopted by Ewing and most other catchers, and by 1890, a padded "Buck Ewing" model mitt was being advertised by sporting goods companies. Switching to the mitt enabled Ewing to catch more games between 1888 and 1890—his last three years of full-time service as a receiver—than in any period of similar length in his career. His regular presence behind the plate in 1888 and 1889, as we shall see, was a major factor in New York's first pennants and world championships.

Another Ewing catching strategy was to study opposing hitters' swings and share the information gathered with his battery mate to try to gain an advantage. "Buck Ewing could point with his finger the batting weaknesses of every player in the National League."[44] He also liked to distract hitters while they were at the plate by striking up conversations with them. Ewing was "known to engage the batter in conversation for no other purpose than to throw him off his stride."[45] This strategy is aptly illustrated by a conversation he once engaged in with Bill Lange, when the Chicago outfielder stepped into the batter's box:

> "Say Bill, that a swell dame I saw you with yesterday," said Buck as Bill stepped to the plate.
> "One strike," shouted the umpire, as Tim Keefe shot the ball over the plate.
> "Any man ought to be proud walking along the street with a fine looking girl like that," continued Ewing.
> "Two strikes," shouted the umpire.

"By the way, Bill, she's in the grandstand now, right back of you," remarked Ewing.

"Three strikes and out," shouted the umpire, as Keefe shot the ball across the plate, while Lange had his head turned, looking for the girl in the grandstand.[46]

When playing behind the plate, Ewing was frequently criticized for employing another strategy that was deemed unsportsman-like. While awaiting a throw from the outfield, he tried to hinder a runner advancing to home by placing his mask on the baseline near the plate. As a result, the runner either was prevented from sliding, tripped on the mask, or at the very least, was forced to hesitate for a second to adjust his stride to avoid the obstacle in the base path. "In the third inning [Pittsburgh's] Miller hurt himself by falling over Ewing's mask at the plate, and the crowd hissed the New York catcher for having, as they believed, purposefully placed it there."[47] Unprofessional as such an action might appear to some today, Ewing was thinking of self-preservation as much as trying to prevent a run from scoring.

In 1878, a new rule was introduced "which clarified that the fielder had to hold on to the ball after applying the tag."[48] As a result, more runners began deliberately colliding with catchers and infielders in an attempt to cause them to drop the ball. After 1883, a catcher's upper body was shielded by a chest protector from such an onslaught, but his legs were not, since shin guards were not introduced until 1907. Additionally, some runners proved to be more menacing than others. In a game between St. Louis and Chicago in 1886, for example, six-foot, two-inch Cap Anson was on third base when Tom Burns hit a fly ball to right field, which was caught and thrown back to catcher George Myers. The lumbering Anson looked to be an easy out, but instead of stopping or sliding, he "went up into the air and threw the force of his 210 pounds against George Myers' 150 pounds. Myers was knocked almost senseless ten feet or more away from the home plate, but pluckily held on to the ball, thus retiring the side. Myers has not yet recovered from the severe shock."[49]

Although Ewing's strategy of leaving his mask on the baseline often helped him avoid such collisions, runners like Indianapolis's Marty Sullivan at times attempted to foil his plan.

Martin Sullivan did spoil Buck Ewing's favorite mask ... and he did it in a manner that created some amusement. The New York Captain has a habit, when there are men on bases, of throwing his beauty protector on the third base line. This inevitably prevents the runner from sliding home, but Ewing finds this particular place the most convenient spot for his mask. In the fourth inning, Myers, Sullivan and Hines were on third, second and first respectively. Bassett smashed a single to left field and Ewing's mask was on the base line in a twinkling. Hines came home safely and Sullivan was making a mighty effort to score from second. Barrister [Jim] O'Rourke [the leftfielder] got the ball, and made a short but accurate throw to the base, and Ewing caught Sullivan about the time that the former Chicagoan discovered the mask. It had prevented him from sliding, and to show his contempt for masks in general and Ewing in particular, he jumped on the cage with both feet, smashing it flat as a pumpkin. Hostilities were then suspended until a new armor [mask] could be procured.[50]

Ewing had lost his mask, but its strategic placement had achieved its aim, for the runner was tagged out.

When Ewing was healthy but not playing behind the plate, he played first base — or second base, third base, shortstop, or any outfield position. He even occasionally appeared in the pitcher's box. Ewing and fellow Hall of Famer Mike Kelly are the only major leaguers who have played at least 25 games at catcher, played every infield and outfield position, and who also pitched.[51]

Ewing appeared as a receiver in a little more than half his career games (636). The bulk of his remaining appearances were spent either at first base (253 games) or in the outfield — primarily in right field (235 games). Next in frequency were his appearances at third base (127 games), second base (51 games), shortstop (34 games) and pitcher (9 games). There are abundant references of both praise and criticism for his performance at each position. His best defensive performances, when not behind the plate, were at first and in the outfield, where his fielding percentages (.974 and .914) rank him at about the mid-point of his contemporaries. He was less successful at the other infield positions, although his fielding average at third base in 1882 (.887) — while achieved in just 44 games — was the highest in the league.

On the infrequent occasions when no pitcher was healthy or otherwise available, Ewing went into the pitcher's box. While his record there was not outstanding, his successes were celebrated in the press.

> With Welch sick, Crane injured, and George and Titcomb out of condition, the Giants were without a pitcher today. Captain Ewing, however, was equal to the emergency. He resolved to do some "curving" himself, and put big Bill Brown behind the bat [as catcher]. When the Boston players saw New-York's Captain in the [pitcher's] box, they regarded the undertaking as a huge joke and got themselves in readiness to lose the ball [hit]. But they didn't. Ewing remained there for nine innings, and although the Boston men hit the ball at times very hard, Captain Ewing of the Giants would not surrender his position, and to the intense discomfort of the 5,900 spectators in the South End Grounds, piloted his club to victory.[52]

Ewing was good enough to have made it to the major leagues playing almost any position, and as we shall see, his peers considered him the greatest all-around player of his era.

Prior to 1886, stolen bases were not counted officially as game statistics.

Consequently, steals usually were noted in the press only in extraordinary circumstances, such as Ewing's steal of home in 1884, or Chicago newspaper reports of George Gore's seven stolen bases in a game in June 1881. Ewing averaged 35 steals per year during the ten full seasons he played after the stolen base was officially recognized. Given his penchant for thievery late in his career, it is reasonable to assume that his early (1880–1885) career steal average matched his later statistics. An 1885 note in *Sporting Life* lends credence to this supposition: "One seldom hears praise for Buck Ewing's base running, and in that particular *he is excelled by few in the profession and none on the New York nine*, as he is fully the equal of Johnny Ward; lacking a trifle of his speed, perhaps, but using as good, if not better judgment"[53] [author's emphasis].

As we have seen, Ewing studied pitchers' deliveries not only to take advantage of the hurlers' weaknesses while facing them at the plate, but also while running the bases. Late in his career, he revealed that he likewise studied the techniques of professional sprinters to improve his base-stealing ability.

> I do not think you can teach a player to become a fast runner. That would be laying claim to something that is impossible. You cannot teach base running. You can take a player so far, but he must plan his leads and starts and do the rest of it. You can improve a base runner's chances by practicing. The success of a player in stealing bases depends chiefly on the kind of start he gets. One foot lost in getting off, a fraction of a second wasted in getting a lead, may prove fatal to your chance at the end of a steal. To be a good base runner you must be going at top speed with the very first step.... If you have ever watched professional sprinters in their training, you will find that most of their time is devoted to getting off their mark.... I have watched some good short distance runners put in an hour of "breaking from the pistol shot." This is what gave me such a percentage in base running. I never was a very fast runner, but I could beat fast runners simply because I got the hunch [jump] on them in getting off their mark.[54]

Ewing's 53 steals in 1888 is the all-time season record for a catcher. Other stolen base records attributed to him are either overly generous or greatly underrate his achievements. *The Encyclopedia of Baseball Catchers*,[55] for example, gives Ewing the nod as the all-time leader in career stolen bases (354) by a receiver. In actuality, about half these bags were stolen while he was playing other positions. On the other hand, the same source credits Ewing with the most stolen bases in a game by a catcher — three. He did indeed steal three while fielding that position in a game — and he did it three times: once in 1888 and twice in 1889. He also stole three bags in a game on eight other occasions while playing other positions. At Boston in early June 1889, however, Ewing stole four bases off Hoss Radbourn and catcher Charlie Ganzel while behind the plate for New York, and he repeated the feat in 1890 while catching for the Players' League Giants. He stole four bases in a game on three other occasions in his career while playing other positions. Ewing's highest stolen base total in a game, nevertheless, exceeds even this number. On May 29, 1888, while taking a day off from catching and playing third base, he stole six bases off Washington's battery of pitcher Frank Gilmore and catcher Jeremiah Murray. This record, verified in game accounts in four different newspapers,[56] has not previously been reported.

Ewing's record of six stolen bases in a game places him in exclusive company. Only four other players have recorded as many steals in one contest: Eddie Collins (twice, in 1912), Otis Nixon (1991), Eric Young (1996), and Carl Crawford (2009). No other catcher has stolen more than three bases in a game, and no receiver has come close to Ewing's record for stolen bases in a season. Chicago's Mike Kelly was the most renowned base stealer of the 1880s. His famous thieving ways became the subject of a popular song, "Slide, Kelly, Slide!" published in 1889, which was an immediate national hit. After a game against Pittsburgh late in Ewing's career, the *Cleveland Plain Dealer* declared him the new base stealing king: "The term 'Slide Kelly Slide' now belongs to Buck Ewing. He will need a new pair of breeches after making three great slides [and successful stolen bases]."[57] Commenting on Ewing as a base stealer at the end of his career, *Sporting Life*'s John B. Foster concluded that "There has never been an example of more scientific base running."[58]

Superstitions among ballplayers are as old as baseball itself, and Buck Ewing was no exception to this rule. Often called "hoodoos" by nineteenth-century players, superstitions could be associated with animals, everyday objects, or humans. Boston's mascot for at least part of the 1886 season, for example, was a "small Maltese kitten."[59] The following year, catcher Charlie Bennett's soiled game shirt briefly served the same purpose for the team. A yellow mongrel dog was the good-luck charm for New York in 1886 until the team went on the road and the dog was captured, sent to the pound, and killed. "Mose," a ring-tailed monkey, was a simian talisman for Buck Ewing's Cincinnati Reds during the 1896 season, sharing the honor with a good-luck turtle that had been donated by a local fan.

A mascot's popularity typically was short-lived — when the team's performance went downhill they were soon discarded. Before a June 1889 contest with Cleveland, for example, Buck Ewing arrived at the Polo Grounds with a temporary mascot — a toy rubber dog that "barked" when squeezed.[60] New York beat Cleveland 17–6 that day, but after a few subsequent losses, the toy fell out of favor as a good-luck charm.

Modern baseball mascots disguised as such personages as the Philly Phanatic or the San Diego Chicken are objects of amusement and entertainment for fans, but are no longer valued by players as good luck charms. Until the

1930s, human mascots were still common in baseball. One of the most famous, Little Ray Kelly, was "discovered" by Babe Ruth in 1921, and remained Ruth's personal mascot intermittently for several years. Eddie Bennett, a sickly lad with a spinal deformity, was considered a lucky charm by both the White Sox and the Yankees during the same time period. Louis Van Zeist, a young hunchback, served as bat boy and mascot for early Philadelphia Athletics teams.[61] Such mascots satisfied the players' superstitious natures, contributed to the amusement of the fans, and provided sports writers with another rich topic for their columns.

During his years with the Giants, Buck Ewing was in the forefront in the recruitment of team mascots. They were all young boys, and their tenure ranged from the length of a home stand to several years. In 1885 for example, the *New York Times* noted "Ewing's mascotte [*sic*], the colored boy who is admitted to the Polo Grounds free of charge to satisfy the superstitions and the whims of the players."[62] In June 1886, the deceased yellow dog, mentioned previously, that had served as New York's mascot, was replaced by "Master Bretsie," a five-year-old boy who knows the rules of the game as well as the players.... Master Bretsie made his appearance on the field yesterday in the full uniform of a National League player."[63] During a mid-season home stand, Master Bretsie was replaced by a mascot known as Master Preston. Returning from a late-season Western tour and finding Master Preston absent from the Polo Grounds, a Giants representative took action.

> Since the return of the New-York Baseball Club, Master Preston, the mascot of the team, had not put in an appearance on the Polo Grounds. Some of the patrons and players were superstitious enough to believe that this was the cause of the club's poor playing. In order to settle the question, Joe Gerhardt, the guardian of the second base, induced Master Preston to play truant yesterday, and he appeared on the grounds in the full uniform of a New-York player. His appearance was greeted with cheers by the spectators and hailed with delight by the players.[64]

On the day of Master Preston's return, New York beat Washington, 4–1.

In mid–July 1888, New York was 4½ games behind first-place Chicago when the team arrived in the Windy City for a three-game series. During the first game, a 14-year-old, freckle-faced street urchin, Fred Boldt, attached himself to the team, but was rebuffed when the Giants lost the contest. After Tim Keefe won both the second and third games of the series, the squad had a change of heart.

> After the Giants lost the first game, they chased Fred away, but Keefe's two victories changed their minds. They slipped Fred on the train to Pittsburgh, where the Giants kept on winning. Fred had to ride the rails to get to Philadelphia, but he finally arrived and the Giants won again. During the remainder of

the road trip, the Giants lost only when Fred was absent. That was enough for Ewing, and he and some of the boys chipped in and fixed Fred up. They had him bathed, got his hair cut, and bought him some clothes. [John] Ward, who lacked the common touch, was one of those who did not contribute, but most of the boys thought that with Fred Boldt on the scene, the Giants could not lose.[65]

It would not have been surprising if Buck Ewing, reflecting on his own early years in Cincinnati, felt a special kinship with fellow Midwesterner Fred Boldt. Although Ewing's youthful circumstances were not as dire as those of the young Chicagoan, delivering barrels of whiskey to Cincinnati saloons at age 14 was far from an idyllic childhood. *The Sporting News* picked up the Fred Boldt story, added the detail that Buck Ewing had bought Fred "some shirts, shoes, and a hat," and then spun the tale as a humanitarian effort on the part of the team: "Aside from the Mascot part of it, the Giants have done the boy a good turn — no home, no parents, a waif on the streets was Fred Boldt. Now he is well-clothed, well-fed, and started, in a small way, in life. Superstition has saved a brand from burning and may start him on the road to make a man of himself."[66]

Fred Boldt *did* "make a man" of himself, as *Sporting Life* reported a month later, but not in the manner hoped for by *The Sporting News*: "New-York's much-lauded mascot from Chicago begged and borrowed clothes, ran up an account at a lunch counter near the Polo Grounds, stole Titcomb's shoes, and eloped."[67]

Thanks to the visual record of photography young Willie Breslin is today the most recognized of Buck Ewing's mascot-protégés (see page 48). The tiny Breslin, one of several Giants good-luck charms between 1884 and 1890, appeared dressed in full uniform with Ewing in a whimsical 1884 photograph, thus providing future generations a permanent visual reminder of the popularity of "hoodoos" and team mascots in baseball's early years. For a short time, Breslin became so famous that he was portrayed on his own Goodwin and Company tobacco card, where he was described simply as the "New York Mascot."

Any nineteenth-century receiver with an aggressive catching and base-running style and a penchant for playing year-round was prone to injuries. Ewing's injuries were so frequent, and on occasion so serious, that they became part of his baseball persona, and an object of concern, criticism, and at times ridicule by fans and sportswriters alike.

Injuries to Ewing's hands began in earnest in the mid–1880s, co-incident with the legalization of sidearm and overhand pitching motions and prior to the adoption of the catcher's mitt. Bone bruises, broken digits, and split fingers (the nail detached from the flesh) often forced him to the bench for days or sometimes weeks. The cumulative effect of such damage was described in an 1887 *Sporting Life* article: "Ewing thinks he will be able to play again within two weeks, but if he gets that horrible looking fist into natural shape in a month he will have accomplished considerable. I have seen some bad base ball bruises, but Ewing's hand is about the ugliest, bruised, battered and swollen fin [hand] I have seen in a long time."[68]

Despite such visible proof of damage to his hands, some suggested that on occasion Ewing pretended that his injuries were more serious in order to save himself for crucial games against significant opponents. Since, until 1889, the opposing team's captain or manager had to approve the substitution of a player for one injured on the other team, Ewing had to convince his rivals of the extent of his injuries in order to be able to leave the game. At times some observers simply did not believe his claims.

> It is "amoosin" [amusing] to see how rapidly Ewing's fingers recover from an injury. In the last Providence game he retired, saying that he wanted to be ready for "that Boston game the next day," which, by the way, was lost [by] the Bostons. In Friday's game, when the New-Yorks had lost the game, he "hurt his finger" again and let Loughran come in and catch, the Bostons consenting. Saturday, Ewing is again behind the bat, having saved his hand through the kindness of the Bostons, and with Welch again defeating the champions. The latter are wonderfully kind to Ewing. Other catchers stand their poundings.[69]

While there is little doubt that the wily Ewing would not hesitate to use a hand injury (or feigned hand injury) to his advantage in a game, his teammates could readily attest to the punishment he took behind the plate prior to the development of the catcher's mitt. Seeking to silence the rumor that Ewing did not play through injuries, Giants outfielder Mike Slattery stated, "I've heard it said in some quarters that Buck was not game. Well, if you saw the condition his hands were in some games he caught you would think he was as game as any man who ever played the game of baseball."[70]

In May 1886, Ewing sustained a serious leg injury — one that would return intermittently for the rest of his career: "Buck Ewing's injury is a strained tendon in his thigh. The hurt is likely to prove a tediously long time healing, and he may not be able to play for weeks. Meanwhile, he is treating himself with a galvanic battery and limping about idly, unable to practice or exercise."[71] Seven years later, when the injury recurred, Ewing gave another demonstration that he was, to use Mike Slattery's term, still "game." An 1893 *Cleveland Plain Dealer* article entitled "Gamey Ewing's Doings," lauded Ewing's performance in a contest against Pittsburgh: "Buck Ewing, whose game leg causes him to limp, made three singles, two runs, and stole two bases, and one was third [base], at that. That was quite a record for the hospital contingent of the nine."[72]

The most serious injury of Ewing's career — one that would effectively end his days as a catcher — occurred in early spring, 1891. While attempting one of his famous snap throws, his arm gave out, idling him until late July and causing him to take some desperate, and at times horrific, means to restore it. His subsequent inability to play aroused the ire of the press, who criticized his high salary and attributed the Giants' third-place finish to the team's refusal to release him.

> About all Buck Ewing does on the bench is to sit and smile and smile. As a smiler Buck has been the greatest success of the season.... New Yorkers blame the loss of the pennant to [on] the continued absence of Ewing.... Had they [the Giants management] dropped the big catcher, and thus restored harmony to the team, the coveted flag would probably once more wave over the Polo Grounds.[73]

Stung by such remarks and by the insinuation of ulterior motives, Ewing angrily responded, "Some critics are making cracks that I am holding off and waiting for the team to get in shape, and then I will jump in and do the catching, and the victories will be attributed to my presence on the team. This is maliciously false. If I could throw I would be behind the bat in every game, for I know how much the team needs me at this time."[74]

Ewing would not catch again until August of 1892, and after a month behind the plate in 1893, his catching career effectively ended. His remaining years in the National League were spent primarily at first base or right field. His detractors were quick to label him with a new nickname, "Glass Arm," to which was added "Glass Leg" whenever the tendon problems in his thigh flared up.

In addition to sore and broken fingers, strained or torn leg tendons and a bad arm, a fourth mysterious, recurring malady afflicted Buck Ewing intermittently for more than a dozen years while in the major leagues, although its presence and persistence is not readily apparent until the entire panorama of his career is reviewed. Beginning in 1886, Ewing was occasionally sidelined with what was vaguely described as "illness," in contrast to the term "injury," which was used to describe his hand, leg, and arm maladies. It was far more common for nineteenth-century players to be felled by illnesses than are modern players. Poor sanitary conditions, careless food preparation, lack of refrigeration and impure water usually were the culprits, and could occasionally have near-fatal consequences. In August 1893, for example, Philadelphia's Billy Hamilton was leading the league in hitting when he contracted typhoid fever from tainted water in Boston. He nearly died from the illness, and did not play again for the remainder of the season. In addition to such maladies, hard drinkers and carousers were frequently felled by hangovers or bouts of syphilis. The press rarely specified the cause of such "illnesses," or if they did, used cover terms such as "malaria" to refer to a broad spectrum of specific diseases or maladies.

While Ewing did occasionally suffer from the typical cold or toothache, he lived a temperate life and was never associated with the "rowdy" players who enjoyed burning the candle at both ends. Nevertheless he did experience intermittent bouts of a generalized "illness" that progressively worsened as he aged.

The first significant occurrence took place during the 1886 season as the Giants began a month-long trip to play their league rivals in the west. On August 18 at Washington, Ewing became "seriously indisposed, and the game was stopped for twenty minutes before he could take his place at the bat in the first inning."[75] The following day the team opened a series in Philadelphia, and Ewing did not play. He returned to action on August 20 and hit a home run to lead the Giants to a 12–3 win. The next day, however, he again left the game sick, and left the team to return to his home in Cincinnati. "Ewing did not accompany the team on the present trip on account of sickness."[76] On August 28, press reports indicated some suspicions with regard to the actual state of his health: "Ewing is still at home, and his long absence has caused a deal of dissatisfaction among the players, who say he is not as sick as he claims to be, and at their request Manager Mutrie to-day ordered him to report for duty at once.... [Jim] O'Rourke ... cannot be expected to do all the work [as catcher]."[77] After missing three games of the Kansas City series and three contests at St. Louis, Ewing rejoined the team in Detroit on September 1, caught the entire game and hit a home run. A few days later, he was again reported ill. "Ewing was unable to catch on account of sickness."[78] He remained out of the lineup until September 18, but afterward finished the season without incident.

While playing for Cincinnati a decade later, Ewing again experienced an illness that kept him out of the lineup for a significant period of time. In July 1896, after stealing a base in a 12–4 win against Washington that left the Reds in second place, Ewing became ill. "I'm not sick enough to go to bed, but for the last few days my stomach has troubled me. I felt too weak to play today. I suppose I will be all right tomorrow. It is a hot [pennant] race and I want to be in it all I can."[79] He took the field against Brooklyn on July 13, but soon had to withdraw. "I felt I was going to fall forward on my face. I was dizzy and sick at the stomach."[80] He attributed his illness to some "green corn" he ate in St. Louis, and affirmed that "Just as soon as my stomach settles, I will be in the game again."[81]

His "green corn" explanation is hardly plausible. Two series, one against Philadelphia and another with Washington, intervened between the end of the St. Louis series and the onset of his illness. In the three games against the

Phillies, he banged out five hits, scored four runs, and stole three bases — not the performance of a sick man. He managed two hits and a stolen base in the first two games against Washington before being taken ill.

After missing two more games, it became apparent that Ewing's illness had worsened.

> His ailment is much more serious than he thought it was. He was so weak when he reached the park yesterday morning [July 16], that he had to lie down. He made a couch in the dressing room and stayed on his back for two hours. He felt well enough ... to go out to the bench and direct the play of the team, but he was too sick to play. "I don't know what is the trouble," said Buck after the game. "For four days I have not eaten anything that would stay in my stomach. I am all right as long as I sit still, but the instant I begin to move about I begin to vomit. I am now under a physician's care but if I don't improve it will be some time before I can play ball again."[82]

Other than two games played against New York a week later in which he sacrificed twice, and participation in a few exhibition games against local Ohio teams in August, Ewing returned to the lineup only once during the remainder of the season.

The following year, 1897, Buck was not in the lineup on opening day, April 22, nor did he play in any contests during the remainder of the month. He did not accompany the Reds on their first road trip in early May, and the *Cincinnati Enquirer*, under the heading "Illness Keeps Buck Home," described the team captain and manager as being "under the weather."[83] As the Reds moved on to Pittsburgh on May 6, the news was still not encouraging: "Captain Buck Ewing is still confined to his bed with illness, and may not be able to join the team for several days."[84] Meanwhile, the Reds lost six straight, and were reported to be "in a chaotic condition" without their "leading spirit."[85]

Ewing returned to the bench on May 13, but clearly was not yet well. Reports of what had transpired during his illness were as vague as they were alarming.

> Captain Ewing was on the bench yesterday and directed the Reds' play. He is still weak from his recent sickness, but is on the road to recovery. His illness was very weakening and he lost considerable blood during his sickness. "I lost no less than twenty pounds during the nine days I was confined to the house.... However, my physician assures me I will have no further trouble if I but take reasonable care of myself. I don't know how soon I will be able to play."[86]

Eleven days later a report noted that "Captain Ewing will play first base [today] if he is able. He is almost entirely recovered from his recent sickness, except that he is liable to be seized with dizziness if he exercises too much."[87] Hope for his full recovery was short-lived: "Ewing made his promised appearance on first base. He was in no condition to play ball. He was sick. In a short time the dizziness that has given him trouble since his sickness was in evidence. He could not see the ball perfectly, and in the sixth inning he gave it up as a bad job and put Holliday in his place."[88]

Ewing went 0-for-1 and was hit by a pitch in those six innings, which were the last he would ever play. His explanation for his condition seems improbable, given the fact that nearly a month had transpired since the onset of the illness, and two weeks had passed since his return to the bench. "Captain Ewing said yesterday that his doctor had told him that the dizzy spells that interfere with his play are caused by the great loss of blood he sustained during his recent illness."[89]

From a modern standpoint, it is difficult to imagine an illness that would cause great loss of blood and a weight loss of 20 pounds in nine days, and yet not require hospitalization. The only logical conclusion is that Ewing was submitting to bloodletting procedures, which, although no longer a common or recommended practice, were apparently still being performed.

Ewing's mysterious illness struck again in 1900, his final year in baseball. Hired as the Giants skipper, his pre-season efforts were curtailed by an unnamed malady. In April 1, he was reported as "still confined to his room in the Sturtevant House [hotel]."[90] His planned return to the team on April 7 had to be delayed until April 9. "Manager Ewing will be on hand to-day; he has practically recovered from his illness, and when he regains some of his strength will get into a uniform and work with the men."[91] An account of the first game of the season at the Polo Grounds, an exhibition match against Columbia University which the Giants won handily, 11–0, noted that Manager Ewing "was able to get to the grounds for the first time in two weeks."[92] Two months later he was fired by the Giants and his career was over.

Details of these illnesses are insufficient to confirm them as early symptoms of Bright's Disease, the kidney malady that would take Ewing's life at age 46. At the very least, however, their repeated occurrences strongly suggest that during the latter stages of his career, Ewing was fighting serious medical issues in addition to his old hand, arm and leg injuries.

Ewing was an inveterate chatterbox on the ball field. While his primary objective always was to beat his opponent, by mid-career he understood well that a game staged before a large crowd was a type of "interactive theater"[93] whose actors included not only the ballplayers, but also the fans and the umpire. Accordingly, his "game plan" regularly involved engaging the spectators, the players on the opposing team, and the umpire in an ongoing dialogue, or subjecting them to his own colorful monologues. His motivations for doing so were two-fold: to amuse and entertain, and to gain a game advantage.

A spring 1889 number of the *Boston Globe*, for example, describes a con-

test between the Bostons and the New Yorks, during which Ewing was "a regular talking machine, and kept up a running conversation between the spectators, the umpire, and his men."[94] Reporting on a September 1892 game
between Brooklyn and the Giants at the Polo Grounds, the *Brooklyn Eagle*,
always critical of the Giants catcher, complained that "Ewing carries on a
conversation with the New York grand stand contingency which is seldom
witty and rarely interests anybody but the Gothamites."[95]

Boston and New York fans were always in for a treat when the two teams
met, since both squads had showmen captains — Mike Kelly and Buck Ewing.
"The running conversation between Mike and Buck Ewing was pleasing. Mike
and Buck are a great team in themselves. They always have lots of fun when
they meet on the diamond"[96]; "Buck and Mike handled their forces right
through nine innings. There was [*sic*] plenty of witty remarks sent out by the
Captains. Buck had new names for all he came in contact with."[97]

Ewing's long-time battery mate, Mickey Welch, recalled many such conversations that were less pleasant for the opposing team's player. "He [Ewing]
used to stay up all night thinking about ways to upset his rivals the next day.
He'd do anything to win. Like [John] McGraw, he'd find out something about
an opposing pitcher's love affairs. Next day, he'd be out there shouting at him,
driving the poor fellow dippy. Like McGraw, his motto was, if you're losing,
knock the other fellow down, rough him up, kick him in the shins ... but
beat him."[98]

There were numerous occasions, however, when such behavior was criticized as being indecorous or downright mean, especially when directed toward
the opposing team's fans. Harry Palmer, a reporter for *The Sporting News*,
noted an incident in Chicago after a close game in which Ewing's sarcastic
comments upset a young female White Stockings rooter. Chicago tied the
score in the bottom of the ninth inning before the Giants came back to win
the game in the tenth. Ewing then mockingly informed the onlookers, "Why
we just let your fellows make that spurt in the ninth just to brace things up
a bit. We can beat you whenever we want — see?"[99] This taunt angered the
young lady. "I just hate that Mr. Ewing. I think the manner in which he
made fun of our boys was positively brutal.... I think that Mr. Ewing was as
mean as he could be."[100] Mean or not, it made for great theater.

Ewing reserved the bulk of his on-field comments for the umpire. When
catching, he would start out by "jollying" him — in other words, congratu-
lating him for his good calls, a strategy that in reality was a double-edged
sword.

> None of them [the catchers of the time period] had the suave tongue of Ewing.
> How quick he could come to the relief of the umpire when the batter started
> to complain. At the first peep from the man with the club [bat] ... the cheery

voice of William would ring across the diamond, "Right over the center" [of the plate].... Then he would make assurance doubly sure by turning around to the press box with his [comment] ... "you couldn't shoot them out of a cannon like that." Some smooth-tongued cajoler that Ewing [was]. If he didn't fancy what the umpire was doing, with a like display of cleverness, he would turn to the press box and shout [ironically] "Oh, no, that one wasn't over! It was just one-quarter of an inch on the outside corner of the outside edge of the plate," and the umpire would glare while the amiable Buck would smile at him and smile at the press box, and the next day the story of the game would tell him that "Umpire Offum never gave Tim [Ewing's battery mate, pitcher Tim Keefe] a corner [of the plate] in the game."[101]

The logic behind this ritual was aptly summarized in a *Sporting Life* column: "Ewing's success with his tricks behind the bat largely depends upon his success in getting the umpire rattled, and in a condition where, to save himself from complete bewilderment, he is apt to favor 'Buck' as much as he can in order to keep that exasperating individual as quiet as possible."[102]

If this strategy failed, Ewing resorted to "kicking" — angrily disputing an umpire's decisions. His continued recourse to this tactic led to fines and ejections, and damaged his reputation among fans and sportswriters outside of New York. Four games behind league-leading Boston during the heat of the 1889 pennant race, for example, he was fined $175 in successive $25 increments by Umpire Curry during an important game against Washington. At the time this was the largest fine ever levied on a player by an umpire. A few days later, "Umpire Baker taxed him $25 and ordered him off the field"[103] for arguing a close play at first base on which he was declared out. The *Brooklyn Eagle* noted that "Buck called Baker 'a robber' and showered him with epithets that would not look nice in print."[104] Since Giants owner John B. Day paid Ewing's fines, there was little incentive to desist, except for the possibility of ejection — which was rare. His behavior did, however, earn Ewing unenviable new nicknames, such as the "Boss Kicker" and the "Prince of Knockers." At this juncture he was considered the worst complainer in the league, since his tantrums now surpassed the famous tirades of Cap Anson: "Buck Ewing now outshines even Anson as a kicker."[105]

A few press reports of the era provide us with some of the specifics of Ewing's harangues. Compared to those of managers like John McGraw a decade later, or to a modern kicker like former manager Lou Piniella, these outbursts seem innocuous. "Ewing kicks to an umpire thusly, 'Put your eyes in the front of your head. Be a man or a monkey; don't be a cross between the two'; 'For heaven's sake, if you're dumb, say so, but don't just stand there like a mummy and say 'ball' when you know it's a strike'; 'I don't think you're a robber, old man, but if this isn't a case of petty larceny, I never was out of jail.'"[106]

Why did Ewing, who in most quarters was considered "good natured" and "affable," resort to criticizing the umpire? First, it was taken for granted that a team captain or player/manager should press an umpire to make decisions in favor of his team. More importantly, in Ewing's case, his "kicks" regularly achieved such aims:

> Although Buck Ewing has the reputation of being the boss kicker, he is not in the same class as [Captains] Faatz of Cleveland and Farrar of Philadelphia. There is always method in Ewing's kicks, and he gains many points for his team, while Faatz and Farrar are kicking for the simple reason that they have been appointed captains and have the idea that kicking and growling will pass for good generalship.[107]

The clearest example of such success occurred in the fourth inning of a contest at Cleveland in August 1889. After Cleveland's Jimmy McAleer doubled to left field, "Powers the umpire also ran to second, and after seeing McAleer safe at the bag, returned to home plate, where he has informed by 'Buck' Ewing that McAleer had failed to touch first base and [then] he [Umpire Powers] promptly called the runner out."[108] A riot then ensued as hundreds of fans jumped onto the field, threatening Powers. With nightsticks drawn, three policemen had to escort him under the stands. After a half-hour, order was restored but play was suspended.

Commenting on Ewing's regular complaints behind the plate in 1889, the *Boston Daily Globe* had to admit that they were often successful: "There is always a method in Ewing's kicks, and he gains many a point for his team."[109] Such successes ultimately led the press to publish tongue-in-cheek game summaries that listed Ewing as the actual umpire of the game. "For New York, Ewing umpired a satisfactory game, greatly assisted by Mr. Daniels [the actual umpire]."[110]

Press criticism of players who objected, sometimes vehemently, to umpire decisions, was selective. Ewing was pilloried for his relatively harmless — but persistent — criticisms, but when his teammate, John Ward, then captain of the Giants, physically attacked an umpire in 1884, he was given a pass by the press and the league. After a game in Buffalo that was called due to darkness by umpire John Gaffney after seven innings, Ward approached Gaffney in the rotunda of the Genesee House Hotel and verbally insulted his umpiring skills. Gaffney returned the insult with regard to Ward's playing abilities. Ward "then struck Gaffney in the cheek, knocking him down into a chair. Before he had time to rise, Ward struck him again over the left eye, opening a deep cut from which the blood flowed freely. The men were promptly separated."[111] Gaffney attempted to umpire the following day's game, but "the mask reopened his wound every time he used it, and his eye was very painful, so he came home. He will not be in condition to umpire probably for a week."[112] Ward, "for unknown reasons, was neither fined nor suspended for his actions,"[113] and the incident drew little response from the press.

When not amusing or enraging fans, umpires or opposing players with his verbal volleys, Buck Ewing liked to hone his conversational skills by spinning preposterous tall tales, delighting in observing how long it took his audience to catch on. In the following example, such a realization must have occurred quickly:

> "But," said Ewing, and not a smile flitted across his face, "talking about accidents that happened on ball fields, one that happened to Conny Yanagan [*yanagan* or *yannigan* was a slang term used to refer to rookies or otherwise inexperienced players] was the most wonderful thing that ever happened in baseball. It happened when I was a kid out in Cincinnati. A great game was being played, and the loss of a player of course meant a great deal. Conny was playing center field, and I hit a terrible drive in that direction, the ball sailing along only a few inches from the ground.
>
> "It struck Yanagan in the left leg and broke that member off as clean as a whistle. A meat axe could not have performed the operation more neatly. Of course Yanagan fell to the ground, but instantly jumped up again, and hobbling over to the fence, he tore off a board, while the rest of us looked on in wonder. We all thought that the injury had unsettled Yanagan's reasoning. He grabbed a board off the fence, strapped it on to the stump where the leg had been, and played out the game."
>
> Everybody set up an incredulous howl as Buck finished this thrilling narrative.
>
> Buck, as sober and apparently serious, as ever, turned to [Giants Manager Jim] Mutrie and said: "Why Jim, you know this man. He is the same man who jumped over Hog river [*sic*] to catch a fly [ball]."[114]

Who was the real Buck Ewing? Was it the hit-and-run specialist, the long-ball slugger, or the accomplished sacrifice bunter? The affable teammate or the irascible umpire-baiter? Was it the stoic who played through crippling injuries or the alleged slacker who did not? The "has-been" with the "glass arm" or the receiver with the strongest arm in the league? Was it the humorous teller of tall tales or the cynic who taunted opposing teams' fans?

The best response to these questions is found in a description of Ewing that was published shortly before the start of the 1889 season: "You cannot measure him: you cannot stop him. [League President] Nick Young would have little trouble classifying 'Buck' as a player; but the man who can classify his personality must be a genius indeed. His disposition is as varied as the color of the chameleon."[115]

Chapter 4

The Giants of New York: 1885–1889

"New-York, with the invincible Buck Ewing, on the South End Grounds tomorrow." —*Boston Daily Globe*, August 18, 1889

In 1885, New York's National League team became competitive for the first time in its three-year history, and it acquired a new nickname — one by which the franchise, today located in San Francisco, is still known. In his fourth full major league season, Buck Ewing hit .304 — his highest average to date, and added to his growing reputation as an all-around athlete by catching, pitching, and playing three infield and two outfield positions. John Day's other team, the American Association Metropolitans, won the Association pennant in 1884, but lost $8,000 in the process, largely due to its admission price of 25 cents — half that of the National League. Seeing the handwriting on the wall, owner Day began shifting his time and resources to his money-making National League franchise. At the end of the 1885 season he sold the Mets to Erasmus Wiman, owner of a Staten Island amusement park called the St. George Cricket Grounds. The Mets played their last two years there (1886–1887) before being replaced in the Association by the Kansas City Cowboys. A major league team known as the Mets would not play again in New York for another 75 years.

Before setting the Metropolitans adrift, John Day and Jim Mutrie conspired to reassign the team's best pitcher, Tim Keefe, and one of its better infielders, Tom "Dude" Esterbrook, to New York's National League team. Keefe, who had logged an unpromising 41–59 record with Troy from 1880 to 1882, blossomed with the Mets, going 78–44 in 1883–1884. Two factors were responsible for this turnaround: the 1883 rule change allowing sidearm deliveries, and Keefe's subsequent development of a deceptive change-up to go along with his blazing sidearm fastball and curve. The durable Esterbrook had played third base in every game for two years with the Mets, finishing the 1884 season with a career-high .314 average.

Even though John Day owned both New York teams, as a signatory of the 1883 National Agreement he was not permitted simply to transfer Keefe and Esterbrook from the Mets to New York. Rather, he was required first to release them from their Mets contracts, and then allow ten days to pass before asking them to sign on with his National League team. He also knew that "other teams would be eager to talk to these players once they were released, and he wanted to keep those teams away during the waiting period."[1]

Day's scheme to guarantee that Keefe and Esterbrook would sign with him was two-fold. First, he transferred Mets Manager Jim Mutrie to the New Yorks. Then, he invited both players on an all-expenses-paid cruise to Bermuda, with Mutrie accompanying them as their "guide." Once aboard the boat bound for Bermuda, Mutrie, with Day's blessing, released them from their American Association contracts. Ten days later, while still at sea with Keefe and Esterbrook, he signed them to New York National League contracts. Incensed by Mutrie's illegal actions, the Association suspended him. The action was to no avail, however, "since Mutrie by this time was no longer a part of the Association."[2]

John Day then acquired another star player, veteran Jim O'Rourke, captain of the Buffalo Bisons. O'Rourke was one of only a handful of players who refused to play under the reserve clause but were still signed by their clubs because of their great talent. The burly O'Rourke hit .347 in 1884, and was a competent outfielder and catcher. He holds two significant baseball records. Playing for Boston against Philadelphia in 1876, he registered the first hit in the National League's first game. Twenty-eight years later, at age 54, O'Rourke was still playing ball in the Connecticut League, and he was invited back for a swan-song major-league performance at the Polo Grounds by Giants manager John McGraw. O'Rourke caught the full nine innings and went 1-for-4 at the plate, thus becoming the oldest player to hit safely in a National League game.

In addition to the acquisitions of Keefe, Esterbrook and O'Rourke, new manager Jim Mutrie made two position changes among the New York team's remaining players. After spending a year in the outfield rehabilitating his sore right arm, former pitcher John Ward was moved to shortstop. Slugger Roger Connor was moved back to first base after a year shuffling back and forth between second base and the outfield. The Waterbury native, now finally settled in a defensive position, responded offensively by leading the league in hits (169 in a 112-game season) and batting average (.371). In future years he would lead the league in fielding at first base four times.

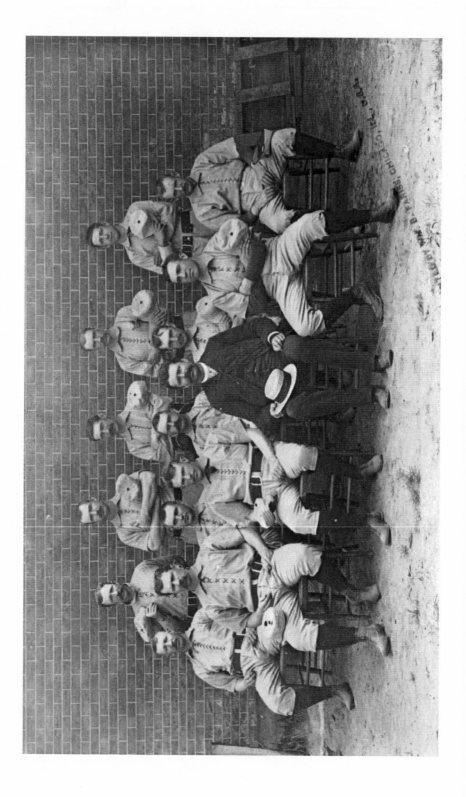

Half the players on the 1885 New York roster were very tall for the era —
three stood over six feet, and three others were close to that height. The tallest,
six-foot, three-inch Connor, was frequently referred to in the press as "the
giant of the team."[3] During the exhibition season in April, the *New York World*
began referring to the entire team as the "Giants."[4] Soon other publications
followed suit, initially setting off the term in quotation marks. By June it had
become standard usage. Nearly 130 years later, it remains the nickname for
the franchise.

In addition to becoming the "Giants" in the press, New York's team
members were rapidly becoming "giants" in the hearts of a large number of
their fans. Three groups among this number were notable. Members of the
New York Stock Exchange were regular rooters, and had their own boxes in
the grandstand. Besides being generous in their praise for the Giants, they
frequently took up collections to reward team members for superior efforts,
either with money or mementos. "Ewing was yesterday presented with a splendid gold medal, the gift of Messers Leavitt and Hallstead, of the Stock
Exchange, for making the best record in the series of [exhibition] games
between the New-Yorks and the Metropolitan [*sic*] last year."[5]

A second significant fan contingent came from New York City's theatrical
community, which had developed a special bond with their fellow "actors"
on the ball field. The entire Giants team and their visiting opponents were
often invited to Broadway performances following their afternoon battles on
the field. "The members of the New-York and Boston Clubs have accepted
an invitation to witness 'The Black Hussar' [an operatic comedy] at Wallach's
[a theater located on the corner of Broome Street and Broadway]."[6] In such
cases the Giants were quick to reciprocate. "Nearly all of the members of the
Black Hussar Company ... were the guests [at the Polo Grounds] of President
Day, and occupied seats in the Director's box."[7] Such arrangements proved
mutually beneficial for the actors and the ball players, since their collective
notoriety among the general populace added to the excitement and the attraction of a game or a theatrical performance.

A third unique New York fan base consisted of an unusually large contingent of female spectators. The *New York Times* took special note of their presence in their report of the season's first home contest against Boston on May 2:

> The first of the League games in this city was played on the Polo Grounds yes-
> terday between the New-York and Boston clubs, and it resulted in a victory for

Opposite: New York team, 1885, the first year they were called the Giants, featuring
six future Hall of Fame players: first row, left to right: Jim O'Rourke, John Ward,
manager Jim Mutrie, and Mickey Welch. Second row, far left: Buck Ewing. Third
row, second left, Roger Connor (courtesy National Baseball Hall of Fame Library,
Cooperstown, New York).

the local nine after a well-played contest. There were fully 6,000 persons present. Every seat was taken in the grand stand, and in the other desirable portion of the ground it was a difficult matter to secure standing room. A noticeable feature of the game was the respectable class of people who attended the contest. The gambling element to be found at other sporting events was missing. There was a large number of ladies present, and the majority of them were armed with pencils and scorecards, and judging from the various questions they plied to their male escorts, they took more than an ordinary interest in the game.[8]

The link between Giants baseball and its increasing number of female and theatrical fans is epitomized in the person of actress Helen Dauvray. Born Helen Gibson in San Francisco, she began her stage career at age five, and by her mid-twenties had amassed a large fortune through astute investments. After training in voice and piano in Italy, learning French, and appearing on the stage in France, she purchased a Park Avenue mansion, established a theater company, and had leading roles in several Broadway productions. A rabid baseball fan, she attended many home games at the Polo Grounds, and in 1887 donated a sterling silver trophy, the Dauvray Cup, to the winner of the post-season playoffs between the American Association and National League champions.

Dauvray's devotion to the game also had a personal motivation. In October 1887, she married Giants shortstop John Ward, a union that was celebrated in the New York press. The marriage was stormy, as Ward was opposed to Dauvray continuing her stage career. It ended six years later when, after a sensational court proceeding covered in lurid detail by the New York press, the actress was granted a divorce from the ballplayer on grounds of adultery.

De Witt Hopper, a youthful member of the aforementioned "Black Hussar" cast, was the local actor most infected by a baseball obsession. He was a regular at the Polo Grounds and organized a theater team that played other amateur squads there when the Giants were on the road. In 1888, Hopper gave the first recital of Ernest Lawrence Thayer's poem, "Casey at the Bat," before a theater audience that included the entire rosters of the Giants and the visiting Chicago White Stockings. The poem became a regular part of Hopper's repertoire, and in the ensuing five decades he recited it publicly more than 10,000 times.

The Giants' bolstered lineup and improved pitching brought the team to the brink of winning its first pennant in 1885. Trailing Chicago by two games in late September, the team arrived in the Windy City for a four-game series that would effectively decide the championship. The confident New Yorkers, who had beaten the White Stockings in nine of their previous 12 encounters, dropped three games in a row before taking the last game of the series, and they left town four games behind and in second place, where they finished the season. Interest in the Chicago series was extraordinary in New

York, as crowds of fans, who would ultimately be disappointed, stood outside of city newspaper offices waiting for telegraphed game reports.

> The interest in this city was so great that it drew dense throngs of people to the street to scan the bulletin boards in front of the different newspaper offices. Printing House Square was so completely blocked that the police could scarcely force a passageway for the horse cars. Then, when the saddening dispatches were posted announcing the crushing defeat of our own representative team, hisses and shouts of derision arose from thousands of throats.[9]

From the onset of the 1885 season, Buck Ewing was plagued by sore hands, a condition that would not improve until he adopted the catcher's mitt several years later. The pounding his hands took from Tim Keefe and Mickey Welch's fastballs, thrown from a distance of 50 feet, reduced his playing time to 81 of the season's 112 games. His hitting and running skills did not falter, however, and his dramatic style of play was drawing national attention. In mid–July, in a contest against Chicago, he stole home for the second time in two seasons: "Ewing hit to centre for three bases and he actually stole home while [catcher] Briody was returning the ball to [pitcher] Boyle."[10] This play capped a three-hit effort on Ewing's part that included a triple and two doubles, with two runs scored. A second daring display of base running against Chicago occurred in early August. With the game scoreless in the tenth inning, Ewing led off with a single. John Ward followed Ewing in the lineup, and the two signaled each other for a hit-and-run play:

> When Clarkson pitched the fourth ball to Ward, Ewing started to steal second base. Ward hit the sphere and it went on a line to right field. Kelly handled it [on the bounce] magnificently and threw New-York's crack base runner [Ward] out at first. While he was doing this, Ewing was on his way to third at his utmost speed. After catching the ball, [first baseman] Anson drove it over to [third baseman] Williamson. Ball and base runner seemed to get there simultaneously, but Ewing, by a headlong dive, gained the base before Williamson had time to touch him.[11]

Pete Gillespie then hit a soft grounder to second baseman Fred Pfeffer, and Ewing took off for home plate. Pfeffer threw home to catcher Silver Flint, and "At that moment, Ewing made one of those slides for which he is famous. The ball, catcher, and runner were hidden in a cloud of dust."[12] Flint, however, had dropped the ball, and "Ewing was carried from the field on the shoulders of a dozen admirers."[13] Ewing's bold scamper was subsequently immortalized in a full-page lithograph that appeared in a number of *Harper's Weekly*, one of the premier magazines of the era, whose circulation numbered in the hundreds of thousands. Such press coverage was making Ewing a well-known figure across the country.

Despite missing nearly 30 percent of the season due to injuries, Ewing's six home runs led the Giants team in a campaign in which Chicago's Abner Dalrymple led the league with 11. Of Ewing's six four-baggers, two were hit in a three-day period off Buffalo's future Hall of Famer, Jim Galvin, and three were hit off Phillies hurler Ed Daily. Two of the latter three came in the same game at Recreation Park in Philadelphia. "Ewing opened up the first inning by sending a high fly over the right field fence, on which he scored a home run, and in the fifth inning he duplicated the effort."[14] In 1885, Ewing was a clutch hitter with men on base. His RBI total of 63 was just two shy of team leader Roger Connor's 65. Connor played in all but two games in 1885, 29 more than Ewing.

On July 5, Ewing did what only a handful of major league players have ever done — he caught and pitched in the same game. By mid-season, total reliance on the arms of Keefe and Welch had taken its toll on both pitchers. Welch was exhausted and Keefe had a sore arm. In the second game of a July 4 doubleheader against Chicago, Ewing, whose hands were sore after seven innings of catching, hurled the final two frames against the White Sox. It was just the third time he had pitched in his major league career, and the results, while not impressive, were not as bad as indicated in the press: "Chicago earned her runs when Ewing, who makes no pretensions as a pitcher, was in front of them."[15] In actuality, three of the four runs that Ewing surrendered were unearned.

In late November, the Giants traveled to New Orleans for a pre-arranged series of exhibition games with St. Louis. The Crescent City's mild winter weather, race tracks, gaming parlors, and raucous night life had been attracting major league teams in the off-season since the early 1870s. Ewing's hitting during the exhibition series gained him more national notoriety and a handsome reward. "Mr. John Curry, a prominent citizen of New Orleans, offered at the commencement of the series of games between the New York and St. Louis nines in that city, a handsome gold medal to the player making the best batting average. Five games in all were played and Ewing won the trophy with an average [.571] considerably in excess of any other player."[16]

During the regular 1885 season, Ewing played a dozen games in the outfield, 60 behind the plate, nine at third base, shortstop or first base, and he took one turn in the pitcher's box. This record now placed him in contention with the superstar of the 1880s, Mike Kelly, for the honor of being considered the best utility player in the game. "Kelly and Ewing are the claimants for the honor of the best all-round player in the league. Opinions differ widely as day and night who is entitled to the palm."[17] By the time both men hung up their spikes, Ewing would get the nod among his peers as having been the best.

The 1886–1887 seasons were near carbon-copy disappointments for the

Giants. After coming close to winning the pennant the previous year, manager Mutrie made few changes to the team's roster. Things had changed in the league, however. The Detroit Wolverines, cellar-dwellers in 1884 and sixth-place finishers in 1885, acquired outfielder Hardy Richardson, veteran Deacon White, and slugger Dan Brouthers from the Buffalo franchise after it folded. In their debut year in Detroit, Richardson hit .351, led the league in hits and tied teammate Brouthers for the lead in home runs (11). Big Dan also led the league in doubles. Detroit additionally had home-grown rookie talent in the person of Sam Thompson, a lanky outfielder who would hit 126 home runs in his career, more than any nineteenth-century player except Roger Connor. Pitchers Charlie "Pretzels" Getzein and Charlie "Lady" Baldwin combined for 72 Detroit victories in 1886, with Baldwin leading the League in wins (42) and strikeouts (323). The Wolverines knocked the Giants out of second place and came within a few games of dethroning the White Stockings as pennant winners.

With the disbanded Union League no longer a threat, and relations between the American Association and the National League stabilized, team owners sought to control their expenses in 1886 by imposing a $2,000 salary limit. Detested by the players, the salary cap would become a prime factor in player discontent that led to the Players' League revolt in 1890. In order to keep some of their stars happy, however, some owners found bizarre ways to circumvent the rule. Manager Mutrie was no exception in this regard.

> Jim Mutrie came here on Christmas eve [sic] with Buck Ewing, and hunted Joe Gerhardt up. After a brief consultation, both Ewing and Gerhardt signed, each receiving the limit of salary. It is said that Mutrie spoke to both men admiringly about the handsome shirts they wore on the field last season. Joe remarked, blushingly, that he valued his shirt very highly as a memento, but would sell it for $750 cash in hand. Ewing offered his souvenir at the same figure. It is said that Mutrie, with tears in his eyes, bought both shirts, and said, "Bless you, my children."[18]

Buck Ewing hit well in 1886, raising his batting average to .309, but nagging injuries caused him to miss more than 50 games. He sprained his ankle in early May, and by mid-month was described as still "very lame."[19] In July a thigh injury kept him off the baselines for three weeks. He finally got back behind the plate late in the month, but in August the aforementioned mysterious illness struck him, and he was in and out of the lineup for the remainder of the season. Given Ewing's injuries, Mutrie in late July established a practice of switching him with center fielder Jim O'Rourke every other game. "O'Rourke and Ewing will alternate in centre field and behind the bat during the remainder of the season. By doing this the New-Yorks will have their strongest batting and base-running team in the field every day."[20]

Despite his injuries — and sometimes because of them — Ewing played all three outfield positions, caught, and played third and second base in his abbreviated 73-game season. In spite of his bad ankle and thigh, he managed to steal 18 bases in the first year that steals were officially counted as a statistic. In the last week of the season, Mutrie revealed that he planned significant roster changes for the 1887: "If money will secure it, I will have a strong club in the field next year.... I intend to infuse new blood in the present nine."[21]

There was some urgency to Mutrie's plan. Polo Grounds attendance had dropped off, and *The Sporting News* reported that "The New York papers have almost abandoned base ball news since the New-Yorks begun [*sic*] their downward slide."[22] Even the State of New York and New York City had some potentially bad news for the Giants:

> At the recent session of the State Legislature, a bill was introduced to cut through one-hundred-and-eleventh street [*sic*], which at present is only an imaginary line running through the centre of the [Polo] Grounds, and every spring such a resolution has been threatened by our Board of Aldermen, and we believe has been before the Committee on Streets and Avenues for some time, but base ball will probably be played there for some time to come.[23]

"For some time to come" would turn out to be one more year, after which John B. Day had to find new quarters in Manhattan for his team.

During the disappointing 1886 season, the Giants franchise came close to making baseball history in another arena. In early September, with starters Keefe and Welch tiring after an arduous campaign, *Sporting Life* reported that "New-York is seriously considering the engagement of Stovey, Jersey City's fine colored pitcher. The question is, 'would the League permit his appearance in a League championship game?'"[24] George Washington Stovey, a Williamsport, Pennsylvania, native of mixed white and black heritage, was a left-handed hurler with a "bewildering array of hard breaking pitches,"[25] a deceptive pickoff move, and a famously bad temper. He posted a 1.13 ERA with Jersey City in 1886, and once struck out 22 batters in a losing cause. While the Giants never took a chance on Stovey, it is tantalizing to think of how baseball and American life might have changed had they done so, and had their decision been upheld by the league.

Major changes to playing regulations were implemented in 1887, requiring significant adjustments by both pitchers and hitters. The high/low strike rule, by which hitters requested a specific pitch location, was abolished. The new strike zone nearly doubled the size of the old one, extending it from the top of the shoulders to the bottom of the knees. The width and length of the pitcher's box was reduced, and the pitcher was now required to keep one foot on the back line of the box during delivery, a distance of 55 feet, six inches

JAMES MUTRIE, MANAGER.

THOMAS DEASLEY, CATCHER.

T. J. KEEFE, PITCHER.

MICHAEL WELCH, PITCHER.

J. H. O'ROURKE, CATCHER AND CENTRE FIELD.

WILLIAM EWING, CATCHER.

Representative New York Stars etching, circa 1886, source unknown, featuring New York's manager, Jim Mutrie, two starting pitchers and three catchers. In 1885, Buck Ewing and Thomas "Pat" Deasley shared the Giants catching duties. In 1886, Jim O'Rourke took over as Ewing's alternate, and Deasley played primarily in the outfield (courtesy Transcendental Graphics/theruckerarchive.com).

from home plate. In compensation to the hitter for the larger strike zone, the number of balls for a walk was reduced to five, walks were credited as hits, and — for the only year in the history of the game — four strikes instead of three were required for a strikeout. As a result, batting averages soared. Even after modern statisticians had adjusted them to exclude walks as hits, they topped their 1886 mark by 18 points.

Giants manager Jim Mutrie made good on his vow to shake up the Giants roster. A few games into the season, second baseman Joe Gerhardt and third baseman Dude Esterbrook were sent to the Mets. Pete Gillespie was moved to left field from right field, which was taken over by power-hitting New Jersey rookie, "Silent Mike" Tiernan. Jim O'Rourke was pulled from the outfield and assigned catching duties, which were to be shared by back-up receiver Pat Deasley.

O'Rourke's place in center field was filled by the acquisition of Chicago veteran George Gore, an old friend of Jim Mutrie who had played with him in New England as a young man. In his prime, Gore was one of the league's outstanding hitters and base runners, and a player whose candidacy for the Hall of Fame has been sadly overlooked. He led the League in hitting (.360) in his sophomore season, hit over .300 eight times, is one of two players to steal seven bases in a game, and one of three men to score more runs than games played in their careers. A left-handed-hitting leadoff man, Gore was a slap hitter who choked up on one of the heaviest bats (50 ounces) ever used. He was an extremely disciplined hitter, leading the league with 102 walks in 1886, a season in which seven balls were required for a free pass to first base. Such discipline was lacking in his personal life, and his talent was often compromised by alcohol and a raucous lifestyle.

Where did Buck Ewing fit in this mix? Jim Mutrie decided to move him to the infield in an effort to keep him healthy and playing daily. "Manager Mutrie of the New-York Club proposes trying Ewing at second base.... O'Rourke is to be played solely as a catcher."[26] *Sporting Life* elaborated on this plan:

> It was deemed advisable to have Ewing's valuable service in every game, which would not be the case were he simply to catch.... Another more potential reason for putting Ewing at second was the fact that hitherto every season the club had been deprived for long periods of his service by reason of injuries he sustained while catching, and these accidents always happened at times when the club needed him the most. At second base he is less liable to be hurt.[27]

It was a year of ups and downs for Ewing. While his offense remained solid (.305 average, six home runs, 26 stolen bases), injuries, position changes and subsequent harsh treatment by fans and the press left him frustrated and ready to leave New York. After an early May loss to Washington, in which he committed two errors at second base, he was lambasted by the *Times* for his "seeming inability to hold balls thrown by the catcher and the lack of general adaptability to the position to which he is now assigned. His errors have been costly.... Ewing's place, were he less lazy, is behind the bat, for he is a good catcher."[28] An angry Ewing responded, "I'll cover the bag all right with a little practice. All these people who are shouting me down now will shout for me before long. I'll give them a second base that'll make 'em dance, and don't you forget it."[29]

A week later he seemed to be making progress, and all appeared to be forgiven by the press and the fans. "Buck Ewing has been covering second base in excellent form recently, and hitting very hard and effectively, thereby reinstating himself in popular favor."[30] Shortly afterward, he injured his hand, and while sitting out for two weeks, utility man Danny Richardson began playing second in fine fashion. "Richardson ... played the base [second] better than it has been played for New York in any previous season."[31]

Injured, unable to catch, criticized in the press and threatened by another player's skill at the second base position, Ewing began thinking that a change in venue might be in order. "Buck Ewing is anxious to get away from New York and try his fortune in pastures new. He will endeavor at the close of the season to cause his transfer to some other League club."[32] Some members of the press, claiming to have special knowledge of Ewing's intentions, asserted he was not catching because of selfish financial motives, and not because manager Mutrie had removed him from the position.

Buck Ewing is tired of New York and anxious to get his release. This is a straight tip, coming directly from Ewing himself. The cause of his trouble is simply this: it appears that he did not get as much salary as he asked for, whereupon he declared that he would not go behind the bat. He has also dictated certain terms upon which he will play at third base, and altogether he is not at all comfortable where he is [New York]. He claims that New York audiences and the press particularly have treated him unjustly, and he will never rest content until he evens up matters. While he is in such a mood he cannot do justice to himself to the club he assumes to play with.[33]

Ewing responded to such ferocious criticism in the way he was best able—with his bat. Returning to the lineup on June 3 and now playing third base, he smacked two hits, including a home run, scored two runs, and played errorless ball. In the ensuing month he went on an offensive spree that included three four-hit

An 1887 Gypsy Queen Cigarette Card, featuring Buck Ewing posing as an infielder. After overhand pitching became legal in 1884, Ewing suffered numerous hand injuries catching overhand fastballs thrown from a distance of 50 feet without the protection of a catcher's mitt. Giants manager Jim Mutrie announced in 1887 that he would use Ewing in the infield in order to keep his bat in the lineup. Ewing played 70 games at third base and shortstop and only eight as a catcher (courtesy Transcendental Graphics/theruckerarchive.com).

games and six three-hit games, and he scored 35 runs and hit three four-bag-gers. Ewing's "Bread and Butter" reputation, however, was unfortunately now part of his baseball persona, and would continue to be referenced for the remainder of his career whenever his on-field performance was questioned.

Given the alleged poor state of affairs between Ewing and the Giants, fans and the press, it came as a great surprise that, in mid–July, shortstop John Ward was relieved of his duties as team captain and Buck Ewing installed in his place. Dire consequences were immediately predicted in *The Sporting News* with regard to this selection: "To a man up a tree, Ewing's appointment to the New York captaincy looks like a big mistake. He is a notable 'weakener.' And if there is one quality a captain needs more than another it is nerve and heart. These qualities make Anson and Kelly great. Ewing lacks them."[34]

Ewing's selection as captain in the face of such criticism calls into question the motives and objectivity of the press, since he would not have been named to the position had he not had the backing of the team, manager Mutrie, and owner Day. A year later, when New York won the pennant and took the World Series from St. Louis under Ewing's leadership, *Sporting News*'s editors would be eating their words.

A few days after assuming his new role in July, Ewing caught for the first time in 1887. "Ewing went in to catch in the fourth [inning] to give Brown as rest and was tremendously applauded."[35] He continued to work intermit-tently behind the plate until mid–August, when he lacerated the middle finger of his right hand. *Sporting Life*, so hostile to him earlier in the season, now lamented his loss, not only for his leadership, but for his "kicking" abilities.

> The unfortunate injury to Buck Ewing has been a severe blow to the team. His services have already been missed, but his absence will be felt even more keenly during the Chicago and Detroit battles here [at the Polo Grounds]. Ewing has developed into quite a captain, and his generalship on the field has been excel-lent. He promises to develop kicking propensities of the Anson stripe, and the Giants will no longer submit to injustice with their former meekness.[36]

There was pleasant news of a personal nature for Ewing in 1887. His younger brother John, who, like Buck, began his baseball career with a Cincin-nati semi-pro team — the Shamrocks — had begun his professional career, playing for the Southern League's New Orleans team. On the advice and with the assistance of his older brother, John had converted from an outfielder to a pitcher with considerable success. "John Ewing, brother to Buck of the New

Opposite: Montage of Major League players, late 1880s, featuring Buck Ewing. This curious selection, which provides no team affiliations for the players, includes eight infielders (Allen, Richardson, Anson, Pfeffer, Nash, Ward, Tebeau and Comiskey) one pitcher (Caruthers), two catchers (Miller and Ewing) and one outfielder (Hanlon) (courtesy Transcendental Graphics/theruckerarchive.com).

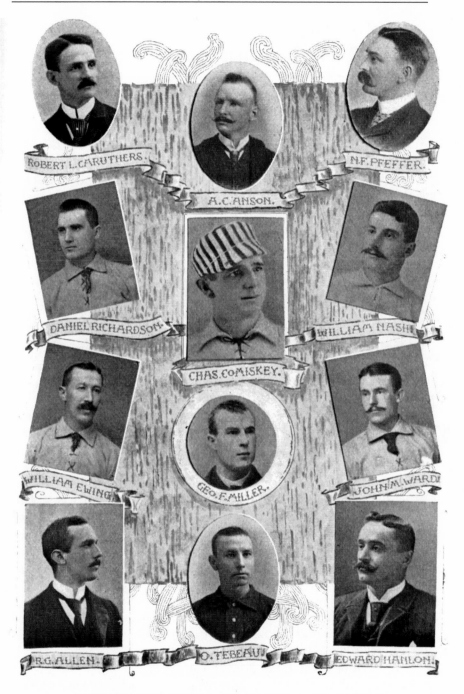

REPRESENTATIVE BASE BALL PLAYERS.

Yorks, and Al Hungler are rivals for being the best pitchers [sic] from the Southern League."[37]

Three years younger than Buck, John, whose six-foot, one-inch height and slender physique earned him the nickname "Long John, " debuted with New Orleans in 1887, and later spent four years in the major leagues — two with Louisville's American Association team and two with the Giants (National League and Players' League), thanks to the intervention of his brother. Like Buck, he died young, passing away from tuberculosis at age 31. At about the same time that Buck's lacerated finger ended his 1887 season, John suffered an injury that ended his own. "The Ewing family is in bad luck. Preceding the accident to Buck in Philadelphia, his brother, the New Orleans pitcher, dislocated his shoulder. The accident happened while practicing Saturday, and he pitched six innings not realizing what was the matter with him. He will be laid up for a couple of weeks yet."[38]

While the Detroit Wolverines were battling the American Association's St. Louis Browns in the 1887 World Series in late October, Ewing and a select group of Giants embarked on a barnstorming tour to the West Coast. Mike Kelly, who had just completed his first season with Boston after having been sold by the White Stockings for the then-unheard-of figure of $10,000, accepted an invitation from the Giants squad to play for them during the undertaking. A Troy, New York, native, Kelly was baseball's first superstar. Like Buck Ewing, he could run, hit, and play any field position, and he was a showman who reveled in entertaining fans and fellow players. Unlike Ewing, Kelly was a heavy drinker and gambler, traits that eventually eroded his athletic skills and left him penniless when he died of pneumonia in 1894 at age 37.

The Giants' barnstorming team stopped first to play five games in New Orleans — where Ewing's "continual grumbling and kicking all through the games the combination played here"[39] earned him bad press reviews. Kelly and Ewing hit it off so well as teammates after the New Orleans series that they took a few days off the tour to do some quail hunting together in Mississippi before rejoining the squad in Texas.[40] Reaching California around Thanksgiving, the Giants took on semi-pro squads in Los Angeles and San Francisco through the New Year's holiday. During the tour, Ewing caught and played first base and the outfield, but he drew the most notice for his work in the pitcher's box. "It will not be astounding to see Buck Ewing occupy the pitcher's box next season. Buck is doing great work in that line this winter on the Pacific Slope. He seems to be as good in one place as another."[41]

On their return east, the Giants stopped off again for a few exhibition games in New Orleans in early February, where Ewing's constant umpire baiting provoked some dire predictions from *The Sporting News*: "Buck Ewing of

Giants team standing in front of the magnificent grandstand at Polo Grounds I on Opening Day of the 1888 season. Located at Park Avenue and 112th Street, at the northern end of Central Park in New York City, the Grounds were demolished by the city at the end of the season in order to create 111th Street, forcing the team to seek new quarters (Polo Grounds II) 40 blocks north in 1889 (courtesy National Baseball Hall of Fame Library, Cooperstown, New York).

the New-Yorks stands in good show [has a good chance] of being lynched if he makes his appearance in New Orleans again."[42]

The next two years, 1888 and 1889, were the greatest Giants seasons of the nineteenth century, and the high water mark of Buck Ewing's career. The team won consecutive pennants and then defeated their Association counterparts, St. Louis and Brooklyn respectively, reigning as world champions. Healthy enough to play nearly every day, Ewing returned to catching full-time, hit over .300, stole 87 bases over the two seasons, and provided strong, steady leadership as team captain. True to form, he continued to use every strategy available to him, be it questionable or acceptable, to achieve his personal and team goals. Likewise true to form, press reports of his performance on the field continued to alternate between lavish praise and vicious criticism.

The 1888 season did not begin auspiciously. Shortstop John Ward and

pitching ace Tim Keefe were holdouts, each demanding more money.
Ward accepted a lower offer in the last
week of spring training, but Keefe
held out until late April, returned out
of shape, and soon had a sore arm.
With Danny Richardson settled in at
second base, Buck Ewing began the
season at third, replacing Dude Esterbrook. He had a rocky start at the hot
corner, but by mid–May his fielding
percentage was .875, second-best in
the league, and he was hitting at a
.337 clip before missing four games
with a mysterious illness.

In the most significant move of
the season, the Giants acquired veteran third baseman Art Whitney
from Pittsburgh in June. A light-
hitting, slick-fielding infielder, Whitney took over at third base for New
York, solidifying the infield that now

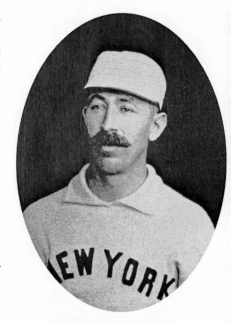

Iconic portrait of Giant Buck Ewing,
mid–1880s (courtesy Transcendental
Graphics/theruckerarchive.com).

consisted of Whitney, John Ward at shortstop, Danny Richardson at second,
and Roger Connor at first. Captain Buck Ewing resumed his old position
behind the plate.

Ewing's position change had an immediate impact on the team. Between
June 21 and July 28, he caught 29 consecutive games (the record at the time
was 44, set by Kid Baldwin in 1887), and the Giants won 22 of them. On
July 31, they took sole possession of first place, and were not seriously challenged again for the rest of the season. *Sporting Life*, which had been so critical
of Ewing during the two previous years, now admitted that his "back-stop-
ping, throwing, batting and base-running have been of immense service to
New-York."[43] The sports journal could not resist, however, declaring that the
Giants' success was due only to the fact that Ewing was now playing what its
editors had deemed his *correct* position. "Ewing is doing wonderful work, and
since he has confined himself to his proper position, the team has materially
bettered its percentage. The best feature is the willingness he shows to go
behind the bat day after day, and this spirit has restored him to his old position
of public fame."[44]

Pitchers Keefe and Welch, with a little help from Cannonball Titcomb,
won the pennant for the Giants. The team ranked fourth in batting (.242)

Above left: Giants Captain Buck Ewing portrayed in a Goodwin Tobacco Card, 1887. Ewing replaced John Ward as team captain in mid–July 1887 (courtesy Library of Congress). *Right:* Studio portrait of Ewing holding a bat. For a portion of his career, Ewing used a 42" bat, the longest length permitted by league regulations (courtesy Transcendental Graphics/theruckerarchive).

and third in fielding (.924), but boasted the league's lowest ERA (1.96). After getting his arm in shape, Keefe reeled off nineteen consecutive wins, and won the pitching "Triple Crown," that is, he led the league in victories (35), ERA (1.74) and strikeouts (335). Welch won 26 games, registering a 1.93 ERA. Titcomb won 14 and the trio combined for 17 shutouts.

A healthy Buck Ewing led the team offense. Batting .306, he placed first among the Giants in hitting and was fifth in the league in that category in a season in which only five players reached the .300 plateau. He also led the Giants in doubles and stolen bases, and finished in the league top-ten in slugging, triples, steals, and extra-base hits. His 53 stolen bases are the most ever by a catcher in a season, and 1888 is the only year in baseball history in which a catcher led his team in steals.

After winning the National League pennant, the Giants played a ten-game "World's Series" against the American Association champions, the St. Louis Browns. While post-season play is taken for granted today, it was a relatively new concept for the Giants and other teams of the period. Until the advent of the American Association, the "default" world's champion was the team that finished in first place in the National League's standings, since no other major league existed. Despite the arrival of a second league in 1882, the National League initially refused invitations from the American Association for post-season series, claiming that the upstart organization was an inferior league. This attitude changed after the league recognized the American Association as its equal in the National Agreement of 1883. In 1884, National League President A. G. Mills accepted Association President H.G. McKnight's challenge to hold a best-of-three series between the two leagues' champions, the National's Providence Grays and the Association's New York Metropolitans. Providence swept the Mets, with the Grays' iron-armed Hoss Radbourn doing what he did frequently during his career — pitching and winning all three games of a three-game series.

Cap Anson's Chicago White Stockings battled Charlie Comiskey's St. Louis Browns in the next two fall classics, which were expanded to a seven-game format. No champion was declared in 1885,

Ewing making contact in this studio portrait, circa 1888. Although self-described as a place hitter who did not swing hard, Ewing led the National League in home runs in 1883, becoming the first player to reach double digits (10) in that category (courtesy National Baseball Hall of Fame Library, Cooperstown, New York).

since the deciding seventh game ended in a tie. The 1886 series was similarly hard-fought, with the Browns winning the Association's first World's Series on a wild pitch by Chicago's John Clarkson in the seventh game.

In the first three series, the winning team shared a $2,000 purse put up by the League and the Association. Beginning in 1887, the participants also competed for physical symbols of victory — a solid silver team trophy, known as the Dauvray Cup, and individual gold badges, with the player's name engraved on the reverse. The Cup and the badges were the gift of actress Helen Dauvray, an ardent Polo Grounds fan who married New York star John Ward while the 1887 World's Series between Detroit and St. Louis was taking place. The usually staid *New York Times* was quick to suggest that Dauvray's motivation for donating the Cup and the medals may not have been completely altruistic. "The generosity of the donor of these prizes was much commented upon at the time they were offered, and many reasons, charitable and uncharitable, were urged [suggested], but among them all not one suggestion of love for an individual player appeared."[45] Regardless of its donor's motivation, the Dauvray Cup is an historically significant award, since it was the first American trophy competed for by professional athletes.

Detroit won the first Dauvray Cup in 1887 by defeating St. Louis in the Browns' third consecutive appearance in the post-season classic. Both leagues now understood the financial benefits associated with the World's Series, but their greed almost succeeded in destroying this golden opportunity to acquire increased revenues. In 1887 and 1888, the Series were expanded to 15 and 11 games respectively, some contests were staged in ballparks other than those of the participants, and both teams agreed to play the full schedule of games, regardless of whether one squad had already clinched the championship. Poor attendance at the final games and late-fall cold weather ended this experiment with an expanded schedule. Mrs. John Ward finally saw her trophy won by the Giants in 1888 and 1889. The Cup was not awarded in 1890, since the series between Brooklyn and Louisville was called after seven games.

Upon the demise of both the American Association and the Players' League, major league baseball once again consisted of a single league whose top team was the default world's champion. Seeking to return to the days of quick revenues from post-season play, Pittsburgh owner William Temple in 1894 offered a silver trophy to the winner of a best-of-seven series between the National League's first- and second-place teams. The Temple Cup series lasted four years, but never attracted the fan interest generated by the previous inter-league competition. It would take another six years and the founding of a new league — the American — before the Fall Classic returned. Major League Baseball today does not officially recognize the nineteenth-century's post-season, inter-league competition as a World's Series.

Posed sliding demonstration by Buck Ewing, circa 1888. In the years after stolen bases were recognized as an official statistic, Ewing averaged almost 35 steals a year (courtesy National Baseball Hall of Fame Library, Cooperstown, New York).

In the ten-game Series between the St. Louis Browns and the Giants in October 1888, Tim Keefe accounted for four of the Giants' six wins, and Buck Ewing, playing in seven games, stole five bases and hit .346, including two triples and a home run. "Ewing's all-around work is largely responsible for the Browns defeat, not only in this game but throughout the series. His presence on the team today went far toward securing the victory, as he not only caught Keefe in masterly style, but he knocked out a home run in the first inning, and with three men on in the third inning, sent them all home on his three-bagger to center."[46]

The naysayers in the press, however, could not resist suggesting ulterior motives for Ewing's work in 1888. Reviewing the successful season, *The Sporting News*, a St. Louis publication that perhaps was smarting from the defeat the Giants had administered to the home-town Browns, claimed that Ewing's outstanding performance was due to special financial incentives he had negotiated with John Day:

> Ward resigned that position [Captain] and Ewing was elected to fill the vacancy. In order to captain the team properly, he was expected to take part in nearly all the games. At first he covered third base with poor results. Then it was thought

best when Whitney was secured to put Ewing behind the bat. The latter and President Day had a long talk together, and Mr. Day made a proposition to him that for every extra game he played he was to receive $25 and an additional $1,000 if the pennant was won. It was agreed that Ewing should play in sixty-five games [as catcher] during the season and that every game over that number should be counted as extra. Ewing played in 103 games out of the 135 games his team was engaged in, for which number he caught seventy-eight. From this it will be seen that he played in thirty-eight extra games, for which he will receive $950. This added to the salary of $3,500 and the extra $1,000 he will get because New York won the pennant will make Ewing's salary $5,450. In addition to this he, as well as the [other] players received $200 for winning the championship.[47]

A week later, the same journal quietly and without explanation revised downward this unsubstantiated estimate of Ewing's 1888 earnings, stating now that his salary was $3,500, that he earned $500 for the captaincy, and another $500 for winning the championship.[48] This total was nearly $1,000 less that the figure they had previously reported. No apology was tendered to Buck Ewing.

In what was described as the "most remarkable campaign in the history of the League,"[49] New York won its second consecutive championship in 1889, edging out Boston on the last day of the season. The Beaneaters had risen from fourth place to pennant contenders on the strength of Dan Brouthers' bat and John Clarkson's arm. Slugger Brouthers, acquired from Detroit, led the league in hitting with a .373 average. Clarkson took the circuit's pitching honors, winning 49 games, 21 more than any other National League pitcher. However, his loss to Pittsburgh on October 5, the final day of the season, coupled with Tim Keefe's New York win over Cleveland that afternoon, clinched the pennant for the Manhattan nine.

In order to finish in first place in 1889, the Giants used different weapons from those they employed the previous year, when pitching and fielding had led the way. Welch and Keefe, who had tallied over 1,800 innings of pitching during the previous two years, performed well, combining for 55 wins. Nevertheless, like the majority of league pitchers in 1889, their strikeouts declined by one-third, and their ERA rose by over one run per game. Keefe and Welch's pitching backups, Ed Crane and late-season addition Hank O'Day, performed well — working in 39 games, they combined for a 23–12 record. They moved to the forefront, however, during the World Series, replacing the exhausted Welch and Keefe and winning all of the Giants' six victories against the Brooklyn Bridegrooms.

The Giants offense secured them the pennant. While only one starter, Buck Ewing, reached the .300 mark in 1888, five did so in 1889, and the team led the league in batting average (.282), runs (935), triples (77) RBI (744)

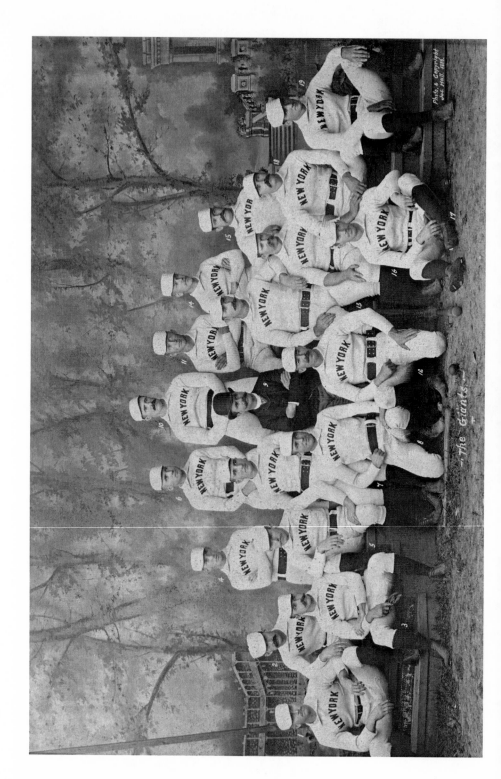

—The Giants—

and stolen bases (292). Buck Ewing caught 97 games, a career high. He hit .327, and stole 34 bases. It was an encore performance that temporarily muted the previous year's press criticism, earning him at last the grudging respect of all.

The Giants were faced with a major challenge even before they took the field in 1889, for they had no field on which to play. Over the winter, New York City made good on its threat to create 111th Street by bulldozing it through the heart of the Polo Grounds. While John Day frantically looked for a suitable location for a new permanent venue, the Giants opened the season playing their first two games at cramped Oakland Park in Jersey City, New Jersey. They then moved to the St. George Cricket Grounds on Staten Island, which had been the Mets home for their last two seasons (1886–1887) in the American Association. After the departure of the Mets, the St. George Grounds had reverted to its original function as an amusement park. Consequently, it was in no condition for baseball even before heavy spring rains turned it into a quagmire. Players were "forced to wear rubber-soled shoes in order to prevent slipping while running for batted balls."[49] A portion of a wooden stage, left over from theatrical performances, protruded onto the field, creating havoc for fielders, since balls "bound by [past] fielders with increased speed after they strike the woodwork."[50]

Challenging playing conditions were not the Giants' only problem, for stars Tim Keefe and John Ward once again were holdouts. Keefe, who had become a partner in a sporting goods store with former Giants reserve pitcher Buck Becannon, bluntly threatened to sit out the season unless his demands were met. "If my terms are not agreed to, I will attend to my sporting goods business and give up the [baseball] diamond until matters are arranged to my satisfaction."[51] As rumors circulated that the unsigned Ward would be sold to Washington or traded to Boston for Mike Kelly, a *New York Times* writer suggested that Ward was not needed in New York; "Ward is a very jealous man ... and he could not bear to see the club winning with Ewing as Captain while he made failures year after year.... I voice the sentiment of nearly all the players when I say that the Giants can play good ball and win the championship without the services of Ward."[52] On the second day of the seasonal play, however, the disgruntled shortstop signed on again with New York.

Opposite: The 1888 New York Giants, including six future Hall of Fame members. Mickey Welch (left) and Buck Ewing (right) kneel in front of manager Jim Mutrie, who wears street clothes and a bowler hat. To Mutrie's immediate right are Roger Connor and Jim O'Rourke. John Ward sits second to the left from Mutrie, and Tim Keefe sits next to Ward, at the end of the row. Relieved of his duties as team captain midway through the previous season, John Ward shows his disdain by facing in the opposite direction of other team members (courtesy National Baseball Hall of Fame Library, Cooperstown, New York).

Two weeks into the campaign, the Giants found themselves without pitchers. Keefe was still unsigned, Welch was sick, and second-year man Ed Crane was injured (Hank O'Day was not acquired until mid-season). It was time for Ewing to demonstrate some of the pitching skills he had shown during winter ball in California. He started in the box against Boston on May 9, and after a shaky start held on for the win. He picked up his second win seven days later against Cleveland, striking out six, walking five, scoring a run and contributing two hits to his 6–3 victory. "His work yesterday was

Rare outdoor action photograph series of Ewing batting, jumping for a high throw, and coming down after making the catch. Ewing introduced the catcher's mitt to the National League in 1888, and ads for Buck Ewing mitts began appearing in sports journals the following year. Here, in addition to the mitt, he still employs a skin-tight glove on his throwing hand (all three courtesy Transcendental Graphics/theruckerarchive.com).

very good, especially when the bases were occupied, when he displayed clever judgment and rare coolness.... Everybody applauded the popular Captain ... and it was agreed that he is the greatest of all general ball players.... The New Yorkers have seen Ewing play every position."[53]

Team injuries and illnesses continued to plague the Giants through mid–June. After finally signing his contract, Tim Keefe returned with a sore arm, which he tried to treat in novel fashion: "Keefe has a new-fangled stocking for his shoulder. It is saturated with mustard and calculated to keep the arm and shoulder in a state of warmth."[54] Shortly afterward, Keefe went on "grief leave," returning to his native Massachusetts to attend the funeral of his sister. Mickey Welch and Ed Crane also had sore arms, and John Ward was out with a similar malady.

Despite such bad luck, the Giants managed to win 10 of 16 games on their first western tour, and by the time they returned to New York in early July they had climbed into third place. During their absence, John Day had secured new grounds for the team at 155th Street and Eighth Avenue, a few yards from an elevated train stop. The new field was part of a large tract of land owned by real estate mogul James J. Coogan. It sloped down to the Hudson River from a steep escarpment that was originally dubbed "Dead Head Hill," but which eventually became known as Coogan's Bluff.

More than 10,000 paying customers were on hand on July 8 for the first game at what John Day had christened "The New Polo Grounds." Since the roof of the grandstand, which sat in the shadow of the escarpment, had not yet been erected, several thousand fans watched the game for free while seated on the slippery slope above or at a nearby beer garden on Eighth Avenue.

> When the gates were closed, those denied admission went across the street to a beer garden and watched the game from the windows. Others occupied positions on a hilly tract of land on the west side of the grounds christened "Dead Head Hill," and they were bunched together as checks on a dude's trousers.... The surreptitious onlookers ... enjoyed themselves to their heart's content.... Several times when good plays were made, and after the shouts of those in the grounds had died away, the echoes of applause from "Dead Head Hill" could be heard distinctly, which proved the onlookers from the lofty eminence could distinguish the fine points of the game.[55]

As the contest began, Captain Ewing was singled out for a special honor, and the details of the brief ceremony reveal the admiration in which he was held by New York's fans:

> All eyes, of course, were riveted on Mr. "Buck" Ewing, the catcher plenipotentiary of the New-Yorks. His appearance on the field was the signal for a big cheer, and hundreds tried to grasp the hand of the clever but modest player. In the first inning several of the Stock Exchange admirers of the New-York

Captain presented him with a gold watch with an inscription. He bowed in acknowledgment of the gift [and] blushed like a schoolgirl.[56]

While Ewing hit just six home runs in 1889, several of them were among the longest of his career. Both four-baggers he hit off the Phillies' Charlie Buffinton are noteworthy. The first, sent over the left field fence on July 24 in Philadelphia, was said to be the longest ever hit at Recreation Park. In an August 2 home game against the Phillies, Ewing drove another Buffinton pitch over the center field fence at the New Polo Grounds. "This home run was worth a green-back century plant [a $100 bill] to the New York Captain, for J. J. Coogan announced some weeks ago that he had that kind of flower [reward] for the man who should knock the ball over the centre field boards."[57]

Ewing's June 22 grand slam off Darby O'Brien at Cleveland garnered the most press attention. The *Times* reported an astounding distance for the blast: "Ewing dropped the ball over the left field fence, 478 feet from the plate, and chased three men home."[58] *Sporting Life* reported that it was the longest hit ever on the Cleveland grounds, but added that the distance to the fence was only 410 feet.[59] Three weeks later, Phillies manager Harry Wright measured the distance and found it to be 123 yards, or 369 feet. Since the ball cleared the high left-field fence by six feet, it was still a mighty blast in that era. Bill Jenkinson, baseball's pre-

Hands cupped together, Buck Ewing demonstrates the proper way to catch a ball during the gloveless era. By the mid–1890s, virtually all players used some form of protection on their hands when fielding (courtesy Library of Congress).

eminent expert on long-ball hitters, has estimated that the blow traveled 430 feet.[60]

Playing in the New Polo Grounds proved to be a tonic for the Giants, and they swept the Pirates and the Cleveland Spiders, and then took two of three from both Chicago and Indianapolis to end the home stand. Their winning ways were due in great part to Buck Ewing's torrid hitting. Ewing collected 15 hits and scored a dozen runs in the 12-game home stand. He twice hit a double and a triple in a game and twice collected three hits in a game. His performance against Philadelphia on July 9 demonstrated the multiple ways he could be an offensive force. He had two hits, sacrificed twice, stole a base and scored four runs.

Ewing often collected steals during the season in the same fashion in which he collected hits — in bunches. More than half of his season total of 34 steals came in just seven games. On June 7, he stole four bases off Boston back-up catcher Charlie Ganzel and pitcher Hoss Radbourn. He twice stole two bases off Indianapolis batteries, and on a third occasion he stole three. Chicago was another of his favorite victims. As was the case with Indianapolis, he pilfered two bases on two occasions, and in another game he stole three. Stealing 18 bases in seven games is a remarkable feat for any player. For a catcher, it is extraordinary.

As the season progressed, Ewing matched his hitting and base-running performances with fine catching, which was described as "a marvel of perfection."[61] While at times he had to sit out games with sore hands due to the addition of hard-throwing Ed Crane to the pitching staff, when injured in other ways he gamely held out as long as he could. "Ewing was struck in the mouth by Carrol's foot in the first inning. As the latter was sliding to the home plate, the spikes in the shoe cut his lip badly, but he caught up to the sixth inning."[62] *Sporting Life*, Ewing's old bugaboo, summed up press opinions of his performance behind the bat by remarking that "Ewing is catching the game of his life."[63]

His leadership as field general was now universally lauded. By mid-season, Jim Mutrie had made it clear to all that Ewing was in charge of the team: "Mr. Mutrie says that Captain Ewing has absolute control of the New York team on the field, and is not hampered in any way, he [Mutrie] preferring not even to sit on the players' bench in order to let Ewing do the work according to his best judgment."[64] Noting that the two games Ewing missed during a mid–August stretch were blowout losses, while the Giants won all the series contests in which he played, the normally staid *Times* waxed poetic, and was effusive in its praise of the Giants receiver: "The Giants without Ewing are like a ship without a rudder.... Ewing is the best Captain in the profession, and his value can only be appreciated when somebody else attempts to fill his position."[65]

The World champion 1888 New York Giants. Captain Buck Ewing stands behind manager Jim Mutrie, who is dressed in street clothes (courtesy Transcendental Graphics/theruckerarchive.com).

With the pennant secured, all team members and administrators were congratulated, but the highest praise was reserved for Ewing:

Every man connected with the club, from President Day to the mascot, can justly claim credit for the success of the team, but the giant's share belongs to Captain Ewing. The genial back-stop played great ball this year. His whole heart was in his work, and his aim was to capture the pennant. He succeeded, but it was difficult task, and it was only gained by remarkable skill and endurance on his part. Day after day he caught the curves of Keefe and Welch, and the speedy pitching of Crane when his hands were sore and painful. But he stuck to his work like a Trojan, and his reward is the proud distinction of being the Captain of the championship nine. Ewing is a great player. It is safe to assert that without his services the Giants could never have won first place.[66]

Ewing's durability behind the plate in 1888 and 1889 can largely be attributed to his adoption of the large, padded catcher's mitt for daily use in 1888. The mitt enabled him to avoid the hand injuries that had plagued him in earlier years. Just as important, the mitt's protection kept his bat in the lineup. Catching without the mitt, Buck caught just 58 games in 1886–1887. Using the padded glove in 1888 and 1889, he caught 165 games. His 185 hits and 44 stolen bases in the earlier two years contrast with his 260 hits and 97 steals during the two championship seasons.

The pennant fever that the Giants had aroused in the Manhattan populace in 1888 was dwarfed by the outpouring of sentiment in New York in 1889. The *New York Herald* captured this spirit in its account of the team's return to town from Cleveland after their thrilling last-day-of-the-season victory:

It seemed as if all the *gamins* of the town had assembled at the foot of Chambers Street to welcome their idols of the baseball world. Hundreds of small boys cheered and stomped and danced in ecstasy until they just about lost their little heads, and the champions had to run the gantlet of all this yelling mob. Proudly, the returning heroes marched up the street, and on every corner clear to the "L" road station, gentlemen stood about and lifted their hats and added to the glorious welcome and joyful hubbub. The president and manager and stockholders came in for their share of good words, but whenever a name in the team was mentioned, hundreds of throats were cracked in vociferous cheers. A crowd followed some of the boys up to Twenty-Third Street, and it was not until the players had scattered to their homes that the excitement subsided. And thus the champions were welcomed home. It was a proud day for the Giants.[67]

A testimonial and benefit for the Giants players was organized by De Wolf Hopper and other New York thespians, and the event took place at the Broadway Theater on Sunday, October 20. Dozens of performers donated their time and talents, and the receipts, including checks sent in by non-attendees, totaled $6,000, all of which was distributed to the 16 men on the team. Several players gave brief speeches of thanks. "There were loud cries for 'Buck' Ewing, the Captain of the team, but 'Buck' modestly declined to deliver an oration."[68]

The Giants defeated the American Association champion, the Brooklyn Bridegrooms, six games to three in the 1889 World Series. Ewing appeared in eight of the nine contests and caught well, but was undistinguished at the plate, hitting just .250, with four doubles and seven RBI. It may be that he was preoccupied by an important impending personal engagement. In a dispatch from Savannah, Georgia, dated December 12, the *Times* reported that

> Capt. [*sic*] Ewing of the New-York Club, the well-known catcher, was married here [Savannah,] to-day. The bride is Annie Caig Sevening. She is a handsome brunette and a resident of this city. A large number of friends of the bride witnessed the ceremony, and the presents were numerous and costly. After the ceremony Mr. and Mrs. Ewing started on a wedding tour. They will stop in New-York for a few days.[69]

The *Times* report mangled the young bride's name. She was Annie L. McCaig, age 21, born in Pennsylvania and living with relatives in Savannah. Her father, Arthur, from Donegore Parish, Northern Ireland, had immigrated to the United States as a teenager, and by 1860 was working in Savannah in the employ of John Gilliard, a grocer, who was from the same Irish village as young McCaig.

A brief notice of Annie and Buck's nuptials that appeared in the Chicago daily, *The Inter Ocean*,[70] claimed that Annie's father was a former Confederate soldier. There is no record of his service in the Army of the Confederacy, but by 1870 he had relocated to Cumberland County, Pennsylvania, where he was employed as a telegraph operator, and where Annie, born in 1868, completed her schooling.

How Annie and Buck met remains a mystery, but the most logical — and romantic — probability is that the encounter came at a Giants exhibition game played in Savannah, which was a popular stopping-off point for major league teams training in the South prior to the start of the regular season. Buck, at this juncture, was one of the most popular and well-known baseball players in America, and it is easy to imagine how the dashing, mature (he was 30, nine years Annie's senior) Giants team captain could have swept the young lady off her feet.

An intriguing, if less plausible, possibility involves the participation of Buck's younger brother, John. For two years, 1886 and 1887, a Savannah team competed in the Southern League, a minor league established in 1885. As we have seen, at this time John Ewing played first for the New Orleans club and then for the Louisville team affiliated with the Southern League. It is possible, though unlikely, that John first made Annie's acquaintance when his league team played in Savannah against the city's league entry, and that he later introduced her to Buck.

Regardless of how the acquaintance began, it was a successful marriage, lasting until Ewing's untimely death 17 years later. After a honeymoon trip to New York, including a Christmas stay at the fashionable Sturtevant House Hotel, the couple settled in Ewing's Pendleton neighborhood in Cincinnati. Arthur, their first-born, named after Annie's father, arrived in October 1890, and a daughter, Florence, followed in June 1891. Annie McCaig Ewing was the opposite of John Ward's celebrity wife, Helen Dauvray. She shunned the limelight, and with two small children in tow during the balance of Ewing's playing career, generally remained in Cincinnati for the season, where he would visit her and the children during his team's western tours. Infrequently, Annie would come east with the children during Ewing's long home stands. When she did, she much preferred staying at her parents' home in Shamokin, Pennsylvania, to living even temporarily in New York City.

Upon the great catcher's untimely death in 1906, Annie's profound influence on his life was briefly noted in the press: "All those who were intimately acquainted with Buck Ewing knew that it was his loving and faithful wife that guided him in most of his successful ventures in baseball. Mrs. Ewing was a very modest little woman, and was seldom seen at the ball games when her husband was a star in the field, but her heart was always in his work and his success was her happiness.["71]

The beginning and the end of the decade of the 1880s were a study in contrasts for Buck Ewing. He arrived home in late fall 1880, as an unknown ballplayer with a few dollars in his pocket to show for his summer's work on the dying Rochester Hop Bitters team, and fervently hoping to be issued a contract to play for the lowly Troy Trojans. He returned to Cincinnati in late December 1889, as a national celebrity, with a comfortable salary as the captain of the World Champion New York Giants, acknowledged by all as one of baseball's greatest stars, and with a beautiful young bride on his arm.

Chapter 5

Fallen Idol: 1890–1892

"A player's reputation lies with the public: he leans on popular favor, and that he may find at any time to be a broken reed." — John Montgomery Ward, "Notes of a Baseballist," *Lippincott's Magazine*, April, 1886

Billy Ewing, the distillery delivery boy from Cincinnati's East End, traveled a remarkable road from the Pendleton sandlots to Manhattan's Polo Grounds and the gaslights of Broadway. By the early 1890s, he was more than a well-known hero of the National Pastime — he was a national icon. During the Giants' slow climb to the top of the league standings in the mid–1880s, a lithograph portrayal of one of Ewing's famous steals of home had appeared in *Harper's Weekly* magazine. It was his first national press exposure beyond mention of him in the sports pages or weekly sports journals. After leading his team to a second world's championship in 1889, *Harper's*, a self-described "journal of civilization," featured an idealized portrait of Ewing on its cover. The top portion of the *Harper's* cover was soon colorized and used as a cigar label with the title, "Buck Ewing: Crack Catcher."

During the championship 1889 season, Ewing accepted an offer from the Guinness Brewing Company to pose for a beer advertisement with Chicago White Stockings player/manager Cap Anson. "Both Anson and Ewing are pictured in their representative uniforms as they take a break from a game to enjoy a refreshing glass of beer."[1] Neither player is named in the ad, a clear indication that their likenesses were recognizable to all. The poster of the two stars, which was circulated nationally, is a further testament to Buck Ewing's notoriety. The Anson-Ewing beer advertisement is "the first documented paid endorsement of any kind by a baseball player. It is also certainly the first advertising piece featuring players in promotion of an alcoholic beverage."[2] Both stars received cash and a case of beer in compensation for their services.

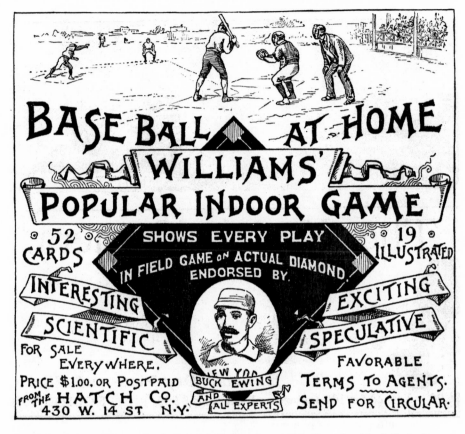

Box lid of the Williams Baseball Card Game, circa 1890, featuring Buck Ewing's image and endorsement (courtesy Transcendental Graphics/theruckerarchive.com).

One report stated that the remuneration was $300 per man, but years later, when Ewing came upon a copy of the poster while traveling, he insisted that he had been paid $500 for his participation.[3]

Ewing was also featured in cartoons. One of them — possibly a tobacco ad — played on the literal meaning of his nickname, placing a sketch of his head, cigar in mouth, on the body of a mature buck with long antlers. A sketch of his likeness and a statement of his endorsement also appeared on the box of a game entitled, "Baseball at Home: Williams' Popular Indoor Game." It consisted of a board, wooden pieces, and 52 playing cards. Nineteen cards contained color profile portraits of players (two per card, one facing up and the other facing down) and game instructions. If the participant drew card Number Four, for example, which featured pitchers John Clarkson and Tim Keefe's likenesses, the instruction was "Batter Strikes Out." Card Number

15, containing portraits of Ewing and Cap Anson, had the highest value. Its possession awarded the fortunate card player with a home run.

Ewing's on-field exploits also became the subject of popular fiction: "Captain Ewing has already figured as the hero of one of the many five-cent novels with which the news counters are burdened."[4] In 1891, Ewing himself became a writer. Asked by the editor of *Ladies' Home Journal*, Edward William Bok, to produce a 2,000-word article on baseball for the "Boy's" section of the magazine, he responded with the essay, "Ins and Outs of Baseball," which provided a brief history of the game and gave pointers on how to form a team and how to hit and field (see Appendix 1 for full text). At the height of Ewing's popularity, it was even seriously suggested that his image appear on U.S. postage:

Buck Ewing/Cap Anson card from the Williams Baseball Game, circa 1890. Drawing the Ewing/Anson card rewarded the game player with a home run (courtesy Transcendental Graphics/theruckerarchive.com).

> It is of little consequence whether the new two-cent postage stamps are green or red. The great question is whose portrait is to adorn them? Will it be that of William Buck Ewing, John L. Sullivan or Corporal Tanner [a double-amputee Civil War hero]? If true genius and representative Americanism were the test it would unquestionably be a toss-up between Sullivan and Ewing. But if statesmanship and ability to tug at the purse strings of the nation is taken into consideration, Tanner ought to get the honor.[5]

Entering his thirties, Buck Ewing had gone from being the toast of New York to the toast of the nation. What could possibly go wrong with his life? Just about everything. Over the next three years he would be served with an injunction by Giants owner John B. Day, be accused by the press of conspiracy and treason against his fellow ball players, suffer an injury that would end his catching career, stand accused of throwing games to Boston to enable them to steal the pennant from Chicago, be relieved of his duties as captain of the Giants, and, after a decade wearing a New York uniform, be traded to the Cleveland Spiders. He survived it all with dignity, although often with frustration, and afterward put in a few more successful years as a player and manager before his career on the diamond ended.

The 1890 season was like no other since the founding of the National League. A large group of players, frustrated by the reserve clause, salary caps, and the blacklisting of those who dared break the owners' rules, established their own organization, the Players' League, setting up shop in eight cities, seven of which already had National League or American Association franchises. The architect of this great rebellion, the last nineteenth-century attempt by players to control their own professional destinies, was Giants shortstop John Montgomery Ward.

Rebus cartoon, circa 1890, possibly a tobacco advertisement, which superimposes Buck Ewing's face on the body of a buck deer (courtesy Transcendental Graphics/theruckerarchive.com).

Ward was uniquely suited to the task. At 14, an age at which other future Giants like Buck Ewing and Roger Connor were already working manual-labor jobs six days a week, Ward was attending the Pennsylvania State College (now Penn State University), taking courses in algebra, geometry, composition, Latin and Greek. Although dismissed from the school for misconduct after his fifth semester (his crime: stealing chickens), he resumed his studies six years later at Columbia College in New York, acquiring a Bachelor of Laws degree in 1885, and a Bachelor of Philosophy from the School of Political Science in 1886. A graceful writer, experienced in the law and practiced in oratory, Ward would prove to be a formidable foe of baseball's establishment.

Ball players had been seeking ways to control their own professional destinies since the demise of the National Association in 1876. For a brief period during the organization of the American Association in 1882, some were able to increase their salaries temporarily by jumping to the rival league. That window of opportunity closed in 1883, when the Association made peace with the National League, and each agreed to honor the other's contracts. Hopes for a league without a reserve clause were dashed for a second time when Henry Lucas's quixotic Union League folded at the end of the 1884 season. Once again unrivaled, the National League and the American Association now felt confident enough to establish a $2,000 salary limit for players in both organizations.

The salary cap rule provoked John Ward to act. In 1885, he and eight other Giants, including Buck Ewing, Roger Connor, Tim Keefe and Jim O'Rourke, founded a union, the Brotherhood of Professional Base Ball Players, and Ward was elected the group's president. During the 1886 and 1887 seasons, the Brotherhood's New York contingent quietly enlisted members from other teams, while Ward, through a series of articles written for national magazines and excerpted in newspapers, sought to bring the ballplayers' plight to the attention of the public and gain recognition of the Brotherhood by the National League.

Although the reserve clause and blacklisting were ongoing concerns of the Brotherhood during these years, the issue that precipitated the 1890 Players' League revolt was the implementation of a new salary restriction code, one that eliminated the loopholes of the original 1885 plan, which, as we have seen, had enabled Buck Ewing to augment his salary by selling his uniform shirt to manager Jim Mutrie. The new plan placed players in one of five salary classifications, ranging from Class A ($2,500 salary) to Class E ($1,000 salary). Adding insult to injury, a player's classification was now based not only on his playing ability, but on the league's assessment of his conduct off the field.

The National League's timing in implementing the new rule was particularly galling to John Ward. At the end of the 1888 season, Ward was one of 20 players who accepted National League magnate Al Spalding's invitation to tour the world playing baseball. As soon as the Brotherhood leader was safely out to sea on the first leg of the tour, the new classification system was enacted. Ward eventually learned of the action, but he was unable to begin to rally his forces against it until he returned to the United States the following spring.

After repeated Brotherhood requests to hold negotiations with the owners on the classification system were ignored in the spring and summer of 1889, union representatives from each team met in July 1889, to form the Players' League. The new league's rules were the antithesis of the National League's policies:

The league would not use the reserve clause; all players would be given three-year contracts and the right to work out transfers to other clubs for themselves. Gate receipts were to be split fifty-fifty among all clubs. After the first $10,000, investors were to share club profits fifty-fifty with the players. The league would be overseen by a board of directors composed of both players and investors.[6]

During the last six months of 1889, John Ward lined up financial backers for the Players' League. Stockbroker Edward Talcott and tobacco magnate E. A. McAlpin were his principal supporters for New York's new team, which would be managed by Buck Ewing. Ward himself became player/manager of the Brooklyn franchise after securing the financial assistance of real estate mogul Wendell Goodwin. Over 100 major league veterans jumped their National League or American Association contracts to play for teams in the new league, including nearly all the top players except Cap Anson, who was a minority stockholder in the White Stockings.

Once the National League understood the seriousness of the threat from the Players' League, it established a War Committee, consisting of Al Spalding, sporting goods magnate and owner of the White Stockings, New York's John Day, and the Philadelphia Phillies owner, lawyer John I. Rogers. The committee developed a three-part strategy aimed at destroying the new league. First, it attempted, with limited success, to bribe top players to return to the National League. It then tried to prosecute high-profile players for jumping their original contracts. Though successfully intimidating the players, this ploy proved a resounding failure in the courts, which unanimously ruled against the reserve clause. Finally, the committee sought to intimidate the Players' League's business partners: "a pattern of economic war emerged, with the league putting pressure on the players' financial backers, hoping to scare away faint hearts. Since all players' teams had capital outlays of at least $50,000, the league strategy was to drive a wedge between the brothers and their financiers, which, it was hoped, would break the back of the rebellion."[7]

It was the latter stratagem that proved successful. By deliberately scheduling its games on the same dates as the Players' League teams, by hiding its own losses, exaggerating its gate receipts and secretly providing financial backing for struggling franchises (New York, for example, only survived the season due to an $80,000 loan from Al Spalding), the National League presented a false façade of economic stability to the rebel league's backers, who were nearly $400,000 in debt. Despite the fact that their league had fielded baseball's best teams in 1890, the Brotherhood's backers, convinced that Spalding's league was invincible, cut their losses and sold out at the end of the season.

The National League War Committee's first retaliatory move against the Players' League was aimed at John Ward. In December 1889, they brought suit against him in New York State court, seeking an injunction to prohibit him from playing with any team except the National League Giants. On January 28, 1890, the request was denied. Having failed at its first attempt to intimidate the opposition, the league then tried to convince star players to defect by offering them lucrative contracts. The hope was that if one or two stars would jump their contracts, others would soon follow. The first man they approached was Buck Ewing.

In mid–February, just as Ewing was preparing to travel east to take charge of the Players' League Giants, John Day met with him for two days at the St. Nicholas Hotel in Cincinnati, and offered him a lucrative three-year contract worth $30,000. Although Ewing turned down the offer, the manner in which he did so, and the fact that he even met with Day in the first place, raised doubts of his loyalty just two months before Opening Day.

> Ewing talked of the interview with President Day, but declared he had not deserted the brotherhood. The tenor of his remarks clearly indicated that he was on the fence. When asked if there was a possibility of him signing with the league, he said, "I told Mr. Day that if he could get Connor, Richardson, Gore and Slattery to sign, I would do the same, because then he would have virtually the old club and there would not be any use of my sticking out by myself."[8]

The *Newark Daily Advocate* suggested that money had been exchanged at the meeting: "Ewing denies that he has signed a contract, but displayed nearly four thousand dollars in large bills."[9] This news created a frenzy among the press, who sought out Ewing in Pittsburgh while he was en route to New York with his wife and Players' League financial backer Al Johnson, a Cleveland streetcar magnate. Ewing reaffirmed his commitment to the Players' League, but noted that recent notable defections to the National League may have inflicted serious harm to the union's cause: "Of course I think that the brotherhood [league] will be a success, but when men like [Boston's Charlie] Bennett desert, it has a very bad effect."[10]

Although in all probability Al Johnson and Ewing were traveling east together to conduct Players' League business, the *Dallas Morning News* drew another conclusion:

> The presence of Johnson confirms the story told last night that the brotherhood leaders had decided that if Ewing was to desert, it would be an almost irreparable injury to their cause, and in order to prevent anything of the sort, they decided to have a trustworthy person [Johnson] stay with Ewing until he was irrevocably committed to the players' league and keep any national league emissaries away from him.[11]

Proof that Ewing had not been convinced to abandon the Players' League, however, came in March, when John Day sued him for breach of contract. Since the National League's suit against John Ward had failed before the New

York State Supreme Court, Day decided to pursue Ewing in U.S. Circuit Court, hoping for a different ruling. His hopes were dashed when Judge William P. Wallace found in favor of Ewing.

The shock of being hauled into Federal Court by men who had been so attentive to him a month earlier had its effect on Ewing, hardening his pro–Players' League stance. As the season started, he vowed, "We'll play for nothing the first year if necessary."[12] He angrily responded to reports circulated by the National League that some Players' League teams were so bad off financially that they would not go west to complete their schedules. "The Players' League will fulfill all its obligations to the very letter.... We will go West and the Western Clubs will come East. Then we will complete the schedule just as it stands."[13] Nevertheless, in late June, Ewing appeared willing to open the door to a possible merger with the American Association, but insisted that in such a collaboration the Players' League would still require a 50-cent admission fee instead of the Association's 25-cent fare, and would refuse to play on Sunday, as Association teams did.[14]

By this time, however, news had circulated that an increasingly desperate Al Spalding had offered Boston's Mike Kelly $10,000 to sign, and had given him a blank three-year contract on which Kelly could fill in any salary amount he wished. Kelly turned down the offer, but Spalding still thought him susceptible, and tried another ploy to sign him that involved Buck Ewing. Reasoning that Kelly might agree to terms if he were told that Ewing was ready to sign, he had Cap Anson arrange a meeting with both men in Youngstown, Ohio. At the last minute Kelly backed out, and Ewing did the same.

In July, amid continuing notices that the Players' League was in financial straits, Ewing reported to Players' League Secretary Frank Brunell that he had again met with John Day, this time in Chicago, and had agreed on Day's behalf to ask the Players' League Giants (specifically, Connor, Richardson, Keefe and O'Rourke) to "use their influence upon the directors of the New York Players' League Club to affect a combination [merger] with the National League Club."[15] This news was not well-received by the named Giants players, and it was reported that gentle giant Roger Connor had given Ewing a "tongue-lashing" after hearing the catcher's presentation.[16] Ewing later strongly denied any conflict between himself and Connor: "In the nine years Connor and I have played together, we have not had a harsh word.... Such stories were circulated to give the public a wrong impression."[17]

Ewing's unauthorized meetings with the opposition were questioned. "Why the New York captain was so often closeted with men like Day and Anson unless willing to listen to propositions, was more than the members of the New York team could tell, and why he didn't come out like Capt. Kelly and ignore all propositions to break contracts made in good faith was a puzzle to the other players."[18] Chastened, Ewing re-stated his loyalty to the Players' League a week later. "Everybody will feel relieved now that Ewing has reaffirmed his loyalty to the Players' League, especially because being a manager, he could, if traitorous, have played both ends against the middle."[19]

Apparently convinced of Ewing's sincerity, his team held a meeting on August 11, and issued a statement of support:

> A rumor credited to an unnamed player concerning the fealthy [*sic*] of William Ewing to the Brotherhood of Ball Players having been circulated in a Sunday newspaper, we, the undersigned members of the New York Players' League Club, desire to say that any such statement is false and malicious, and does an injustice not alone to Mr. Ewing, but to the organization which he represents.
>
> The item published in the same paper that any player of this club desires the release of Mr. Ewing is also untrue. We are not only satisfied that he is true to our cause, but appreciate the hard, honest, and remarkable work he has done on and off the field for us this season. Signed T. J. Keefe, Roger Connor, Daniel Richardson, George F. Gore, Daniel Shannon, M. J. Slattery, W. Brown, H. Vaughn, G. Hatfield, H. M. O'Day.[20]

After the Players' League owners had surrendered to their National League counterparts at the end of the season, Ewing was once again pilloried in the press for alerting his team's financial backers to make a deal while they still had some leverage. As a result, Talcott and McAlpin received National League Giants stock in exchange for allowing their players to be absorbed by their rivals. Ewing later explained his actions in this regard to the press:

> I saw a disposition on the part of every club in the Players' League to quit, and each club was working to get all it could out of it. I went to Mr. Talcott and Colonel McAlpin and told them of the things I had heard, and, being in their employ and having a friendly feeling for them, I did not like to see them lose any more money.... At the meeting held here in New York after the season closed ... I urged Mr. Talcott and Colonel McAlpin then to get things settled as soon as possible, and because they got fixed first, there was a great cry.[21]

Coming out of the "peace conference" meetings between the leagues that were held at the St. James Hotel in New York City in mid–October, an exasperated Ewing summed up his feelings about the great Brotherhood experiment, stating, "I am tired of stock-holding players and player-directors. They are a failure, and I will never play again with a team which is made up of them."[22] *Sporting Life* could not resist a parting shot at the beleaguered catcher: "Buck ... is a big success riding two horses at a time."[23]

Ewing's behavior during the Players' League rebellion was not heroic, but neither was it villainous. Recently married and with his first child on the way, he resisted the temptation to jump his contract, even though he was promised more money for three years of future service than he had earned since joining the National League a decade earlier. When it became obvious that the rebel league was in serious financial trouble, he entertained the idea of defecting — but only if most of his fellow Giants followed suit. When this option failed, he presented John Day's offer to consolidate both Giant squads to his teammates. Finally, when he became aware that the rebel league's dissolution was imminent, he alerted his team's financial backers, allowing them to get the best terms from the National League.

If the actions of players who signed with the Brotherhood's league were placed on a continuum, its polar extremes could be represented by Boston's John Clarkson and New York's Roger Connor. After signing with the Players' League Boston team, Clarkson sold out to the team's National League counterpart for $25,000. Connor, on the other hand, shunned all lucrative offers to jump his contract, condemned backsliders like Clarkson, played the last months of the season without being paid, and was still speaking optimistically of the Players' League's second season when it surrendered to the National League.

Buck Ewing belongs at the mid-point of this continuum. Ultimately, "Bread and Butter" Buck, the consummate poker player, played the hand that he had dealt himself. In modern baseball parlance, his actions during the Players' League revolt were another example of Buck being Buck.

The Players' League Giants' first task in 1890 was to secure a playing field. Real estate mogul John J. Coogan rented them the large parcel of land that lay adjacent to the National League Giants' Polo Grounds for $4,000. Fans could reach the field, known as the Brotherhood Grounds, by taking the Sixth or Ninth Street

This baseball game card, circa 1888, featured generic poses with facial features unique to each player. In 1887, Buck Ewing spent most of the year at third or second base, on orders of manager Jim Mutrie, who declared him too valuable to risk injury as a catcher (courtesy Transcendental Graphics/theruckerarchive.com).

elevated railroads and de-boarding at the same station that was used to reach the National League grounds.

Buck Ewing allowed himself one luxury in his new role as manager. He was an avid dog lover, who, as previously noted, was once fooled into believing he had been given the gift of a pedigreed canine, only to discover in front of Polo Grounds fans and his teammates that the gift animal was actually a goat. At Brotherhood Park, new skipper Ewing brought along all his canine friends.

> Anyone who enters the club-house on these [Brotherhood] grounds, and who knew Manager Ewing under the old regime, would at once perceive a difference. Lying in recently built kennels or tied to convenient posts, are no less than five dogs, four of them the property of Ewing.... At the Polo Grounds, Buck was only allowed one dog, and that had to be securely housed. Now, before the Summer [sic] is ended, it is likely that a separate club-house will be required by Ewing and his pets.[24]

With few exceptions, the Players' League Giants' roster closely resembled that of the 1889 World's Champion team. Mickey Welch and Mike Tiernan were absent, having decided to stay with Jim Mutrie's National League Giants, and John Ward was now the manager of the new Brooklyn Players' League team, which was immodestly nicknamed "Ward's Wonders." The remaining players, Gore, Connor, Keefe, O'Rourke and company, made up a team that was very familiar to fans, and which was still considered the "authentic" Giants team. This perception had its effect at the gate, as attendance for the season at the Brotherhood Grounds was twice that of National League games played a few yards away.

Pitchers Keefe, O'Day and Crane were all on board, and Buck Ewing used his influence as manager to find a replacement for Mickey Welch. He chose his brother John to fill that vacancy — a decision that caused considerable controversy, especially given the younger Ewing's prior major league record. For two seasons, "Brother John," as he would be known in New York, had toiled for the American Association Louisville Colonels — arguably one of the worst teams in baseball history. For the seventh-place 1888 Colonels team that finished 48–87, he won just eight of 21 contests, but registered a solid 2.83 ERA. In 1889, the Colonels became the first team to lose 100 games in a season. John Ewing lost 30 games and won just six, but led his team's pitchers with 155 strikeouts.

Early reports that the younger Ewing would join his brother in New York were greeted optimistically. "Ewing and Ewing ought to prove a winning battery.... [John] Ewing is young and has plenty of speed, is a good fielder, and with a man like Buck Ewing behind him, he will be in the front rank."[25] Midway through the pre-season, however, *The Sporting News* was writing him off: "John Ewing is being battered pretty hard in the exhibition games of the

Allen & Ginter Buck Ewing tobacco card, circa 1888. The Richmond-based Allen & Ginter Company produced the first color tobacco cards (courtesy Library of Congress).

Players' League. It looks as though the company was too fast for him."[26] On April 21, the Ewing battery debuted in the second game of the regular season, becoming one of a small number of pitching/catching brothers working together in the same game in major league history. Boston pitcher Will White and catcher Jim "Deacon" White were the first such combination in 1877. Los Angeles' Norm and Larry Sherry were the last in 1962.

John Ewing lost his first three games in a Giants uniform, and his troubles were exacerbated when he was out for two weeks after breaking his thumb while trying to stop a wild throw from outfielder Jim O'Rourke.[27] After a 19–7 shellacking by Brooklyn in mid–June, the *Times'* critique of John was merciless: "Perhaps 'Long' John Ewing thinks he is a pitcher. The Brooklyn Players' League team says he is of no earthly use in the box. Likewise sayeth [*sic*] the Philadelphia team."[28]

As the season progressed, however, Tim Keefe developed a sore arm and

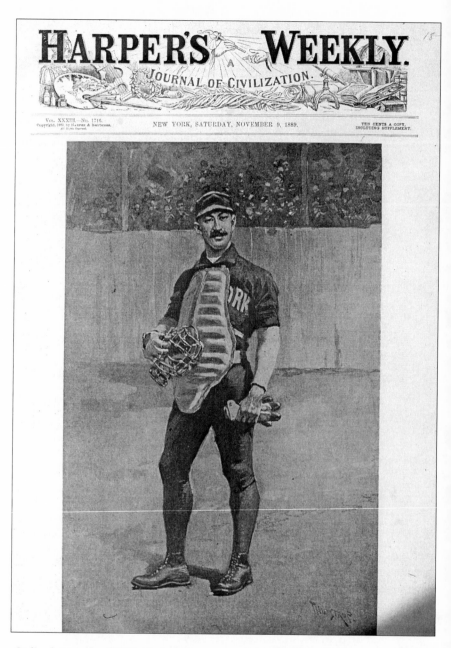

HARPER'S WEEKLY.

JOURNAL OF CIVILIZATION.

Vol. XXXIII.—No. 1716.
Copyright, 1889, by Harper & Brothers.
All Rights Reserved.

NEW YORK, SATURDAY, NOVEMBER 9, 1889.

TEN CENTS A COPY,
INCLUDING SUPPLEMENT.

Stylized portrait of Buck Ewing that appeared on the cover of *Harper's Weekly* in November 1889 after the Giants, under Ewing's guidance as team captain, won their second consecutive pennant and world championship. The Giants' form-fitting black uniforms were introduced in July 1888 and were designed by Tim Keefe's Manhattan sporting goods company, Keefe & Becannon. In the portrait, Ewing still uses the old style catcher's gloves. In reality, he switched to the more protective large catcher's mitt in 1888 (courtesy Transcendental Graphics/theruckerarchive.com.

Ed Crane's alcoholism was making him "perfectly useless to the New-York team."[29] Meanwhile, "Brother John" was starting to pitch effectively. After blanking the Cleveland Infants, 5–0, in late June, the *Times* began to have a change of heart. "Buck Ewing went behind the bat ... at Cleveland yesterday, and he succeeded in steadying his brother John so well that the Clevelands made only four safe hits off him."[30] As Long John first matched, and then surpassed Tim Keefe in the win column, *The Sporting News* now praised him, and chided the New York dailies for their early criticism of the younger Ewing's pitching, conveniently forgetting that a few months earlier, it had also done the same. "Buck Ewing's obstinacy in holding on to his brother John, despite the jeers of the New York press, is being justified, as John is coming up fast and pitching fine ball now. After all, Buck knows a good deal more about practical ball than the reporters who theorize about it."[31] As the season drew to a close, John, like his brother Buck before him, began to understand the fickleness of the Big Apple's press, which now confidently affirmed that "with another pitcher like Ewing, the New-Yorks could win the championship."[32]

Behind the pitching of Hoss Radbourn and the slugging of Dan Brouthers, Mike Kelly's Boston Reds finished in first place at the end of the Players' League's only season. John Ward's Brooklyn squad landed in second place, doing justice to their nickname, "Ward's Wonders." The Giants, who led the league in fielding and placed second in hitting, finished a respectable third, eight games behind Boston. They loved Brotherhood Park, going 47–19 there, but they won only 27 of their 65 road games. The latter total proved doubly significant at the end of the season, since 19 of their last 20 games were played on the road.

Buck Ewing's first season as a manager was no picnic. Since new owners Talcott and McAlpin had no prior baseball administrative experience, they relied heavily on Ewing on the business side of the operation as well as on the field. Following the Harry Wright managerial model, Ewing set the lineup, established game strategy, recruited and signed new players, supervised practices, and enforced discipline among the players, but he also was in charge of salaries and budgets, equipment, grounds and travel arrangements. When two architects sued the team over compensation for their services in designing the Brotherhood Grounds grandstand, for example, it was Ewing, not Talcott or McAlpin, who was called upon to explain the matter to the press: "Manager Ewing says they did not attend to their business properly, hence the objection to paying so large a sum."[33] In mid–June, Ewing's role as part-time groundskeeper at the Grounds resulted in an injury that kept him out of the lineup for most of the rest of the month: "Buck Ewing hurt his back while doing some heavy lifting in preparing the grounds for the Yale and Princeton boys. He could not go to Philadelphia on that account, or the returns [results] would have been different."[34]

Ewing's outstanding on-field performance in 1890 is all the more remarkable when considering his myriad off-field responsibilities and the constant, savage criticism heaped upon him by the press throughout the season. Playing in 83 games, 81 of them behind the plate, he led the league in fielding his position (.949). Hitting second in the lineup behind George Gore, he had career highs to that point in runs (98), RBI (72), batting average (.338), on-base percentage (.406), and slugging (.545), and he stole 36 bases. His eight home runs were two shy of his career high. One of them, the first ever hit over the Brotherhood Grounds left field fence, earned him a new suit as a bonus.[35] He had two four-hit games, and in one of them he slugged two home runs. On July 9, catching his brother John, he collected a home run, a triple, and two singles in an 18–4 win over Buffalo. In Pittsburgh on July 30, his three hits were a triple, a double and a home run. Against Cleveland in an August game, he stole three bases. In October he stole four in a game against Buffalo. In his tenth year in major league baseball, Buck Ewing put up the best numbers of his career thus far.

In October, during the peace conference between Players' League and National League representatives, wonderful news for Ewing arrived from Cincinnati: "While in attendance upon [sic] the conference meeting Wednesday at the Fifth Avenue Hotel, Buck Ewing was informed of the birth of his first heir — a boy."[36] Annie and Buck named him Arthur, after Annie's father.

The following spring, with the league wars over, the consolidated Giants prepared for the 1891 season. Although still the titular owner of the team, John Day was nearly bankrupt. Having spent most of his fortune trying to keep the team afloat, he was now forced into an alliance with his enemies, the former owners of the Players' League Giants. Jim Mutrie stayed on as manager, but his long-time allegiance to John Day had made him vulnerable. It would be his last year as a major league skipper.

One remnant of the Players' League revolt endured as a permanent reminder of the struggle: "The new group of owners decided that the Brotherhood Grounds, now without a tenant, was the superior facility in Coogan's Hollow, and moved the New York National League team into it for the 1891 season."[37] The park's new name had a familiar ring: the Polo Grounds. For another 67 years, until the franchise moved to San Francisco after the 1957 season, it would be home to Giants with names like McGraw, Mathewson, Bresnahan, Hubbell, Youngs, Ott and Mays.

As the 1891 season opened, an uneasy truce existed between members of the Giants who had chosen different sides in the Players' League revolt. Jim Mutrie tried to alleviate the tension on Opening Day by staging a symbolic pre-game

Chromolithograph cigar label featuring Buck Ewing, circa 1890. Ewing's image here is a slightly retouched version of the portrait that appeared on the cover of *Harper's Weekly* in 1889 (courtesy Transcendental Graphics/theruckerarchive.com).

ceremony. As a band played the song, "When We Were Comrades," the former Players' League men lined up opposite their National League rivals. At a signal, the groups approached one another: "Coming near the home plate, they wheeled and marched to within a few feet [of each other] and tipped caps. There were no smiles or hugging. The players were evidently trying to swallow a bit of medicine, and did it with the best grace they could muster."[38]

It was the end of an era. Welch and Keefe, the pitching stars of the 1888 and 1889 champion teams, were now on their last legs. Both returned out of shape, and together they pitched in just 30 games. Keefe was sold to Philadelphia in August; Welch retired the following spring after a disastrous first outing. Owner Day would be gone within a year, and Connor, Richardson, O'Rourke and Ewing would follow in another 12 months.

Burke Beer poster featuring Cap Anson and Buck Ewing, circa 1890. One of the earliest paid endorsements by baseball players, this chromolithograph features the two stars sampling stout and ale as a game transpires in the distance. Copies of the poster were distributed to saloons across the country by the Guinness Brewing Company, owners of the Burke Beer brand. It is noteworthy that the two stars were so well known that no mention of their names is made in the advertisement (courtesy National Baseball Hall of Fame Library, Cooperstown, New York).

The 1891 Giants managed their third-place finish thanks to the pitching of John Ewing and a 20-year-old fireballer named Amos Rusie. In his last season in baseball, Long John won 21 games and led the league with a 2.27 ERA. Rusie, an Indiana native, had begun his career at age 18 with the Indianapolis Hoosiers in 1889, and was acquired by the Giants in 1890 when the Indianapolis franchise folded. Blessed with tremendous speed, he was as wild as he was fast, winning 33 games in 1891, and leading the league in both strikeouts and walks. Rusie pitched another six seasons with the Giants, accumulating 246 wins, enough to earn himself a plaque at the Baseball Hall of Fame in Cooperstown.

The big news story of the Giants' season, however, was the loss of Captain Buck Ewing due to an arm injury that idled him for all but 14 games, and that left the baseball world wondering whether his storied career was over. Confusion exists in the historical record with regard to this incident. Prior researchers agree that the injury occurred, but most date it from the 1892 season. This error probably derives from Ewing's 1906 *New York Times* obituary, which stated that during a spring exhibition game that year, "Something snapped in his shoulder. He never recovered the use of his throwing arm afterward."[39]

The injury actually occurred in a May 1891 contest against Boston. After the physically and emotionally draining Players' League season, Ewing laid off all winter, doting over his new-born son. He reported to spring training out of shape, and then caught the flu. He missed most of spring training and the first two weeks of the season because of back and arm issues. "Buck Ewing is already lamed up [*sic*] with a sore back and sore arm."[40] Initially he sought relief with a poultice; "In order to keep Buck Ewing's arm warm, his physician has secured a pad filled with red pepper and ginger, in which his arm is now encased."[41]

On May 7, he went behind the plate at Boston and caught the first two innings without incident. The arm gave out in the next inning. "Buck Ewing threw [pitcher John] Kiley out at second in the third inning, and with it went his arm. How Buck did twist with pain, but pluckily remained at his post to the end of the inning."[42] Ewing caught in just five more games in 1891. A series of bizarre and painful treatments enabled him to catch 30 games in 1892, but only briefly at or near his previous performance level. He caught just one game, his last, in 1893.

After resting the arm for a week after the injury, Ewing returned to the field at Cleveland, but was forced to retire. "Buck Ewing started to play to-day, but only lasted half the game. He called upon O'Rourke to relieve him. He appeared to be all right, but he suddenly collapsed and claimed that he was unable to work."[43]As in the past, some believed that he was not really hurt. Stung by reports that he was faking the injury, he reacted in late May:

> Some critics are making cracks that I am holding off and waiting for the team to get in shape, and then I will jump in and do the catching, and the victories will be attributed to my presence on the team. This is maliciously false. If I could throw I would be behind the bat in every game, for I know how much the team needs me at this time. I am confident that my arm will be right, for it is improving slowly and the muscles don't pain me half as much as they did two weeks ago.[44]

The injury did not improve. Unsettled by the critics and now seriously worried that his catching career might be over, Ewing tried another poultice on the shoulder for a week, to no avail. He then took a desperate move, allowing a veterinarian to perform a procedure on him that was normally used to treat horses. In late June, the *Times*, now conceding that Ewing was indeed actually injured, offered a full report of the barbaric process:

> Buck Ewing will be able to go behind the bat July 4 in Cincinnati. It had been thought by many that he was shamming and that his arm was not sore. But it turns out he really was forced into idleness. His arm is now in good condition, with the exception that it needs a little strength, due to the fact that he had an operation performed on it which will cause a good-sized sensation.
> A veterinary surgeon went at his arm and handled it something like a horse is treated when its tendons are strained. He first put a plaster on Ewing's arm, and then produced an iron which was placed on the plaster, burning the flesh. Much pain and suffering was attached to it, but "Buck" stood it heroically. He winced under the intense agony several times, but knowing that if successful it would bring his arm around all right, he held on tightly. Ointment was then rubbed on the arm, after which it was done up in a heavy bandage. A mark will be left on his arm for life. The result of this treatment was to loosen and expand the muscles. Ewing said yesterday that he is in trim now and he was the happiest person imaginable when he said it.[45]

The horrific treatment failed to bring the hoped-for results. After a month's recovery, Ewing reported that he was experiencing no pain, but that "the arm lacks strength due to its long disuse."[46] He did not catch again, putting in eight games at second base during the last two months of the season. His inactivity sparked more negative comments in the press. "About all Buck Ewing does on the bench is to sit and smile and smile. As a smiler Buck has been the greatest success of the season."[47] In late August, *Sporting Life* blamed him for alleged discord on the team: "They [the Giants' players] say that Ewing's management is rapidly breaking the team up so badly that, instead of winning the championship, it will be lucky to make a respectable finish."[48] After the Giants were statistically eliminated from winning the pennant, all blame was placed on Ewing's inability to play: "New Yorkers blame the loss of the pennant on the absence of Ewing. Had they dropped the big catcher and thus restored harmony to the team, the coveted flag would probably have once more waved over the Polo Grounds."[49]

While Ewing's injury and the scorn of the press were difficult blows for him to endure, yet another controversy surfaced when the season ended. In the last weeks of the campaign, Boston and Chicago were in a heated battle for first place. After taking two games of a three-game series in Brooklyn, the Giants arrived in Boston for the start of a three-day, five-game series against the Beaneaters. Early season rainouts had mandated the difficult schedule of a single game followed by back-to-back doubleheaders. The Giants lost all five games, scoring just 22 runs to Boston's total of 56. After being pulverized by the Beaneaters, New York closed out the season at Brooklyn, losing two of three. Boston took the pennant, beating out Chicago by 3½ games.

Chicago's President, Jim Hart, and player/manager Cap Anson cried foul, claiming that New York had "purposely weakened the ... team so that Boston would have no trouble winning."[50] At Chicago's insistence, National League President Nick Young opened a formal investigation of the affair on October 10. Chicago's specific complaint was that several players, including Amos Rusie, John Ewing, Roger Connor and catcher Dick Buckley, were either absent or deliberately benched during the series. Manager Mutrie and captain Ewing provided detailed explanations for all the allegations. Catcher Buckley had injured a finger, John Ewing sprained an ankle in the Brooklyn series, and Rusie had been hit in the leg by a line drive and was too injured to play. Returning to the club after being granted a day off, Connor's train had been involved in a wreck, further delaying him. The circumstances, while extraordinary, were verifiable, and the Giants were exonerated. That did not convince Cap Anson, who blamed it all on Ewing: "Buck Ewing, who is a player and a manager, has all the say."[51]

As the League Committee met to examine the allegations, further charges against Buck Ewing were leveled by Art Irwin, a former National League infielder who managed Boston's American Association team: "While the New Yorks were in Boston, 'Buck' Ewing and Mike Kelly made no secret of the fact that the Bostons were to win all the games. They talked it over in the dressing room, and Ewing fixed up his team in Kelly's presence and talked and laughed over it in the presence of others.... There is no secret that 'Buck' Ewing gave the signs of the New York pitchers to Mike Kelly."[52] Although Irwin claimed that the allegations could be proven by "reputable witnesses who were in the dressing room,"[53] he failed to name them, and when asked if he would be willing to testify if an investigation were held by the league, he backed down, saying, "I don't know.... It's the League's funeral and let them settle it among themselves."[54]

Engraving, circa 1890, of Buck Ewing heading for first base (courtesy Transcendental Graphics/theruckerarchive.com).

Irwin's claims and Chicago's allegations left a cloud of suspicion in the air at the end of the season, with all fingers pointing to Ewing as the culprit. As the Giants prepared to leave on a post-season barnstorming tour of New England, the injured and disheartened captain had no interest in the trip or in remaining a Giant, and asked for his release. John Day responded by placing him on the team's reserve list for 1892, and by sending him a tersely worded note: "You will accompany the team, Mr. Ewing."[55]

Aside from John Ewing's pitching success, there were two other bright spots in the gloom of the 1891 season for Buck. In June, his second child, a daughter, Florence, was born in Cincinnati. In the same month, his essay, "Ins and Outs of Baseball," appeared in the *Ladies' Home Journal*.[56] Books and articles about baseball were still relative novelties in the late nineteenth century. There were two early varieties of such writing: autobiographies and "how to" volumes that taught the finer points of the game. Mike Kelly's *Base Ball: Stories of the Ball Field*, the first player autobiography, was published in 1888. The *Brooklyn Eagle*'s Henry Chadwick, a British-born exponent of the game — although he had never played it himself — published two early guide-books, *The Art of Batting* and *The Art of Fielding*, in 1885.

Capitalizing on their on-field experience, enterprising players soon began writing instructional books. Among the earliest was John Ward's *Base Ball: How to Become a Player*, published in 1888. After an introduction that traces the origins of ball playing back to ancient Greece, Ward's elegantly written volume devotes individual chapters to each field position and to hitting and running. In his chapter on receivers, Ward, who had lost his captaincy to Buck Ewing the year before, still named Ewing baseball's top catcher, although acknowledging that he was injury-prone. "Ewing, of New York, combines with wonderful skill and judgment the ability to stop a ball well and throw it quicker, harder, and truer than anyone else, and therefore, I consider him the 'King' of all catchers — when he catches."[57] Ward also praised Ewing in his chapter on hitting, including a woodcut illustration of him swinging a bat, and observing, "The accompanying [wood]cut of Ewing is an excellent representation of a batter, in the act of hitting. He not only swings the bat with his arms, but he pushes it with the weight of the shoulders. This position is a picture of strength."[58]

John Ward likewise introduced the practice of publishing baseball-related articles in national magazines. His "Notes of a Base-Ballist" appeared in *Lippincott's Magazine* in 1886, and the essay, "Our National Game," appeared in *Cosmopolitan* in 1888. Lacking Ward's broad educational background, Buck Ewing was understandably anxious about his own writing skills, as the introduction to his first baseball essay nervously relates. "I have often been asked to write about base-ball, but I have never done so for the reason that I know where my forte lies. However, I have undertaken this article at the persuasion of the Editor of the *Ladies Home Journal*, who assures me that his boy-readers will be interested in what I say. If I don't succeed, it will be his fault, not mine."[59]

While structurally and thematically paralleling Ward's book, Ewing's short essay is distinctive because it is the first such article written by a player that is directed to young boys, and not to older players seeking pointers from a major leaguer. Given its target audience and the type of magazine in which it was published, the sentiments expressed in some of the essay's introductory passages may seem overblown or pedantic to the modern reader:

> For my part, I consider baseball to be the best and healthiest form of recreation man or boy can indulge in.... But the game is not only advantageous as a means of physical training: besides strengthening the muscles, brightening the eyes, and knitting the whole frame of the body into a firmer soul, it produces a corresponding higher plane of morals. When the blood flows in coursing streams of health through the veins, there is a like healthfulness of the moral nature that alone would suffice to put baseball in the front rank of outdoor games for boys and men.[60]

Ewing informs his young readers that the two hardest positions to play are those of pitcher and catcher, and that the latter "must be a man of quick judgment, a hard thrower, and a good backstop. To be an accurate thrower is the principal thing."[61] His discussion of shortstops praises John Ward above all others for his intelligence, agility, speed and daring: "Ward, especially, is a heady player. He is nimble and accurate. He takes great chances, and no player in the country can beat him at stealing bases. He is a good winning man."[62]

Facing the challenges he experienced on and off the field during the 1890 and 1891 seasons, Ewing's final words of advice to the young readers of his essay might have also served as words of encouragement to himself: "Practical success in life depends more than you think on physical health, and a man who played baseball in his youth will meet reverses more calmly and take life more easily that the man who didn't."[63]

The last victim of the Players' League revolt, the American Association, ceased operations at the end of the 1891 season, and for the first time in a decade there was only one major league. Five of the Association's nine teams were disbanded, and the remaining four added to the National League. The press coined a new term, the "Big League," when referring to the league's now bloated, 12-team composition.

The Senior Circuit had finally restored its baseball monopoly, but the price it paid was high. The league itself and most of its franchises were broke. Teams were ordered to turn over ten percent of their gate receipts in order to pay for the debt incurred from buying out a quartet of Association teams. By season's end, that rate had increased to 16 percent. In June, team rosters were trimmed to 13, and salaries were cut 30 percent. Powerless, the players could do nothing but comply.

In New York, manager Jim Mutrie was replaced by Pat Powers, whose major league experience consisted of one year as skipper of the Association's Rochester club. John Day remained the voice of the team's owners, even

Woodcut, circa 1889, of Buck Ewing using a catcher's mitt on his left hand and a padded glove on his right hand. The Giants' black uniforms, which created a sensation when introduced in 1888, were called *Nadjy* uniforms by the New York press, a reference to a popular Broadway play of the era in which an actress created an uproar by appearing onstage clad in nothing but a black leotard (courtesy Transcendental Graphics/theruckerarchive.com).

The 1891 New York Giants with mascot. Tensions were high on the team, which included men from the now-defunct Players' League, others who had played in the National League during the Brotherhood Rebellion of 1890, and a few who had originally signed with the Players' League but later deserted to the National League (courtesy Transcendental Graphics/theruckerarchive.com).

though his Players' League rival, E. A. Talcott, now was the team's majority shareholder. Over the winter the Giants traded veteran slugger Roger Connor to Philadelphia and announced that Buck Ewing would take his place at first base. Fans and the press blamed the departure of the popular Connor on Buck Ewing. John Ewing developed a debilitating respiratory illness in the off-season, and was not fit to play when spring training began. In March 1892, he was diagnosed with consumption (tuberculosis), and the news circulated that "he will never play ball again."[64] Veteran hurler Charles "Silver" King replaced Long John in the rotation. Mike Tiernan, George Gore, Jim O'Rourke and Buck Ewing were the last remnants of the old Giants team reporting for duty in March 1892. Only Tiernan would be back the following year.

Manager Pat Powers' solution to the team's financial problems was to fill the bench with minor leaguers who worked for half the salary of his established players. Twenty-three men wore the Giants uniform over the course of the season, and the squad finished a dismal eighth in the 12-team league, 31½ games behind first-place Boston.

Determined to correct the impression that he was now a "back number," Buck Ewing journeyed to Hot Springs, Arkansas, in late January to start his own training regimen before the Giants' spring training began. Known for the healing powers of its thermal water springs, Hot Springs became a popular spring training site after Cap Anson's White Stockings spent the pre-season there in 1886. With his injured arm encased in a liniment poultice, Ewing followed a demanding training regimen, daily running a challenging ten-mile route through the Ouachita Mountains with Cincinnati second baseman Bid McPhee and New York utility infielder Shorty Fuller, and then finishing the day with a session at the hot baths.[65]

On the recommendation of several local doctors at the Springs, Ewing underwent a series of mechanical massage and electricity treatments on his arm. Each session on the machine lasted 15 minutes. Its movements were far from gentle. "It works with such force that Buck's entire body shakes and one can see the muscles and veins bulge out as the machine does its work"[66] These sessions were followed by painful electric shock treatments.

The description of this process and the supervising physician's assessment of Ewing's injury are powerful reminders of medicine's primitive state in the Ewing era:

> After the massage, Dr. Moore takes Ewing into a side room and applies the electricity. It is not the old shock, but a smooth current, applied with sponges. There is not a whimper from Buck as the sponges run over his arm, but just as soon as he raises his arm and the electricity touches the spot that was sore [,] Buck pulls away from the current as the pain passes through his arm. Dr. Moore is of the opinion that the grip [a cold] settled in Buck's arm and at the same time one of the deep muscles was sprained. That caused the blood to coagulate, and there is a poisonous spot the size of a quarter which has caused him all the trouble.... The poisonous spot ... is bound to disappear, and Dr. Moore agrees [*sic*] to send him away with a powerful well arm. Buck is happy over his luck, and this season, will no doubt find him as great as ever captaining the New-Yorks.[67]

The winter snow was still on the ground when the baseball pundits began to wonder if Buck Ewing's inactivity during the previous season would be repeated in 1892. The prevailing opinion was that his bench time might again be significant. "Buck Ewing is said to have patented a comfortable eiderdown cushion and pillow, which he will use in case his 'game' arm necessitates his holding down the bench this summer."[68]

By late March, the report from the Giants' spring training camp in Virginia was that Ewing had "regained his old form."[69] Except for his throwing arm, the report was accurate. Although the pain in his arm was gone, he could not yet throw a ball across the diamond. New treatments temporarily brought back his arm strength, allowing him to catch 30 games, though only occasionally with his accustomed past efficiency. He played 73 games at first base, finishing the season in the bottom third of the league at that position in fielding average (.974). Manager Powers made it clear that Ewing's bat was keeping him in the lineup: "He does fairly well at first, and we cannot afford to have him out of the team on account of his batting and run getting."[70] Over the course of the campaign he again struggled with illness and injury, the later due primarily to his aggressive base running, but at season's end he led the team in triples (15), home runs (8), RBI (76), stolen bases (42), batting average (.310) and slugging percentage (.473).

On the field, when healthy, he played almost like the Ewing of old. His primary struggles were in the clubhouse. Having captained or managed his team for the previous five years, Ewing was accustomed to complete autonomy in his on-field decision-making. New manager Pat Powers, with just two years' major and minor league managing experience — and none as a player — had no intention of giving Ewing such leeway under his command. By mid–May reports were surfacing that there was a "conflict of authority in the New-York team, and that Powers and Ewing are working at cross-purposes."[71]

The conflict divided the team into pro–Ewing and pro–Powers factions. By the end of May there was word of a scheme on the part of the New York players "to oust Powers from the management of the club and install Buck Ewing in the position."[72] A week later, with the Giants struggling in seventh place, the *Times* blamed the losses on an anti–Ewing faction:

> There appears to be a clique in the club, and from all appearances the object is to injure Captain Ewing. When he is playing, three men on the team never exert themselves, and from their actions, they don't care a snap whether the team won or lost. They all draw big salaries, and it is about time the officers of the club took some action. Ewing, as a ball player, a batter, a base runner and a Captain is the equal of any man in the profession, but he cannot win games unless all the men work together in harmony. If they don't care to work under Ewing, it behooves the Directors of the club to make some changes. If Ewing had a lot of conscientious ball players, he would probably make a better showing of the team.[73]

The controversy did not affect Ewing's play. By the end of June he had seven three-hit games and had stroked five home runs. Against Philadelphia on June 24, he stole four bases off catcher Jack Clements and his old battery mate, Tim Keefe. His second four-bagger of the season, a three-run blast, was hit at Cleveland off a tall, powerfully built right-hander from Gilmore,

Ohio, named Denton Young, who was in his second full major league season. Young's nickname, "Cy," was short for "Cyclone," a tribute to his blazing speed. Cy Young won 36 games in 1892. In his 23-year career he would amass a victory total of 511, which was 94 more than his closest competitor, Walter Johnson.

While the controversy with manager Powers was simmering, Ewing had an off-the-field run-in with Giants second baseman Charlie Bassett. During the 1891 season, Ewing had complained to John Day that Bassett was leading star pitcher Amos Rusie to drink. A year later, his campaign against Bassett was alleged to have created factions on the team. "Ewing is said to be trying to get Bassett fired from his position at second base, and this has torn up the club from catcher to center field, and put every director in fighting humor."[74] Biding his time, Bassett was out for revenge. During a chance encounter on the street in Harlem on the evening of June 27, "Bassett approached Ewing and warned him to defend himself. Ewing did not move. Then Bassett hit him a clip over the eye that almost sent him to the grass. Ewing retaliated with his umbrella, and then, it is said, turned tail and ran."[75]

The press, which had regularly derided Ewing as a slacker and a traitor, now declared him a coward. It is not likely, however, that Ewing would have fled in fear from the Giants' second baseman. He was an inch taller than Bassett, outweighed him by 30 pounds, and, as indicated in Chapter Three, was considered an excellent boxer. The more likely story is that Ewing had determined to get Bassett's release from the Giants and realized that retaliation would not help achieve his aim. In much the same fashion as he did during the famous "fixed" poker game years earlier, Ewing allowed himself to appear to lose, only to win in the end. Immediately after the incident in Harlem, he reported it to John Day and Bassett was released.

By mid–July, the Giants were mired in tenth place in the new 12-team league. After announcing the league-prescribed salary cuts, manager Powers began experimenting with Eastern League substitutes for his injured players, prompting the observation that the Giants now had "a minor-league tinge,"[76] due to the presence of so many fringe players. *Sporting Life* blamed the team's decline not on Manager Powers, but on the "utter incompetence of Ewing as Captain."[77] In the meantime, the struggle between Powers and Ewing intensified. After his manager pulled him out of a game for "sulking,"[78] Ewing retaliated by removing himself from a contest for unspecified reasons. As he struggled with a hip injury and a bout of illness, the press complained:

> The actions of William Ewing have caused considerable talk recently. The man appears unable to play two games in succession without a break in his physical mechanism.... His frequent injuries ... and the half-hearted way in which he conducts himself, have about worn out the patience of the local cranks [fans]....

His actions strengthened the belief of many that Buck is simply trying to freeze out Powers, with the hope of getting the management of the team.[79]

Ewing's illnesses, injuries, and unfavorable press reviews gave Powers the opening he needed. In late July, John Day turned over on-field control of the club to him, and reports surfaced that "Buck Ewing has been advised to permanently resign his New York captaincy, and with it whatever managerial ambitions he may possess."[80] Sports writer O. P. Caylor then wrote a humorous eulogy for the ex–Captain:

> The great and only Buck, who but a few seasons ago held the throbbing base ball public in the hollow of his gnarled and horny hand, is of little more interest to base ball as it is now played in New York than the ground keeper [sic] — hardly as much. Buck has been laying off for ten days, having his corrugated leg ironed out, getting his arm straightened, his feet trimmed and taking a general overhauling.[81]

The report of Ewing's professional demise was premature. On August 8 in Philadelphia, catcher Jack Doyle suffered a finger injury, and the following day, his replacement, Jack McMahon, dislocated a finger. A week after relieving Ewing of his responsibilities as team captain, John Day and Pat Powers now asked him to catch. He buckled his chest protector, put on his mask and went to work.

Ewing caught his first game of the season on August 10 at Eastern Field against John Ward's Brooklyn Bridegrooms. The rivalry between Ewing and Ward had begun when Ewing replaced Ward as Giants captain in 1887. It intensified during the Players' League revolt. While Ward never mentioned Ewing by name, he made numerous disparaging general comments about those whom he felt had betrayed the Brotherhood. Consequently, the competition between Brooklyn and New York was intense, and every game became "a battleground."[82]

In Ewing's return as a receiver, the Giants beat the Bridegrooms, 4–1, and he put on an exhibition that stunned the naysayers, throwing out Ward and two others on the base paths with what had been thought to be a "glass arm."

> For two innings the Brooklyns did not have an opportunity to steal any bases, but in the third, "Johnny" Ward tested Ewing. He was on first, with one out, and after getting a good start, he dashed to second. Ewing sent the ball like a rifle shot and when the Brooklyn Captain got to his destination, [second baseman] Fuller was waiting for him with the ball. Ward got up, brushed the dirt off his uniform, and looked at Ewing in surprise. The latter laughed, and remarked, good naturedly, "Simplest thing in the world."[83]

In the sixth inning, right fielder Oyster Burns made an effort to steal second, "but, like Ward, he fell easy victim."[84] When pitcher Ed Stein tried to go from second to third on a short passed ball, "he was put out for his foolhardiness."[85] Under the headline, "A Shattered Idol Restored," O. P. Caylor, who a week earlier had essentially written Ewing's baseball obituary, now marveled at his recovery: "The result can be hardly estimated in its general effect upon the game. It is the most promising surprise of the season. His [Ewing's] work behind the bat in support of Rusie, Crane and King will greatly strengthen the New York team."[86]

Ewing caught 29 more games during the remainder of the season, and the Giants averaged over .500 in the won-lost column, reversing the .419 mark of the season's first half. Ewing attributed the restoration of his arm strength to the efforts of a new Russian massage therapist.[87] It was

Studio portrait of a dapper, mature Buck Ewing, circa 1892 (courtesy The New York Public Library).

an imperfect solution to his problem. On bad days, his work was classified as "unsteady."[88] On good days, he appeared to have fully recovered.

> Ewing again proved that he is king of all catchers. Behind the bat he was like a stone wall, and his throwing to the bases was of the very best character. His coaching, too, materially benefitted [pitchers] Crane and King. Ewing knows the weak points of batsmen about as well as anybody, and he used his knowledge for all it was worth.[89]

After Ewing caught a doubleheader at Cleveland, *The Sporting News* waxed nostalgic about his performance, even though it was less than perfect: "Buck caught both games ... and he did it fairly well. It seemed like old times to have Buck there to chaff [chat] with the audience behind the backstop. He threw to second badly once or twice, and threw perfectly once or twice also. His presence behind the bat adds life to the team."[90]

He played through most of his injuries when able, and when not, took a day or two off. After throwing out seven St. Louis runners in a three-game series in early September, he missed five games with a sore arm. When he returned to the lineup, Charlie Bassett, who had been picked up by Louisville after his release from the Giants, and who still had a grudge against Buck, tried unsuccessfully to return him to the bench. "On the recent trip, Buck Ewing received a split hand, a blow to his throwing arm, and a spiking in the leg by Bassett, which Ewing thinks was intentional"[91]

Offensively, Ewing soared above his teammates in the second half of the season, batting .372 and collecting three hits in a game five times. His performance against St. Louis on September 13 was the highlight of the season: "Ewing yesterday gave a very pretty exhibition of ball playing in the field and at the bat. His record is one to be proud of. He scored two runs, made three singles and a three-base hit, accepted eight chances without making an error, and stole four bases."[92]

After a two-game layoff and a game spent playing first base, Ewing closed out the season behind the plate at Philadelphia on October 15. It was his last game in a Giants uniform. As his good fortune rose during the last months of the campaign, the New York franchise was undergoing a slow process of disintegration. Jim O'Rourke, released in September, blasted Pat Powers, asserting that he was detested by the majority of the team and had been "a monumental failure as a manager."[93] Amos Rusie, Shorty Fuller, and Mike Tiernan were released on October 7, after they refused to take a salary reduction from the original figure stated in their contracts. No team salary checks were issued for September or October, and the players were sent home with promissory notes from the club, which had lost $25,000 in 1892.[94] John Day resigned his position as spokesperson for the owners, although he kept a small amount of stock in the club. Pat Powers was fired, and never managed a major league club again.

Amid the chaos and controversy of the last months of the season, the Giants overlooked the efforts of a promising young local rookie whom they had brought in from the Eastern League in October. He played his first game for the team on October 2, and his arrival was noted by *The Sporting News:* "The New-York club has signed W. T. Keeler, late the third baseman of the Binghamton Club. Keeler is a Brooklyn boy, who first played professionally during the current season. He is said to be a very good bat man and third baseman."[95] Born William O'Kelleher, and nicknamed "Wee Willie," the diminutive (5'4") Keeler was sold to Brooklyn after playing seven games in 1893, and then sold to Baltimore. In 1894, his first full major league season, he hit .371 for the pennant-winning Orioles. Keeler would play another 15 seasons, compiling a lifetime batting average of .341 and earning a place in the Hall of Fame.

In November 1892, Ed Talcott, the former owner of the Players' League Giants, assumed full control of the National League Giants and announced plans to bring back Roger Connor and John Ward in 1893, and to sign Mike Kelly. Regarding Buck Ewing, who had led the Giants in almost every offensive category and who had intervened to help the magnate avoid financial disaster when the Players' League dissolved, Talcott tersely stated, "Ewing can go if a good trade can be made."[96] Responding to a rumor that the Washington Nationals were after Ewing, *Sporting Life* observed that "Some people ... consider him a back number [washed-up]."[97]

In mid–February 1893, John Ward was named manager of the Giants. Contacted at his home in Cincinnati, Buck Ewing stated that he had not heard from the team, that he had no objection to playing under John Ward, and that he would sign for a "respectable" salary, but would retire before accepting an "absurd cut" in wages.[98] On February 28, he was traded to the Cleveland Spiders for infielder George Davis.

There is an element of Greek tragedy in the story of Buck Ewing's career from 1890 to 1892. It is a tale of a great and famous man laid low, brought down by circumstance, the rants of the press, his own hubris, and time's effect of his body. Like the Greek myth of the Phoenix, however, Ewing would rise again from the ashes, and for a few more seasons confound his critics and amaze his friends with his exploits on the diamond.

Chapter 6

Spiders and Reds: 1893–1899

"Ewing seems to have found Father Time the kindest doctor he ever had." — *The Sporting News*, August 28, 1897

Cleveland's professional baseball roots run deep, dating from 1871, the first year of the National Association of Professional Base Ball Player's League. The Forest Citys, as the Cleveland team was then known, lasted until mid–1872 in the Association before folding for financial reasons. A second Cleveland nine, the Blues, represented the city in the National League from 1879–1884. After a four-year hiatus, a new Cleveland team nicknamed the Spiders returned to the league in 1889.

During the 1890 Players' League revolt, the Spiders competed for fans in their home town against a Players' League team, the Infants. The Infants' ranks included future Hall of Famer Ed Delahanty and slugger Pete Browning. Browning's .349 lifetime batting average, the fourth-best all-time, exceeds Delahanty's mark (.346), but Browning still lacks a plaque in Cooperstown, by most accounts because of his poor fielding (.880). Both 1890 Cleveland teams fared poorly, both finishing seventh in their respective leagues. In 1892, however, the National League Spiders climbed to second place, thanks to the pitching of Cy Young (36–12) and George Cuppy (28–13), and the hitting and run-scoring ability of second baseman Cupid Childs (.317 average and a league-leading 136 runs scored).

On-field rule changes and events on the national scene significantly impacted the 1893 baseball season. A week after Opening Day, the World's Columbian Exhibition, or World's Fair, opened in Chicago. A celebration of progress and modernity, the Exhibition soon found its lofty ideals tarnished by economic reality. Four days after its opening, the bankruptcy of a major U.S. business, the National Cordage Company, sparked a financial panic, and "within weeks, hundreds of banks failed and hundreds of thousands of men lost their jobs. The worst depression the country had ever seen enveloped the land for the next four years. Few were spared hard times."[1]

The National League's first response to the dire economic climate was to hold the line on player salaries:

> The players were squeezed again at 1893 contract time. By March it was apparent that the owners were clinging close to a $2,400 maximum on salaries, and holding total payrolls to around $30,000, as they had planned. The maximum was not established formally, as in the 'eighties, and there were exceptions, but $2,400 was the unofficial limit through the 1890s.[2]

The reserve clause was continued, teams still were under no obligation to pay players who were ill or injured, and team rosters were pared down. As in other sectors of the nation's economy, many baseball men were out of work, and those players who still had jobs after the downsizing from 25 to 12 major league teams in 1892, worked for less pay and fewer benefits, and remained at the mercy of team owners with regard to their contracts.

Hard economic times and player frustration contributed to a new ethos on the diamond: baseball became coarser, rougher, and at times even dangerous.

> The 'nineties may have been gay in some respects, but big league baseball was anything but. Hoodlumism and dirty playing if anything were worse than ever. There was scarcely an issue of *The Sporting News* that did not tell of kicking [arguing] and wrangling with umpires, fights among players, indecent language, and incidents of rowdyism in general.[3]

The rowdy spirit of the decade was epitomized by the behavior of two players, Cleveland's Oliver "Patsy" Tebeau, and Baltimore's John McGraw, whose foul language, physical intimidation of umpires and violent on-field behavior were notorious. Compared to the antics of such team leaders, Buck Ewing's past on-field behavior was tame.

In 1893, the final chapter was written in the 20-year attempt to establish equilibrium between hitters and pitchers through rule changes. Since 1887, pitchers had been required to start their delivery with the back foot on the back line of the pitcher's box, 55'6" from home plate. Yielding to the anemic offense that had characterized the game for years, team owners abolished the pitcher's box in 1893 and required the pitcher to throw with one foot planted on a 12-inch by 4-inch rubber slab located 60'6" from home plate. The effect of the rule change was immediate. Under the 1892 pitching distance rule, the top team batting average was .262. Under the 1893 rule, all but two teams beat that average, and two hit over .300.

An indirect consequence of the increased offensive production that followed the implementation of the new rule was the disappearance of the bare-handed fielder. "Five or six years ago not a single fielder outside the first base-man and catcher ever dreamed of wearing a glove except in case of injury."[4] Even baseball's last barehanded holdout, Cincinnati's veteran Bid McPhee, now found it necessary on occasion to protect his often injured left hand. "McPhee of the Cincinnatis played with a glove last Wednesday for the first time in his life."[5]

Buck Ewing, now 34 and starting his 13th big league season, was well aware that his playing days were nearing an end, and he was taking measures to insure his family's financial security.

> Buck Ewing is investing his money in real estate in the East end of Cincinnati. Besides owning three or four nice dwelling houses, he now has a force of work-men engaged in putting the finishing touches on a four-story building. There will be three store rooms on the ground floor and flats in the upper stories. It will cost from 10,000 to 12,000 [dollars].[6]

Apparently, Ewing felt the need to insure that he would always be near a ball field, since all his Cincinnati properties were "within plain sight of the scene of the late lamented Kelly's Killers."[7] The "scene" referred to here was the ballpark used by Mike Kelly's ill-fated 1891 American Association team. Located in Cincinnati's East End, it was erected on the site of Buck Ewing's childhood sandlot field, the Pendleton Grounds.

George Davis, a Cohoes, New York, native who was 11 years Ewing's junior, made his major league debut with Cleveland in 1890. After playing center field for two years, he moved to third base in 1892. Davis was a young switch-hitting prospect, but not yet a star, and was coming off his worst offensive season (.241 batting average) when he was dealt to New York for Buck Ewing. Ironically, when Ewing returned to New York to manage the Giants in 1900, it was Davis who successfully led a movement against him on the team, and when Ewing was fired in early July of that year Davis took over as manager.

Having come so close to winning the pennant in 1892, Cleveland fans and the Forest City press wanted no changes in the 1893 squad, and the Ewing/Davis trade "caused both the press and cranks [fans] at Cleveland to howl in opposition to the move, as Davis is regarded to be one of the finest all round players in the League."[8] Their complaints were echoed in the national press, which, despite Ewing's standout 1892 season, was ready to write him off as a has-been, just as it had done two years earlier. Former league player Sam Crane, for example, apparently was ignorant of Ewing's fine 1892 offensive statistics when he wrote, "For the past two years, 'Buck' did very little work for the home team. A 'glass arm,' he claimed, was responsible. Occasional flashes of his old-time ability came only in fitful flashes. He will leave here with the good wishes, however, of all the old timers, who will remember him only as the most brilliant player of his time."[9] *Sporting Life*'s headline read, "Ewing's Case Shows How Evanescent Is Baseball Fame."[10] *The Sporting News* claimed the New York fans had given up on the Giants' former captain: "Buck's usefulness here was a thing of the past. He became very unpopular with the Polo Ground cranks [fans] during the latter part of the second season, and at one time was almost booted from the field.[11]

After signing with Cleveland's president, Frank Robison, Ewing embarked on his own publicity campaign, first seeking to re-establish his reputation as a sought-after player. "Buck says that every club in the League without an exception asked about his services next season. They all wanted him, but of them he was anxious to come to Cleveland."[12]

Once this objective was accomplished, "Bread and Butter" Buck provided an extended, self-effacing, gracious commentary on the trade that would have disarmed the most hostile Cleveland critic:

> Cleveland has always treated me royally, and I am confident of a warm reception there. My arm feels good as ever and I believe I can play as good ball as ever I could. I will do it if I can. Other players have been afflicted as I have and have recovered, and I do not think this ailment is permanent. There is no person in the city of Cleveland who takes to heart the release [trade] of Davis with more sorrow than I do.... I dislike greatly to think of supplanting a man who is so valuable. I have nothing to say against those who criticize me so harshly, but I shall endeavor before the year is over to earn their good will. I will play hard and I want to help Cleveland win the pennant, which I think Cleveland can win. This city is the one above all others in which I wanted to play. There may be some people who call me a back number, and perhaps I am, but last year when at bat I could see the ball just as well as ever, and it never tired me much to run the bases. I don't know where I am to play. [Manager Patsy] Tebeau will fix that and I respect his base ball ability as much as that of any man in the country.[13]

Written off by nearly everyone, Ewing would once again confound his critics. Playing right field in his first season with the Spiders, he set individual-season highs in games played (116), at-bats (500), hits (172), runs (117), doubles (28), RBI (122), and batting average (.344).

Led by their cantankerous and foul-mouthed player/manager, Patsy Tebeau, the 1893 Spiders were a mix of up-and-coming and established players. Most were Midwesterners. Pitcher Cy Young, catcher Chief Zimmer, center fielder Jimmy McAleer, shortstop Ed McKean, and right fielder Buck Ewing were all Ohio natives. Pitcher George Cuppy hailed from Indiana, and first baseman Tebeau was from St. Louis. Backup pitcher John Clarkson and third baseman Chippy McGarr were Massachusetts-bred, and left fielder and future Hall of Famer Jesse Burkett was from West Virginia. Clarkson, also a future Hall of Fame member, was now in the twilight of a remarkable 328-win career that included seasons with 51 and 49 victories.

There was a macabre aspect to this team that did not become apparent for another two decades. An inordinate number of these men came to early or untimely ends. Cupid Childs and Buck Ewing died of Bright's Disease (kidney failure) in their mid-forties. George Cuppy succumbed to the same malady in his early fifties. Chippy McGarr passed away at age 41 in a Massachusetts insane asylum, and John Clarkson was just 47 when he died of pneumonia in a psychiatric hospital in the same state. Patsy Tebeau owned a bar after his baseball career ended, and in 1918, he "was found dead by suicide in his saloon, with a revolver tied to his right wrist." The former Cleveland manager was 54.[14]

The Spiders spent the 1893 pre-season playing local teams in Georgia, South Carolina and Ohio. After unexpected and embarrassing losses to some of these semi-pro nines, Patsy Tebeau blamed the defeats on the poor physical condition of his out-of-shape ballplayers. His criticism didn't include Buck Ewing, who reported to camp ready to play, 20 pounds lighter that his weight the previous season. By April 1, *The Sporting News* was already up to its predictable mischief with regard to Cleveland's newest acquisition, suggesting by its headline, "Will Ewing Roll Tebeau?"[15] that Ewing was plotting to replace the Spiders' manager.

In response, Ewing let his field work do the talking. Reporting on Cleveland's 16–8 loss to an Atlanta semi-pro team, *Sporting Life* marveled that "Ewing, he of the 'glass arm,' threw out a man at the plate from deep right field."[16] Two weeks before opening day, *The Sporting News* expressed its own surprise at the caliber of the veteran's performance: "Ewing's play is a revelation to those who thought Buck's usefulness had gone for keeps, for he is batting with his old time vigor, and his fielding, they say, is immense."[17]

The Spiders opened the season at Pittsburgh in late April, with their star pitcher, Cy Young, on the mound. Standing 6'2" and weighing 210 pounds, the 26-year-old Young was said to send "terror to the hearts of timid batsmen when he shoots the ball over home plate with cyclonic force."[18] Nevertheless, it was the veteran Ewing who took the laurels in his first game with Cleveland. Starting in right field, he banged out three hits, scored three runs, and stole three bases. "Ewing, whom the New York reporters have written down as a back number, was the star performer of the day. He knocked the ball at will, ran the bases with excellent judgment and much daring, and gave other evidence that he is still one of the best players in the League."[19]

Although his home run count dropped to six in 1893, Ewing's four-bagger in his home debut for Cleveland left no doubt that the old slugger was still in the game. In a 21–4 rout of Cincinnati on May 18, Buck went

3-for-7, and "set the crowd by its ears [on its ear] by knocking the ball clear over the high left field fence when he came to bat in the sixth inning. The hit was the finest ever made on the grounds. Two years [actually four years] ago, Buck put a ball over in about the same place, but that was before the addition had been put to the fence."[20] The "addition" mentioned here, as explained by a note in *The Sporting News*, was actually lattice work attached to the rear of the left field fence, adding sufficient height to prevent onlookers seated on high perches beyond the fence from watching the game for free. "Buck put a ball over the left field fence the other day, the first hit made over that wall since the lattice work was put on to shut off a pirate stand in the adjoining lot."[21] As mentioned in Chapter Three, the 1889 home run, hit before the height of the fence was increased, was estimated by long-ball expert Bill Jenkinson to have carried 430 feet.

In 1904, two years before his death, the long-retired Ewing would recall (with some facts altered) this blast as one of his most nerve-wracking and memorable achievements:

> I've been in many tight places in base ball ... and there has been many a game that I was eager enough to win to fight for it, if it came down to a question of an exchange of courtesies, but I never walked to the plate more anxious to win a contest than one in which I played when a member of the Cleveland nine.
>
> I had been traded from New York to Cleveland in exchange for George Davis. I was all in as a catcher and was to play right field for Cleveland. There had been no end of a howl in the Forest City because Davis had been let go, and it was up to me to make good with the bat or lose my grip in Cleveland.
>
> In the first game in which I played on the Cleveland ground we were behind when we came in for the last half of the ninth. I don't know whether it was one run or two, and it doesn't make much difference anyhow. When I came to bat we had enough men on bases to win if a long hit was forthcoming. I had hit a few in my time — although, if I remember well, I had hit little or nothing that afternoon — and as I made my way to the plate I said to myself, "Here's my chance." Before I got to the box I had stage fright. I fairly shook, and a strike got away from me as I settled down. I can't think now who the pitcher was, but after another ball had been called he gave me a low one over the side corner, just where I wanted it, and I landed the ball over the centre fielder's head and won the game.
>
> Luck? Yes. But what a dead one I would have been if I missed it.[22]

While Ewing's narrative is spell-binding, it is clear that time had clouded his memory. His first home run as a Spider was the aforementioned May 18 blast, occurring in a 21-7 rout of the Reds. The nearest actual equivalent to his 1904 description is the four-bagger he hit in Boston on August 28. While occurring in the ninth inning, this home run failed to win the game, which Boston took by a 4–3 score. "Buck Ewing stepped to the plate, carefully poised his bat, looked at young Nichols down in the box, and waited. The ball came whizzing toward the eager [catcher] Bennett, but it never reached him, for 'Buck' had hit it, and far away in the blue ether it sailed, and calmly dropped on the further side of a passing train."[23] Several months after the 1893 season had concluded, another perspective on the August 28 four-bagger in Boston was offered by an eyewitness, Edwin Phillips, *Sporting Life*'s Portland (Maine) correspondent: "I see that [*Boston Globe* sports reporter] T[im] Murnane says that Buck Ewing made the most sensational hit of last season on the Boston grounds. I was present at that same game and made up my mind to the same effect. It was the greatest hit that the undersigned ever saw."[24]

It did not take much time for the perennial Ewing critics to take another swipe at a player who was having a banner season. After a fine early-June performance in a 12–10 loss to Boston, in which he made three hits, scored three runs and stole a base, the *Cleveland Plain Dealer* remarked, "Ewing was in the game with both feet, his hitting and base running were great, and many wondered why Buck did not work as hard for New York last season."[25] *Sporting Life*'s commentary was even more outrageous:

> Buck Ewing's good work for Cleveland is evidence that he was in fitter condition while with New York than he pretended to be. It is therefore reasonable to conclude that Buck played a confidence game on the New York Club and public, and drew salary that he wasn't really entitled to. Other players have done this thing in the past, but Buck's case is the most flagrant of record.[26]

For good measure, in its next issue, *Sporting Life* started a rumor that Ewing was trying to replace Patsy Tebeau as manager of the Spiders, concluding that if that were to happen, it "would just about ruin the Cleveland team."[27]

Shortly after these diatribes, Ewing injured his leg stretching a double into a triple in a game at Baltimore, and played infrequently for the next few weeks. When in the lineup, he gamely attended to his craft. "Ewing limped around but that did not prevent him from making two catches [of balls] that had the appearance of triples. He was generously applauded ... for his work."[28] The *Cleveland Plain Dealer* observed that Ewing was running "like a spavined [lame] horse on account of his game leg,"[29] but that did not stop him from stealing two bases in a 13–9 win against Washington on June 27, and getting three hits the next day. After a game-winning, tenth-inning triple against Philadelphia on July 1, it was reported that "The smite [hit] was to right center and was good for three bases, even for such a limpy [limping] Moses as Buck."[30]

By mid–July, Ewing had recovered from his injury and was helping the team move from fifth place to a tie with Pittsburgh for third. Now hitting fourth, he collected five hits in a win at Chicago on July 31, three the next day, and a double and a triple the following day. He repeated the double/triple combination, a hallmark of his offensive repertoire, in an August 9 win against Louisville. As a clean-up hitter, Ewing did not disdain the sacrifice, collecting four in six games in mid–August. The most exiting of these was a suicide squeeze against St. Louis in the first game of a doubleheader on August 12, in which he bunted home Ed McKean, who had tripled.

Instead of praise for his remarkable performance, *The Sporting News* responded with vicious sarcasm. In a front-page article in late August, the St. Louis sports weekly published a tongue-in-cheek poem, allegedly penned by Ewing:

A Ball Player's Song

A happy man is the base ball star,
Who has good eyes and whose foot is fleet:
It's luck he isn't driving a car
Through the loudsome smells of a crosstown street.

There was a time in my younger days
When bread was scarce and butter was dear;
But I played the game in such a way
That I soon drank wine instead of beer.

Then gold and silver they came my way,
And seldom a man in better luck
For never a player could equal the play
Of Ewing, called "Bread and Butter Buck."

But eyes grow week and arms take in glass
We can't stay young and agile too:
And maybe I'm falling out of my class,
For I don't quite bat as I used to do.

The new star comes like a swelling bud
On a tree in the early days of spring,
It will not be long before some young-blood
Will have my job; ring off; ting-a-ling.[31]

There was no "young-blood" yet able to take Ewing's place in Cleveland. Although still bothered by the leg injury, by the end of August he was hitting .363, piling up sacrifices (35 total), and making fine defensive plays like the "running catch of an apparent home run,"[32] made in Brooklyn in early September. Throwing from the outfield with his shoulder rather than his forearm, he was able to surprise many who challenged him on the base paths. John Ward, now back with the Giants, was among those who gambled and lost in this manner. "Ewing's arm is in great form. He is throwing men out [from right field] with regularity and precision. [John] Ward was one of his victims last week."[33]

As an aging veteran, Ewing's skills were constantly challenged by opponents, several of whom were old friends and former teammates. Playing against Washington in late September, he got a chance to turn the tables on Jim O'Rourke. O'Rourke had taken over as manager of the lowly Senators after being released by New York in 1892. He was in his last big league season. After Ewing singled, O'Rourke, who was catching, yelled out to him, "'Now go down to second' ... [and] as soon as [pitcher] Stephens doubled himself up to deliver the ball, he [Ewing] scooted for second, arriving there ahead of O'Rourke's throw, whereupon the ex–Giant laughed at the ex–Giant."[34]

Three days later against Philadelphia, Ewing went behind the plate for the last time in his career. There had been many requests for him to catch, but manager Tebeau had resisted, knowing that Ewing was needed in right field. He finally relented on September 30. Ewing's battery mate, John Clarkson, was two dozen games away from finishing his own career, and at this juncture was relying primarily on off-speed pitches and luck. Ewing put in six innings behind the plate in most unusual fashion: "Ewing caught without a chest protector, because Clarkson didn't pitch the ball fast enough to have won in a contest with a club of females. Ewing's return of the ball was speedier than the pitching."[35]

The Spiders finished in third place, and Ewing had proved, at least to the Cleveland press and fans, that he was "far from the has-been ranks."[36] In his own review of the campaign given to *The Sporting News*, the veteran once again tried to quell the persistent rumor that he was angling for Patsy Tebeau's captain/manager position:

> I've had a first class season in Cleveland.... I like Cleveland and have been splendidly treated there and wish you would say that all the talk about my assuming the club captaincy is pure buncome [*sic*]. I don't want it. Captain Tebeau is the ideal captain. I don't know a better one. I am satisfied to play wherever he assigns me, and am glad to work for a President like Mr. Robison and a manager like Captain Tebeau.[37]

The Sporting News apparently took him at his word: "Buck Ewing is conceded to be one of the best field captains the League ever had. Buck knew when he had enough, however, and is not again hankering for the position."[38] However, the season did reveal that when not in the position of captain or manager, "boss kicker" Buck Ewing largely desisted from an action habitually thought by the press to be innate in his behavior — baiting the umpire.

Back in Cincinnati at season's end, Ewing had one more cause for amusement. He had bet his former boss, Giants owner Ed Talcott, two suits of clothes that the Spiders would finish the season ahead of New York. Under John Ward, the 1893 Giants finished fifth, seven games behind third-place Cleveland. The former Giants captain looked dapper all winter in his new wardrobe.

Ewing proved unable to repeat his first year's success with the Spiders in 1894. He spent the winter umpiring indoor baseball games and running five miles a day to keep in shape,[39] but his arm failed to respond to any and all treatments. At the end of spring training, which the team spent barnstorming in the Southeast, Ewing reported that "As long as I keep throwing it's all right [his arm], but when I stop and it's all chilly, I can't do anything. The warm weather will bring it around all right."[40] His prediction did not prove accurate.

After taking two of three games at Louisville to open the season, Cleveland traveled to Cincinnati, where Ewing was warmly received. "'Buck' Ewing's popularity was demonstrated by the applause given the old war horse every time he went to bat in Cincinnati."[41] His defensive work seemed solid; "Buck Ewing covered himself in glory in the right garden [right field], and pulled down a number of hits that looked like two-baggers."[42] Nevertheless, he "was pitiful when obliged to throw the ball back to the infield."[43] Worse still, he was not hitting. The 60'6" rule raised league batting averages 35 points in 1893. In 1894, they would jump another 29 points, to an all-time high of .309.[44] Ewing's final 1894 average, in contrast, plunged 93 points to .251, the lowest mark among Cleveland's starters. By mid–May, he was still hovering around .230,[45] and when the Spiders won only nine of their 23 games in June, pressure began to mount on the old veteran. After a 5–2 loss to Chicago on June 19, in which he dropped a fly ball, leading to the team's defeat, the Cleveland Plain Dealer announced that "Buck Ewing is in a bad way. He has lost his ability to throw and is rapidly losing his ability to bat and catch."[46] Ewing's final stroke of bad luck occurred on July 2, while hitting against New York: "Ewing sprung his 'charley horse' in the fifth while at bat, and [Jake] Virtue took his place in right."[47]

Although described as a "charley horse," the injury proved to be much more serious than simple leg cramps. Ten days later, Sporting Life reported that Ewing's "leg is still in terrible shape, and seems to get worse instead of better."[48] A week later, he had not improved; "his leg is in awful shape, and he can't run the bases."[49]

During the first week of July, the stumbling Spiders lost six consecutive games at home — three to New York and three to Boston, and attendance, which normally ranged from 2,000 to 3,000, dropped to 250 for the last game with Boston. Owner Frank Robison and manager Tebeau promised that a team overhaul was at hand, and on July 13, veteran hurler John Clarkson was sold to Baltimore and Buck Ewing was released. The news of Ewing's departure was reported dramatically in some quarters: "Thus descends the burnt out stick of that magnificent rocket which blazed in the baseball sky only a few years ago."[50]

It would take another five months for the sporting press to realize that their eulogies for "the old war horse" were once again premature. *Sporting Life*, however, which twice previously had written Ewing off, had finally learned its lesson.

> Buck Ewing plunged [gambled] a little on the grand circuit racers [horse races] last week and was quite successful in guessing the winners. The amounts the old veteran laid down on each event [race] did not indicate financial embarrassment as a result of his temporary retirement from the game. I use the term "retirement" advisedly, for I am very sure that before many days the once king of catchers will be hitting out home runs for some club in the big league.[51]

A week before Christmas, Ewing signed a contract to manage and play first base for Cincinnati. After 15 seasons, he was coming home to play ball in his own backyard.

Cincinnati had fielded a major league team (either National League, American Association or Union League) every year since 1876 except one — 1881, when they were expelled from the National League for playing ball on Sunday and selling liquor at the games. As an American Association team (1882–1889), they finished first once, in 1882. The city's National League teams (1876–1880; 1889–1894) never finished higher than second in the standings, and in the past half-dozen years had not risen higher than fourth place.

Cincinnati's player/manager for the 1892–1894 seasons was Charlie Comiskey, a tall, lanky first baseman from Chicago who had been the architect of the St. Louis Browns' four consecutive American Association pennants from 1886 to 1889. When his contract expired with the Reds, Comiskey purchased a franchise in the Western League, an organization that would in a few years declare itself an equal to the National League and change its name to the American League.

The departure of Comiskey meant that Cincinnati's owner, John T. Brush, needed to fill two vacancies — field general and first baseman. He found the perfect candidate in Buck Ewing, who not only could manage the team and handle first base, but who was also the greatest player ever produced by Cincinnati and wildly popular with the city's fans. For Ewing, the new job was a dream come true. Now 35 and starting his 16th full season, he could play in front of his friends and extended family, and spend more time with wife Annie and children, Arthur (age four) and Florence (age three).

His first order of business was to convince owner Brush to fund several weeks of spring practice in a warmer climate. Under his predecessor, Comiskey, the Reds' pre-season preparation was rudimentary, consisting of a "week or so of ball-tossing at the home park."[52] Ewing could attest first-hand to the benefits of spending a few weeks in the South before the start of the season, and with Brush's approval, the Reds made Mobile, Alabama, their spring base camp.

Other than Ewing at first base, there were few new additions to the Reds team. The remaining infielders, Arlie Latham at third base, Bid McPhee at second, and shortstop Germany Smith, had played together in Cincinnati for four years. The speedy and scrappy Latham, who previously had spent four years in the St. Louis Browns' infield, had earned the reputation as "the greatest comedian in the game,"[53] due to his on-field antics: "He was a clown and a prankster, and was an accomplished tumbler who incorporated acrobatics into a game on more than one occasion."[54] Latham's opposite, second baseman John "Bid" McPhee, was "quiet and sedate ... and quietly proud of never having been ejected from a game."[55] One of the last infielders to put on a fielding glove, McPhee led the league in fielding his position nine times, and is the only second baseman in history to record more than five hundred putouts (529) in a season. George "Germany" Smith, a Pittsburgh native, was a light-hitting, strong-armed shortstop who had recorded over 500 assists four years in a row (1891–1894) while with the Reds.

Two of the three outfield starters, Bug Holliday and Dusty Miller, were lifetime .300 hitters, and the third, Billy "Dummy" Hoy, posted a .288 mark over 14 seasons. The diminutive (5' 6") Hoy, a deaf-mute, was an outstanding fielder, one of three men in baseball history to record three outfielder-to-catcher assists in one game (1889). The Reds' weakest link was the pitching staff. Returning hurlers Frank Dwyer and Tom Parrott combined with newcomers Frank Forman and Billy Rhines for a 59–57 mark in 1895, with a few remaining wins and losses tallied by part-time hurlers. Ten-year veteran Harry "Farmer" Vaughn, from Ruraldale, Ohio (hence his nickname), did most of the catching for the Reds. At 6' 3" he was one of the tallest men in baseball.

During spring training in Mobile, Ewing's leg injury that had plagued him the previous year appeared to have healed. "Captain Ewing showed that his 'bad leg' is all right in yesterday's game, when he ran at full speed and scored a three-bagger."[56] The new manager's training methods were calculated to dispel the Reds' reputation as an undisciplined team, which they had earned under former manager Comiskey. "Early to bed and early to rise has been Captain Ewing's motto.... No form of dissipation has been indulged in by anyone."[57]

Taking a page from Dummy Hoy, Ewing schooled his team in a new way of receiving instructions while on the field:

Captain-Manager Buck Ewing of the Reds has adopted a code of signals by which he directs the movement of his men on the field. It is said that he does not have to get on the coaching lines and shout his commands to the players, as Comiskey and Latham have done in years gone by. He simply works a string of signals, something after the style of the deaf and dumb language.[58]

The "rejuvenated Porkapolitans"[59] returned to Cincinnati on March 31, and the next day played their first home game, an exhibition contest against Indianapolis. Queen City interest in Ewing's Reds was enormous. Between 6,000 and 7,000 fans turned out for the game, hoping to see a better team than the tenth-place finisher of the previous season.

All eyes were on Buck Ewing, and he did not disappoint:

> It was a proud moment for him when he went to the bat the first time. There were very few in the assemblage that didn't either clap their hands, stamp their feet, or in some way demonstrate their kindly interest in the Cincinnati boy the first time he ... started for the rubber [plate]. The greeting he received bordered on an ovation. Captain Ewing had to doff his cap twice before they would let up in their efforts to show they were with him.... Three balls and one strike were called, and then Buck sent the blood coursing through the veins of his admirers.... He brought his bat around with a terrific swish and the next instant the regulation Spalding [ball] was speeding through the air with a through ticket for centre field. It carried on the fly to the embankment, not a foot from the bottom of the fence. It was a great hit, and Buck made two bases on it.... Captain Ewing's record speaks for itself. A two-bagger, a single, and a stolen base for a man with a dead arm, a glass leg, and in the last stages of baseball decrepitude is pretty fair, thank you.[60]

In a rematch with the Hoosiers the following week, "Twice Buck put the ball against the fence embankment. [Once} It [the ball] went out with such force that it stuck in the soft ground in the place that it hit."[61]

As luck would have it, the Reds hosted Ewing's previous team, the Cleveland Spiders, on Opening Day, and Patsy Tebeau was already lamenting the loss of the old veteran: "If I had my way he would still be on the [Cleveland] team. I would not have released him. He is a great ballplayer."[62] The now-retired Long John Reilly — the man who had first recommended Ewing for major league play, was on hand to see Ewing's Cincinnati debut. "Long John rarely ever attends a game.... However, [he] will forget his resolve today, and will come down from the East End with the rest of the Ewing rooters."[63]

Ewing's "Braves," as the Reds were then often called in the press, defeated Cleveland, 10–8, and Ewing collected two hits and stole a base. His statement after his first Cincinnati win made clear the significance that the game held for him:

> I have had some very bright spots in my life. When I piloted the New-Yorks to the pennant twice and won the World's Championship on two different occasions with that team, I had reason to feel happy, but I say without equivocation that this is the proudest moment of my life. It pleases me to be able to please so many of my friends and neighbors.[64]

Ewing banged out three hits, including a triple, and scored two runs in the second game of the series, which the Reds won, 14–9. Two days later, an enormous crowd of 17,436 packed Cincinnati Park, drawn by news of Ewing's stellar performance in the first two games, and the hope of sweeping the Spiders. In attendance was DeWitt Hopper, the New York actor and Ewing's friend from his glory days with the Giants. Hopper's opera company was in town for a series of performances, and the actor, "who was such a Ewing fan that he named his favorite horse Buck Ewing,"[65] invited the entire Reds squad to his company's show that evening.

Ewing put on his own show that afternoon in a 12–3 win over Cleveland. He stole two bases, scored two runs, and made two hits, one of which was a four-bagger.

> The hero of the assembled 17,000 was Captain Buck Ewing, the Cincinnati boy now in charge of the home team. They cheered him every time he came to bat, and when, by a supreme effort, he sent the ball sailing over the York Street fence for a home run, they simply became delirious with joy."[66]

Ewing's own joy and satisfaction in his first week with the Reds was interrupted by tragic personal news. During morning team practice before the Reds game with Pittsburgh on April 23, he received word that his brother, former pitcher Long John Ewing, had died of tuberculosis in Colorado. "Captain Ewing took the news very hard."[67] Soon after he was diagnosed with consumption in spring, 1892, John moved to Colorado Springs, hoping that the pure mountain air would cure him. "He was getting along all right at that place, but the yearning to be with old friends was so strong that he could not resist it. He thought to work home by easy stages. He started to Denver, hoping to get acclimated. That change in base proved fatal."[68]

The tactless sports writer O. P. Caylor had few good words to say about "Brother John" upon his death:

> John Ewing was never more than a fair pitcher, but his brother believed in him. It was Buck's opinion alone that kept Long John in the major ranks. Had he been the brother of a less admired player, Ewing junior would not have drawn six months' salary out of the treasury of any National League club."[69]

Caylor had evidently forgotten about John Ewing's last season with the Giants, when he led the league in winning percentage (21–8; .724) and ERA (2.27).

It took all of Ewing's skills as a player and leadership abilities as a manager to lift Cincinnati up two notches from tenth to eighth place in 1895. Six games into the season, steady outfielder Bug Holliday went out with appendicitis, and after he finally returned to the team in mid-season, he suffered a "split finger"[70] that kept him on the bench for the remainder of the year. A cut hand from a spiking early in the year and a sore throwing arm late in the campaign sidelined Bid McPhee. Temperamental third baseman Arlie Latham was benched for poor fielding in August, and complained to the press of unfair treatment by manager Ewing, forcing Ewing to reply that "I never let my feelings enter my government of the team. I am looking for the man who can do the most good."[71] In September, Latham and catcher Farmer Vaughn aired their differences in a fistfight in the dugout during a game at Pittsburgh, and the *Cincinnati Enquirer* complained of too much quarreling on the team, with Latham "the bone of contention."[72]

It was evident by mid-season that the team's pitching was weak, and Ewing subsequently drew criticism for "not trying out some young pitchers."[73] Since owner Brush was unwilling to bankroll such an experiment, Ewing had to ride out the year with the staff he had inherited. The Reds loved Cincinnati Park, going 42–22 there in 1895, but they lost nearly two-thirds of their away games (24–42). They finished 66–64, which was 21 games behind the league-leading Orioles.

In his last great season as a player, Ewing did all he could to try to keep the Reds in contention. While his defensive play was just adequate (.976, in the bottom third of first basemen), he hit .318, drove in 94 runs, smacked 24 doubles, 13 triples and five home runs, and stole 34 bases. All could agree with the assessment that "For an 'old charley horse stiff,' a 'glass arm back number' and a 'paralytic,' Buck is doing pretty well, thank you. Buck has heaped bushels of live coals on the heads of his defamers."[74]

Soon after the 1895 season ended, Ewing traded troublemaker Arlie Latham and pitcher Tom Parrott to St. Louis for catcher Heinie Peitz and pitcher Red Ehret. Ehret was a gamble, since he had gone 6–19 the previous season, although with an admittedly terrible St. Louis team that won only 39 games. He collected 18 victories for the Reds in 1896, and returning veterans Frank Dwyer and Frank Foreman combined for 38 wins. Peitz and returning catcher Farmer Vaughn shared the duties behind the plate, with Vaughn also putting in 57 games at first base, filling in for the injured or ill Buck Ewing.

The Reds' firepower in 1896 was supplied by their speedy outfielders. Eddie Burke, who was Bug Holliday's backup the previous year, started in left field, hit .340 and stole 53 bases. Right fielder Dusty Miller stole 76 bases and hit .321, and center fielder Dummy Hoy stole 50 sacks and hit .298.

The "bad boys of Baltimore," including John McGraw, Joe Kelley, Hughie Jennings and Willie Keeler, had battled Patsy Tebeau's Cleveland team for the 1895 pennant, with the Orioles taking first place by three games over the Spiders. The two teams were expected to again vie for the championship in 1896, but they were joined by Buck Ewing's surprising Reds, who led the league until a disastrous 11-game losing streak on the road in late August and early September did them in. The Orioles claimed their third straight title, with Cleveland claiming second place and Cincinnati third.

The 1896 Reds were a spectacular 51–15 at Cincinnati Park, but a dismal

26–35 on the road, and they had the misfortune of playing only two of their last 29 games at home. A description of one of the team's travel odysseys during their 11-game losing streak, a journey from Boston to Washington, illustrates well the disadvantages of playing on the road during the 1890s.

On August 21, the team lost a tough afternoon contest, 10–9, at Boston. Due to the length of the game, the players were forced to dress at the ballpark and hurry to catch a train instead of returning to their hotels and showering before leaving town. They caught a train to Fall River from Boston, arriving in the early evening. In Fall River they boarded a boat for an uncomfortable and largely sleepless overnight ocean trip to New York City. Arriving in New York with time for "only a sandwich for breakfast," they boarded a train for Washington. Arriving finally at the capital in time for their afternoon game, they lost a 9–2 blowout to the Senators. Commenting on the team's listless performance against Washington, the *Cincinnati Enquirer* conceded that their grueling travel route "may have had some influence on the Reds' play."[75]

For the first month of the 1896 season, Buck Ewing appeared to be picking up where he left off in 1895. Now 36, he nonetheless still managed to keep pace with his young outfielders on the base paths. During the first week of play he stole four bases in two games against Pittsburgh and two more in the next contest against Louisville. He stole two against Cleveland on April 21, four against Chicago on April 27, and three against Baltimore on May 9. He was also receiving high praise for his work at first base. "Buck picks low throws out of the ground and picks them out of the air. His capture of Lange's long foul yesterday was a beauty"[76]; "Buck Ewing played first base as well as it was played by anybody in this city."[77]

This productive streak came to an abrupt halt in mid–May. During a game against Washington he was hit on the knee by a pitch, and then sidelined with a "bad cold ... that has settled in his throwing arm."[78] A week later, his own prognosis for his return was not good:

> I am unable to say whether it is the rheumatism that is bothering me or whether I strained my shoulder when I tried to get back to first in that game with Washington in the rain.... I was pretty near all right until I went in this afternoon. When I tried to hit that high ball I gave my arm a twist, and it hurt me like a bad case of toothache. I will go in the game if I am able to stand it at all.... We need every game we can get.... I will miss very few games if I am able to play.[79]

Shortly thereafter Ewing did return to the lineup, and on June 13 at Boston hit the last home run of his career off hurler Jim Sullivan, an eighth-inning solo shot that reached the railroad tracks beyond the left field fence. Ten days later he was again sidelined with a "charley horse."

There was clear indication now that his body was in further decline, for the injured leg was "not the leg that gave him so much trouble in Cleveland, but the other leg."[80] To these afflictions were soon added a wrenched ankle and a bout of his mysterious illness, which was now recurring with greater frequency. He played in only a handful of games for the remainder of the season, and only infrequently was able to perform as in the past. At Philadelphia on September 1, as the Reds lost their 11th straight game, he achieved the last double/triple combination of his career. He "hobbled around first base in a painful way, owing to his sore ankle. His batting, however, was a feature of the team's work."[81] During the last month of the season he played in just one more game.

Age and illness had finally caught up with the "Duke of Pendleton," just as they had with many of his teammates from the 1880s. His manager at Troy, Bob Ferguson, died in 1894, as did his California barnstorming pal, Mike Kelly. That year, John Ward, Danny Richardson and George Gore retired. By the time Ewing buried his brother in 1895, Mickey Welch was tending bar in his saloon in Holyoke, Massachusetts, and Tim Keefe was living off his real estate interests in Cambridge. Jim O'Rourke bought a team in the Connecticut League and player-managed there for another decade. Before the 1896 season was over, Ed "Cannonball" Crane, another of Ewing's battery mates from the 1888–1889 championship seasons in New York, committed suicide. Roger Connor, the Giants' first baseman whom Ewing replaced in 1892, and Cap Anson, Ewing's beer poster partner, would hang up their spikes in 1897. Mike Tiernan was the only starter on the championship 1888–1889 Giants teams who was still a regular starter, and he would retire after the 1898 season. It was the end of an era.

Cincinnati held its spring training camp in New Orleans in 1897, where fuel was "added to the interest in the Reds' stay ... with word that Buck would play."[82] Preliminary reports indicated that Ewing was working hard to get in shape: "Ewing for a time was in the heat of the exercise [batting and fielding practice]. Then he withdrew, and from the players' bench watched the boys."[83] At the conclusion of each day's practice, the players ran laps, making "the circuit of the park.... Everybody made the circuit from four to a half-dozen times.... Ewing reeled off ten [circuits]."[84]

The attractions of New Orleans proved too powerful for many players in their off hours. Upset with their frequent "riotous indulgence,"[85] manager Ewing assumed the role of a stern father with his squad. "In order to keep good watch on his men, Ewing has had his belongings transferred from the room he had occupied to another room on the third floor. It is situated so that every player is compelled to pass his [Ewing's] door to reach his individual bed, and hereafter the player keeping irregular hours will call forth a lecture that will not be complimentary or kindly."[86]

Ewing's major acquisition in 1897 was left-handed pitcher Ted Breitenstein, who over the last four years had averaged 21 wins and 26 losses a season with the St. Louis Browns. During those years the Browns had not finished higher than ninth, and Ewing knew that, with better support, the lefty's record would improve. Breitenstein's signing with Cincinnati reunited him with his former Browns battery mate, Heinie Peitz. These two German-heritage players were known in baseball as the "Pretzel Battery." According to Peitz, the nickname

> originated at the Golden Lion saloon in St. Louis. After a game at the Mound City [St. Louis] one day, Breitenstein and Peitz were at the Golden Lion, sitting in a back room cooling off in an appropriate manner. On a table before them sat a bowl of pretzels. A fan strolled in, saw who was sitting in the back room, and shouted to ... the customers at the bar, "Hey look who's back there. It's that pretzel battery, Breitenstein and Peitz."[87]

The Pretzel Battery did great work for Cincinnati in 1897. Peitz hit .293, while Breitenstein led the pitching staff with a 23–12 record and himself hit .266, banging out six triples and driving in 23 runs from the ninth position in the batting order.

Starting the season at home, the Reds won their first six games, but Ewing, suffering from a bout of his "illness," was not in the lineup. He was too sick to accompany the team on their first short road trip to Cleveland and Pittsburgh, where the Reds promptly lost four of five. "Without Buck, matters are in a chaotic condition. The players have more than enough signs, but without the leading spirit to control and direct, signs or nothing else are of avail."[88]

Ewing was back on the bench when the team returned home, and the Reds promptly won ten straight. On May 27 against Boston, he went in at first base for the first time. Dizzy and weak, he was 0-for-1 at the plate, reaching first once when hit by a pitch. In the third inning "he could not see the ball perfectly,"[89] and muffed an easy throw from short, allowing Herman Long to reach base. Disgusted with his performance, he benched himself after six innings. It was the last major league game he ever played.

All evidence suggests that Ewing knew that his playing days were over. At the beginning of the season, his plan was to alternate at first base with backup catcher Farmer Vaughn. A few weeks before his last game, both legs hurting, his arm and his hitting eye gone, and perhaps becoming aware that the recurring pattern of sickness was an indication of a serious condition, Ewing began scouring the league for a first baseman to take his place. His choice was veteran Jake "Eagle Eye" Beckley, a lifetime .300 hitter, who had spent seven seasons with Pittsburgh but was sold to New York early in 1897 after his average dropped dramatically. Beckley "didn't hit well in New York either, and the Giants released him in May."[90] He signed with the Reds on the same day that Ewing played his last game. He spent the next seven years with Cincinnati and hit .308 for his career. In 1971 he was elected to the Baseball Hall of Fame.

Cincinnati played decent ball with Ewing on the bench, but their troubles on the road continued. They were 49–18 at home, but 27–38 away from Cincinnati Park. Injuries took their toll. Bid McPhee was out for a month after gashing his knee with his own spikes while sliding, and Heinie Peitz had a nail torn from his finger during practice. Intent on defeating their traditional rivals, Cleveland and Baltimore, the Reds, along with the rest of the league, were overtaken by the surging Beaneaters of Boston, whose pitching trio of Kid Nichols, Fred Klobedanz and Ted Lewis combined for 78 wins. The Orioles finished second, and Amos Rusie's arm led the Giants to a third-place finish. Cincinnati finished fourth.

Bench manager Ewing soon reverted to his old behavior with the umpires. "He was the same Buck of old, wearing the same old smile and up to the same old tricks of 'jollying' the umpire.... It was rather odd to see a man not in the game roaming around the home plate one-quarter of the time, discussing some baseball problem with Prof. Hurst [the umpire]."[91] During a game in Philadelphia, Phillies star Ed Delahanty threw an old ball out of the park in order to get a new one put into play before he went to bat. Delahanty was fined $1.25 for his action, and Ewing fired off a letter of protest to President Nick Young, complaining about the small amount of the penalty: "Think of a fine of $1.25 to pay for a good chance to win a game. At that rate, players would take all kinds of chances of beating the other side. I think Kelley is a good umpire, with the one exception that he is not severe enough"[92] The press christened the old veteran with two new nicknames, each a play on his original one, "Buck." He was now called "Buchanan" Ewing,[93] and Captain "Buckingham" Ewing."[94]

Ewing was well enough in late July to have some fun with his players. During a series at Chicago, the team, lodged at the Leland Hotel, was awakened each morning at six o'clock by an opera singer from the Schilling Opera Company, who started the day by opening her window and bursting into song. After a team meeting, the players decided to fight back; "a few minutes after six this morning, the notes of one of the songs of 'Il Trovatore' rent the air. With a bound, Buck Ewing was out of bed, and running to the window, sang, in a fog-horn voice, 'Oh, I Wish You Had Ne'er Come Back.'"[95] The diva countered with another song, and then the rest of the team opened their windows and offered their own musical selections in response. The singer and the ballplayers had a "glaring confrontation"[96] in the hotel lobby later in the day, but the following morning the unwelcome serenades had ceased.

In August, with the team not hitting and mired in fourth place, Ewing, apparently concerned over the renewal of his contract, began a familiar ploy —

he "casually" let it be known that his services as manager were being sought by another club. While in Philadelphia, he reported a conversation he had with Phillies owner. Al Reach: "He [Reach] asked me how I would like to come to Philadelphia [as manager].... I told him that Cincinnati was my home, and that I intended to stay there if I can come to terms with the Cincinnati Club officials."[97]

Since his overall health had improved, he likewise aroused the press's interest by suggesting the possibility of his own return to the lineup:

> Because Buck Ewing was on the bench all this season does not signify that he is out of the game for good. He expects to play ball again. He will not carry an extra outfielder next season, but will get in condition himself, and if any of the regular outfielders get hurt, may take their places. Buck may try his hand as an outfielder in the present Eastern trip. He is in condition right now, and can get in and play at a half hour's notice.[98]

He did return to the diamond briefly, but only in a few exhibitions games against small-town semi-pro clubs in Ohio and Maryland.

Like every other major league team in the nineteenth century, the Reds took advantage of any open dates in their league schedule to play exhibition contests with amateur or semi-pro squads to earn extra cash. After dropping two of three games to Chicago at home in mid–August, Cincinnati headed east to start a tour in Philadelphia, and on the way scheduled two games in Ohio against local opponents, with Buck Ewing in the lineup. "Captain Ewing will play second base or the outfield in the games at Wilmington [Ohio] and Hillsboro [Ohio]."[99]

At Wilmington, the 1,500 fans who had gathered "were entertained before the game by a fine exhibition of fungo hitting by Captain Ewing and Heinie Peitz,"[100] and then watched the old veteran knock out two hits and play errorless ball at second base during the game. He collected three hits and scored three runs the following day at Hillsboro. It was not his game performance that made news there, but rather a startling personal revelation made by the Reds manager:

> The greatest result of the visit [to Hillsboro] was the development of the fact that Buck Ewing is a Highland Countian [*sic*], born within four miles of Hillsboro, at Hoaglands [*sic*]. The popular superstition has always been that Buck was a Millcreek [Cincinnati] product, but he gave the secret away today, being reminded of his old home by a train passing only a few rods [yards] from the house. The fact will make Hillsboro root harder for the Reds, and from now on Buck will divide honors with Senator Foraker as the two most distinguished products of Highland County.[101]

Ewing himself, of course, had for years insisted that he was born and bred in Cincinnati's East End. It was both poignant and fitting, however, that at the end of his playing career he returned to his true birthplace to play one more game.

Ewing experienced mixed success during his last two years as a bench manager for the Reds. A near-miss at winning the pennant in 1898 was followed by a drop to sixth place in 1899. Cincinnati won more than 90 games (92) for the first time in franchise history in 1898, and the team's success was at least partially due to manager Ewing's seemingly uncanny ability to trade players whose careers were on a downward trajectory for others who suddenly became more productive. For example, in November 1897, he sent starter Billy Rhines and backup catcher Pop Shriver to Pittsburgh for outfielder Elmer Smith and pitcher Pink Hawley. Rhines subsequently was 12–16 for the Pirates while Shriver hit .229, and both men retired at the end of the season. In contrast, Hawley led Reds pitchers with a 27–11 mark, and Smith hit .342.

Ewing's successful trades had administrators from other teams trying "to ascertain how it happens that Buck can trade for such players as Elmer Smith and Pink Hawley and not find them dead ones as soon as he gets them. Perhaps Ewing is a Svengali when dealing with other owners."[102] Now in his fourth year as the Reds manager, he was gaining increasing recognition for his abilities in that role, and his ideas about team management were becoming better known. He gained grudging praise, for example, for unorthodox experiments with team lineups:

> Manager Ewing has branched out as a second wizard of Menlo [a reference to inventor Thomas Edison].... Buck has tried a number of experiments this season in running a ball team, and seems to have made as great a success as the kinetoscope [an Edison invention]. For one, he has shifted the batting order whenever he pleased. The leader off one day would be down in the bottom of the batting order the next. A catcher who might have made a home run to-day would be benched in favor of another tomorrow. A sub[substitute] who made three hits yesterday might be tending the water cooler to-day ... but the Reds keep on winning.[103]

Ewing's Reds manufactured runs by playing what today is called "small ball"—stealing bases, sacrificing, and using the hit-and-run play. His hitting advice to his players was similar to Willie Keeler's famous dictum, "Hit 'em where they ain't." Cincinnati's manager believed that "In order to make batting thoroughly effective, it is necessary to spring surprises on opposing fielders—hit where they don't expect you to hit. If the opposing fielders are looking for a bunt, the ball should be hit out, if they are looking for a hit to right field, give them something else, and so on."[104]

While leading the Reds' spring training camp in San Antonio, Texas, in March 1898, Ewing was asked to discuss his approach to getting players in shape after a winter layoff. He responded by emphasizing the importance of pacing during training.

> I make it a rule not to work my men over three hours a day when we are in training. With the pugilist it is the aim of his trainer to get him at his best for a certain day. To have him on edge so as to be at his very best just as he enters the ring, the pugilist has to prepare for the [single] event. With a ball player it is different. In training a ball team you must bear in mind that there is a long siege of playing ahead of them. It won't do to bring them to their best to get them "an edge." On the contrary, you must aim to have them robust and fast, and down to weight without getting them so fine that a continuous siege of playing may cause them to fall off weak.[105]

Ewing's specific drills contrasted with those of more traditional methods: "Instead of practicing at 'fungo,' which is often the rule for a team in training … [Ewing's] players are divided into two nines, and a game is played every day. This brings points into play that never come up in 'fungo' hitting, and the men always have an opportunity to improve their team work."[106]

Despite his age and well-publicized injuries and illnesses, the Reds skipper still found leading his men by example to be the best practice:

> I am training just as hard as I ever did. It is far better to lead and let your players follow than it is to sit still and order your men to go on and train. They do not feel that they are imposed upon when you do [not] ask them to do more than you are willing to do yourself. I feel better when I train. I have trained hard every season since I have been in the business, and I do not intend to change my tactics at this late date.[107]

A Cincinnati Enquirer report detailed the specifics of Ewing's personal routine and his team's training regimen during home stands once the season started:

> Captain Ewing has a standing order that all players must report at the park every morning at 10 o'clock.… Captain Ewing is usually there an hour before this time. Buck has a good trotter and a stylish buggy. He drives the rig from his house to the Cincinnati park every morning. He does not return for luncheon, but a few sandwiches from the café under the grandstand is usually his noonday meal. Buck does not take off his uniform from reporting time until he starts for home after the game. While he is mild mannered and always pleasant and affable, the Reds' Captain is not an easy mark for delinquent players to load up with excuses. Buck has been a ball player long enough to know all the ins and outs. He is almost as strict a disciplinarian as [Chicago's] Captain Anson. Like the big Chicago chief, he has a way of enforcing orders that commands respect and at the same time does not interfere with his popularity. Buck has the good will of all his players.[108]

In the skipper's estimation, training was meaningless without team cooperation and harmony.

No captain or manager, be he ever so great, can make a team win ball [games] when there is lack of harmony. If there are two or three men who are not speaking to each other, and who are continually talking about shirks and mumbling and grumbling, it is impossible for them to play good ball. They may capture a game now and then, but they cannot be depended upon. Every man in the team should stand ready at any moment to do his best to make his nine win. It is out of all reason to expect your men to do what you cannot accomplish yourself. Harsh language has done more to ruin prospective players than any other cause.[109]

Despite such encouraging rhetoric, an incident between Ewing and one of his players that occurred near the end of the 1898 season gave indication that the manager's good relationship with at least some of his players had broken down. The Reds led or had been near the top of the league standings through early September, but their hitting production then suddenly slowed, two pitchers, Pink Hawley and Bill Hill, developed sore arms, and a third, Frank Dwyer, was seriously injured. Dwyer won 16 games for the club before being knocked unconscious at Philadelphia by a blow to the back of the head from a batted ball. It was a career-ending injury. He was out for the remainder of the season, and after going 0–5 in 1899, he retired from baseball.

From September 10 to September 19, Cincinnati dropped eight of nine games, including doubleheader losses at Baltimore and Philadelphia. At the start of the downward slide, manager Ewing's illness returned, but he rallied after a week in bed and re-joined the team in Baltimore. Suspecting that heavy post-game drinking was affecting team play, he called a team meeting in the clubhouse after the double losses to Philadelphia on September 19, and announced: "We are now at the most crucial stage of the race, and I want every man on the team to cut out the booze. No drinking except a glass of beer or two after the game."[110]

For the first time since becoming the Reds' manager, his authority was challenged. After a moment of silence, outfielder Dusty Miller spoke up: "Look here, Mr. Ewing, you don't have to tell me when to drink and when not to drink, and, just to show you that I am game, I will just about mop up five steins of beer when I leave the dressing room."[111] After Miller's comment, "Buck's face darkened, but he didn't say a word. His silence spoke volumes."[112]

Amid the dissention and the injuries, the Reds rallied to win five straight near the end of the season, but it wasn't enough to catch Boston or Baltimore, who finished first and second respectively. Boston's nine, described by historian David Nemec as the "greatest team of the 1890s,"[113] was led offensively by outfielder Billy Hamilton, who hit .369 and stole 54 bases. Manager Frank Selee's squad featured the first four-man pitching rotation, and it came within one game of being the first such rotation ever to have four 20 winners (Kid Nichols, 31 wins; Ted Lewis, 26; Vic Willis, 25; and Fred Klobedanz, 19).

Public and press opinion in Cincinnati turned against Buck Ewing's leadership in 1899. He managed to recruit two exceptional rookies, but the remainder of the squad "had begun to show signs of wear and tear."[114] Frank "Noodles" Hahn, a 20-year-old left-hander from Nashville, won 23 games for the Reds and led the league in strikeouts (145). The other starters, Hawley, Breitenstein and Phillips, combined for just 44 victories. After his confrontation with Ewing, outfielder Dusty Miller hung on for most of the 1899 season before being released in August. He finished the year with St. Louis, but never played major league ball again. In early September Ewing signed a rookie outfielder, Sam Crawford, to replace Miller. Crawford hailed from Wahoo, Nebraska, and his hometown's unusual name became Crawford's nickname for the remainder of his career. "Wahoo Sam" hit .307 for the Reds during the last month of the 1899 season, banging out 39 hits, seven of them triples, in 31 games. He would add another 302 three-baggers to that total before his career ended in 1917, and he remains baseball's all-time triples leader.

The Brooklyn Bridegrooms, tenth in the league in 1898, won their first pennant in 1899, after Baltimore manager Ned Hanlon and Orioles Vice-President Harry Von der Horst bought a controlling interest in the Brooklyn franchise and transferred most of Baltimore's best players there. Cincinnati wintered in Columbus, Georgia, got off to a slow start and played streaky, inconsistent ball for the entire season. After a seven-game losing streak in June that left the team at 24–24, Ewing was called to Indianapolis for a conference with team owner John Brush. A week later Cincinnati newspapers polled their readers on who should manage the team the following year, and Ewing finished last. Support for him, however, came from an unlikely source: his old nemesis, *Sporting Life*:

> The efforts of a few disgruntled spirits to drive Buck Ewing out of Cincinnati are amusing to an outsider. Where, for instance, do these misguided ones imagine the Reds would be were it not for Ewing? Tenth [place]? Perhaps they would [be], but not much higher. Ewing put baseball on its feet in the Queen City, and has got surprisingly good work out of a very indifferent team.[115]

As rumors began to circulate that Ewing would be fired, the team caught fire, winning 14 consecutive games in late July and early August, including sweeps of Brooklyn, New York, and Louisville. They then promptly dropped five in a row, and sank back into the middle of the standings. At season's end the team had won 82 games, but finished in sixth place. Although Reds owner John Brush initially insisted that Ewing "positively"[116] would manage the team in 1900, a week later at the Reds' annual stockholders' meeting he announced that Ewing would not be retained, because he "failed to land the club on top."[117] Brush followed his announcement with a statement of unusual praise for Ewing, a tactic that suggests that he was not in agreement with the other shareholders' decision: "I consider Ewing the peer of any manager in the business. There is not a part of the game in which he is not thoroughly competent. He has been a hard working and faithful employee.... I know of nobody in the business more competent to get good results than Ewing."[118]

In his second year after taking the reins in Cincinnati (1896), Ewing had moved the team up to the first division in the league, where it stayed for the remainder of his tenure, placing third twice and establishing a team record for victories (92) in a season. The Reds would not win 90 games in a season or gain first place in the standings for another 19 years.

Chapter 7

The Last Hurrah: 1900–1906

"To the end, without a moment of complaint or wavering, Buck maintained a courageous spirit." — *Cincinnati Enquirer*, October 22, 1906.

As the twentieth century dawned, major league baseball again was entering an era of transition. In 1900, the National League ended its eight-year experiment with a 12-team format — the "Big League" — by eliminating the four financially weakest franchises — Cleveland, Louisville, Baltimore and Washington. The decision cost the League $104,000 in payments to owners of the four dissolved teams, a sum that was recovered by requiring the eight remaining franchises to surrender five percent of their gate receipts during the season.

Player morale remained low, primarily due to frozen salary levels. "The average league salary, about $2,000 ... stood nearly exactly where it had been in 1878."[1] In an action reminiscent of the Brotherhood movement of the mid–1880s, Chicago pitcher Clark Griffith, Pittsburgh catcher Chief Zimmer, and Brooklyn shortstop Hughie Jennings responded to this state of affairs by forming a new players' union, the Protective Association of Professional Baseball Players, in the spring of 1900. League owners scoffed at the union — just as they had 15 years earlier when the Brotherhood was born — but players soon had another league to which they could offer their services in exchange for a higher salary.

In 1894, Cincinnati sportswriter Byron Bancroft "Ban" Johnson formed the Western League, a minor league of franchises spread throughout the country's heartland. In 1900, Johnson changed the organization's name to the American League, added the National League's defunct Cleveland team to its rolls, and, in accordance with procedures established in the National Agreement, asked permission to expand further by admitting clubs from Washington, Baltimore and Philadelphia. The National League refused Johnson's request. Undaunted, he soon began recruiting National Leaguers for the 1901 season, offering them higher salaries and official recognition of the new players' union. When the American League opened for business in 1901, nearly two-thirds of its players had prior National League experience. Two years later the two leagues signed a new National Agreement, establishing the basic two-league organizational structure that persists today in major league baseball.

Rumors that Buck Ewing would manage the Giants in 1900 surfaced even before his release by Cincinnati. They were bolstered by comments made by Reds owner John T. Brush, who was also a minority shareholder of the New York franchise, and who saw no inconsistency in firing Ewing for not winning in Cincinnati and then asserting that "If the New York club secures Ewing, they would have the right man in the right place."[2] Shortly thereafter Ewing signed a contract with Giants owner Andrew Freedman to return to New York after a seven-year absence.

Freedman (originally Freidman), a millionaire real estate mogul with close ties to Tammany Hall, purchased a controlling interest in the Giants from E. B. Talcott in January 1895. He holds the dubious honor of being considered the "most loathsome owner in baseball history."[3] During his eight-year ownership of the team, he managed to arouse the disdain and disgust of fans, players, sportswriters and fellow team owners. In his first two years with the Giants he waged war against New York sportswriters who dared criticize him, physically assaulting one writer, barring another from the Polo Grounds, and severely restricting the number of free press passes for games.

His most famous campaign against one of his own players began when he withheld $200 from pitcher Amos Rusie's last 1895 paycheck, for "dissipation and failure to give his best toward the end of the season."[4] Rusie, the team's star player, sat out the 1896 season rather than pay the fines, and he hired John Ward to represent him in a legal action against Freedman. Ward brokered a deal for Rusie from the league's Arbitration Board. He had to sign with the Giants for 1897 under Freedman's terms ($3,000 salary), but league owners compensated him $5,000 as a reimbursement for his year's lost wages, legal costs, and owner Freedman's original $200 fine. The Giants owner was outraged at the terms of the settlement.

A second incident with another player did little to improve Freedman's reputation. During an 1898 game at the Polo Grounds against Baltimore that was attended by the controversial Giants owner, Baltimore outfielder Ducky Holmes, a former Giant, yelled an ethnic slur at Freedman ("Well, I'm damn glad that I don't work for a Sheeny [Jew]"[5]). Freedman ordered the umpire to remove Holmes from the game, and when he refused, the Giants' owner pulled his team off the field, forfeiting the game and incurring a $1,000 fine.

The National League Board of Directors upheld the fine and suspended Holmes for the remainder of the season (August through October). A few days later, however, after Holmes secured an injunction requiring Baltimore to play him despite his suspension, the league reversed itself and reinstated the Baltimore outfielder.

The league's financial support of Amos Rusie and its reinstatement of Ducky Holmes enraged Freedman, who undertook a complicated and expensive plan of revenge. Since many of the financially distressed league teams depended heavily on the shared gate receipts they received from playing the Giants at the Polo Grounds, the New York owner deliberately set about to discourage attendance there by harassing his own players to distraction in order to negatively affect their performance. Salaries were cut across the board and players routinely fined at Freedman's whim. The blanket salary reduction was the last straw for Amos Rusie, who had averaged 29 wins over the previous eight seasons, and he "refused to sign and retired from baseball."[6]

Freedman's plan was successful. Attendance at the Polo Grounds in 1899 was half what it had been the previous season, and at season's end, as we have seen, the National League jettisoned its four most vulnerable franchises. The machinations of the Giants' owner also devastated his own team, which finished last in 1899, winning 60 games and losing 90, the worst record to that point in franchise history.

Buck Ewing had an opportunity to experience Freedman's arbitrary and arrogant behavior first-hand while with Cincinnati in 1897. At the time, the Reds were in the middle of a long eastern tour and had been rained out at Baltimore and Philadelphia. It was raining in New York when the team arrived to start their series, and Freedman canceled the first game due to wet grounds. The sun soon began to shine, however, and manager Ewing decided to use the free time to get in some much-needed practice at the Polo Grounds. To his surprise, the team was denied access to the Grounds by Freedman. "You, as visitors, are entitled to the privileges of the grounds on days of games, but not at any other time. As I have declared the game off for to-day, I insist that you and your men leave the grounds immediately."[7] Incredulous, Ewing responded, "But, we are the visiting team ... and are entitled [by National League rules] to some privileges on the grounds."[8] Freedman's stinging response was, "You are no visitors of mine ... and for the last time, I tell you to leave."[9] The Reds took their revenge on Freedman the next day when Ted Breitenstein outdueled Amos Rusie, 2–1.

By agreeing to manage the Giants in 1900, Ewing had accepted a nearly impossible challenge. Now entering his forties, he was well-off financially and able to retire comfortably. What would prompt him to take the reins of a last-place team owned by a man with a reputation like Andrew Freedman's? First,

Only 11 of the eventual total of 23 players on the 1900 Giants appear in this early-season photograph with manager Buck Ewing. Shortstop George Davis, standing, far left, was the ringleader of a group of team veterans that plotted successfully to have Ewing ousted as manager in mid–July (courtesy Transcendental Graphics/therucker-archive.com).

he believed that he could improve the team through a series of trades. Second, what better place to attempt such an improvement than the scene of his greatest achievements on the diamond? Ewing greatly overestimated his ability to effect change in New York. Signing with owner Freedman was the last decision he made in his long and storied baseball career. It was also his worst.

Ewing convinced the usually stingy Freedman to underwrite a few trades by assuring him that the men he had in mind were either utility players who would earn their salary playing multiple positions, or men who could be acquired for a small outlay of funds. He made his first trade before the Giants left for their spring training camp in Charleston, South Carolina, acquiring the multi-talented George "Win" Mercer from the Washington Nationals. Although used primarily as a pitcher, "Mercer was such a fine hitter [.291 lifetime] and excellent all-around player that in between pitching assignments he saw frequent duty at third base and shortstop as well as in the outfield."[10] He played all of these positions for New York in 1900.

In a series of trades in March, Buck acquired 6'2" catcher Frank Bowerman from Pittsburgh, and two of his former Cincinnati players, pitcher Pink Hawley and outfielder Skip Selbach. Hawley was just 14–17 with the Reds in 1899, but had three 20-win seasons previously under Ewing's tutelage. Selbach took over in left field at the Polo Grounds and hit .337. Finally, the new Giants manager purchased Charlie "Piano Legs" Hickman from Boston. Hickman had pitched and played both the infield and the outfield for the Beaneaters. As New York's full-time third baseman in 1900, he hit .313. The remaining Giants were team veterans: George Davis at shortstop, Kid Gleason at second, Irish-born "Dirty Jack" Doyle at first base, outfielder George Van Haltren, and pitchers Bill Carrick and Ed Doheny.

During spring training, Ewing again suffered a severe bout of his now-customary illness, and while confined to his bed when the team returned to New York, he penned an essay on "team harmony." It was his second on the theme, and was published at the start of the regular season. Given the events that would occur on the team over the next few months — events that would lead to Ewing's resignation in July — his essay topic was highly ironic:

> Teamwork is the whole thing in baseball.... Without teamwork no baseball club can win.... I would rather take a team of the veriest [*sic*] novices and train them into my ideas of strategy and tactics than be put in charge of an all star combination [team].... In the latter case it is an army of generals, all with individual schemes of play, and each with his idea that his particular play is the best for the emergency. In the former instance, however, it is the trained man who realizes that he is part of the plan of attack, and whose duty is to carry out that part to which he is assigned with fidelity to his comrades.[11]

The Giants' manager then detailed the need for cooperation among players in specific game situations, such as the hit-and-run play, concluding that "Every man on my team must know to a dot what the other man is going to do and what is expected of him in the plan of action."[12]

A group of returning players on the team had other ideas. George Van Haltren and George Davis were seven-year Giant veterans, and Kid Gleason and Jack Doyle had completed five and three seasons respectively with New York. Thanks to Andrew Freedman's wrecking-ball philosophy, seven different men had tried to manage the team under his vindictive rule. Among the seven were Davis and Doyle themselves, and these veterans, accustomed to doing things their own way during such administrative chaos, had no intention of working "harmoniously" according to Ewing's direction.

The die was cast when Davis, the team captain, assumed interim managerial control of the nine during the final two-week pre-season practice sessions at the Polo Grounds while Ewing was still bed-ridden. By the time Ewing returned, the veterans had formed a unified front against him, with the intention of substituting Davis as manager. It took them until July, but their plan finally succeeded. With player loyalties divided between the veterans and Ewing's new hires, the Giants could not win. They were 6–16 by mid–May, but then managed to play .500 baseball until disaster struck. Riddled with internal strife and weakened by the temporary absence of Davis due to a knee injury, the Giants were swept successively by Boston, Brooklyn, and St. Louis, and later by Chicago. When the team returned to New York on July 12, Ewing tendered his resignation and George Davis was appointed the new manager.

A bitter Ewing aired his views to the press:

> Ewing claims his resignation was due to the fact that he could not make the team win, owing to a clique of the old players on the team against him in the interest of George Davis. The clique, Ewing says, was composed of Davis, Doyle, Gleason, Warner and Van Haltren, as against the new men — Selbach, Smith, Hawley and Bowerman — put into the team by Ewing.[13]

George Davis garnered no immediate support among the press, since it was suspected that he had faked his leg injury to complicate matters for Ewing. "Davis was reported with an injured knee, and more than one hint was thrown out to the effect that Davis was taking things easy while Ewing was piloting a poor team on a Western trip.... However, the symptoms of that serious malady disappeared with remarkable rapidity when Davis was appointed manager. He jumped into the first game under the new conditions."[14]

After taking a parting shot at Andrew Freedman for refusing to provide financial backing for more trades that he had brokered, Ewing indicated that

> he was glad he was out of it. He gets his full salary for the year and returns to his Cincinnati home fully convinced that he was the victim of a conspiracy. The public is convinced that if Ewing could have had the support of the club to the extent of a few thousand dollars, he would have made the New York club a factor in the race. But the material [money] was not at hand and the success of the clique that forced Ewing out was made possible because the club did not back up its manager.[15]

George Davis was unable to heal the schism that he had fostered on the Giants team, and New York finished in last place in 1900 with a 60–78 record. The following year they were 51–85, finishing seventh under his command. A trio of managers successively ran the team in 1902, Freedman's last year as owner. The final member of that trio remained the team's skipper for the next three decades and led the Giants to ten World Series appearances and three championships. His name was John McGraw.

After his departure from New York in July 1900, Buck Ewing disappeared from the national sports scene and led a quiet life in his beloved East End, in Cincinnati. In 1901 he partnered with Charles W. Murphy, sports editor of the *Cincinnati Enquirer,* to create the Cincinnati School for Baseball Players, also known as The Buck Ewing School. Instruction was conducted by correspondence, and the school enjoyed a brief successful run. An instructional volume, *Buck Ewing's Advice to Young Players,* was also planned, but never materialized.[16]

Rumors periodically surfaced that Ewing was getting back into the game. Five months after leaving New York, *Sporting Life* hinted that he might replace Bob Allen as Cincinnati manager.[17] In 1902 he declined an offer to manage the Saginaw team in the Michigan State League: "I am very much obliged for the remembrance ... but I don't believe that I want the Saginaw club."[18] Two years later, the *Dallas Morning News* reported that "Buck Ewing turned down a managerial offer for 1904, but he may be at the head of a National League team in 1905."[19]

The sad fact, however, was that Ewing's health had been rapidly failing since he left New York in 1900. In 1898, *The Sporting News* specified the cause of his original illness: "Buck Ewing's continued illness is malarial fever — a very troublesome disease."[20] While malaria was a catch-all diagnosis for a host of maladies during the period, several of Ewing's self-described symptoms — vomiting, nausea, fever and anemia — mirrored some of those brought on by the disease. Malaria, caused by a parasite transmitted by a mosquito, was extremely common in nineteenth-century America. Over a million cases were diagnosed among soldiers during the Civil War, and 10,000 Union deaths were attributed to the disease.[21] Liver or kidney failure are two possible serious complications for malaria patients. Buck Ewing was diagnosed with the latter malady — then termed Bright's Disease — in 1903.

Sudden, unexplained weakness and extreme weight loss were the first symptoms of the disease that he experienced. A consultation with the Cincinnati Reds' team physician confirmed the diagnosis. He then tried other doctors and many kinds of remedies, but to no avail. In February 1906, the baseball world was informed of the seriousness of his illness:

> All lovers of baseball, particularly the elder, will regret to learn that "Buck" Ewing, the famous veteran catcher, is dangerously ill with Bright's disease at Cincinnati. He has been a sufferer for a number of years, but kept his feet until recently, when he broke down completely. Attending physicians say he cannot recover. The dying man was, all things considered, the greatest catcher the game ever produced. He was a superb backstop, a perfect thrower, a grand hitter and a very crafty base runner.[22]

In the ensuing months, he gradually grew weaker, but a friend later reported that he

> retained his genial good nature and happy mode of living to the last. He loved no place like his little home in the East End, where friends were always royally

entertained on their visits. During his illness the butcher, the grocery keeper and all the tradesmen who knew the former ball player in his prime made special efforts daily to get him some appetizing dish or serve his wants in the most satisfying manner. From the daily papers he gained his information on the progress of the baseball season, and was deeply interested in the outcome of the recent world's series. He loved to discuss with East End fans the great players of the day, and every sensational play made on the diamond filled his heart with enthusiasm.[23]

Although in his last days he was no longer able to leave home,

> he kept his nerve and was always brave and cheerful, refusing to recognize the close and certain approach of the grim reaper. Friday [October 19, 2006] was the first day since his decline began that found him unable to rise from his bed in the morning. Previous to that day he had been up and around the house, though not strong enough to do more than walk from his bedroom to the parlor downstairs. But he insisted on being up and dressed every day and on taking his place at the family table.... But on Friday Buck was unable to rise at his usual hour. He grew weaker throughout the day and at midnight lapsed into a state of unconsciousness from which he never emerged.[24]

Death called for the great catcher at two o'clock in the afternoon on Saturday, October 20, 1906. Last rites were held at his East End home on Worth Street, with the eulogy given by close friend Judge Howard Ferris, a fellow member of the Elks. Ferris had gained notoriety a few years earlier by heading a syndicate — possibly including Ewing — that unsuccessfully endeavored to purchase John T. Brush's interest in the Cincinnati Reds. The pallbearers selected by the family were two close personal friends, two representatives from the Cincinnati Lodge of Elks, one of whom was Frank Bancroft, Reds Business Manager during Ewing's tenure, and two Cincinnati Reds who had played under Ewing: second baseman Bid McPhee and pitcher Frank "Noodles" Hahn. McPhee played the last five years of his 19-year career with Cincinnati under Ewing, and during that time the two roomed together on all the team's road trips. A Nashville native, Hahn enrolled in the Cincinnati Veterinary College in 1903, and when he retired from baseball in 1906 he became a federal government veterinary inspector in the Queen City.

Cincinnati native and long-time Ewing friend, Long John Reilly, also was in attendance. The grieving Reilly was "another one of Buck's boyhood friends who is heartbroken over Ewing's death. Mr. Riley always regarded Ewing as the greatest ballplayer of his day, and says he could hardly name one who is his equal among the present day celebrities."[25]

During their years together with the Reds, Frank Bancroft and Ewing became close friends. Both were stalwart members of the Elks, who had supported the Brotherhood during the 1890 Players' League revolt, and together they frequently attended the organization's local, state and national meetings.

When Bancroft received word of Ewing's death, he urged that all Cincinnati ball players honor the great catcher's memory by attending the funeral. As the hour drew near, "hundreds of ballplayers ... wandered to the home, and, after offering their services and sympathies, waited outside for the comrades, and finally when all were gathered they proceeded to prayer and paid the last worldly respect to the man that all realized was their peer in their chosen profession."[26] When the services at the home concluded at two o'clock, the large procession of over 500, consisting of family, friends and fellow ballplayers, began its slow journey by horse and carriage to the cemetery in the nearby village of Mount Washington. "Mainly on account of the large number of friends to assist her, the widow bore up under the terrible strain with great fortitude, and it was not until she had entered the closed carriage that she broke down and wept."[27] Floral tributes to the former Giants great had arrived from across the nation, and it took several special carriages to convey them to the grave.

At the time of his death, Ewing's age was listed either as 46 or 47. We will never know for sure which age is correct. As has been previously mentioned, birth certificates were not issued in Ohio until 1880. During his tenure with the Reds, Ewing gave his birth date as December 25, 1860, partly to dispel rumors that he was over 40. Another motive may have been to ingratiate himself with Reds investor Albert Johnson. "There has been some dispute going the rounds of the press about Captain Ewing's age. A little conversation that came up during the [Eastern tour] trip settled the point. Both Johnson and Ewing were Christmas gifts. Both were born on the 25th of December, 1860. This puts the stories about Captain Ewing being up in the forties to rout."[28] In his self-reported 1900 U.S. Census data, however, Ewing listed his birth month and year as March 1860, but provided no specific date for the event. On his father Samuel's 1860 Census report, recorded in July of that year, the future baseball great is listed as a one-year-old. Upon his death, Cincinnati papers gave his birth date as October 27, 1859. As we have seen, Ewing managed to keep his actual birthplace, Hoagland, Ohio, a secret until 1897, always proudly insisting he was a native-born Cincinnatian. He took his actual birth date — if indeed he ever knew it himself— to his grave.

Of the many contemporary tributes and eulogies to the deceased Giant, the most unusual was delivered in Cincinnati on October 22 by the Reverend Don G. Tullis, of the Poplar Street Presbyterian Church:

> The shades of evening are beginning to fall upon the diamond of life, the game is almost ended. Breathless, the crowd sits awaiting the end.
> The score is a tie. Everything is in the balance.
> This day will decide, not the world's championship, but the greater struggle of eternity.

One there is among the war-scarred veterans upon whom all eyes are fastened. He has won many a game before. He has heard the plaudits of thousands and received the applause of millions in his day.

Will he be able to win this game?

The shadows descends [*sic*], the crowd is breathless.

All depends on him.

It is no time for a single.

He has made them before, and has won many a game with them.

A base on balls will do no good.

It is no time for a sacrifice.

There is but one thing will count in this closing moment — a home run.

Can he do it?

Death hurls the ball toward the batter.

"Strike one," the umpire cries.

Again the sphere flies by while the batter stands unmoved.

"Strike two," comes the voice through the gloom.

There is but one more chance...

He pulls himself together, his frame like iron.

His features are unmovable: the ball once more speeds toward the plate.

With one supreme effort he swings the stick and sends the ball to a distant corner of the field, and the dauntless Ewing starts upon his last circle of the bases.

One, two, three — the ball is being rapidly returned.

Will he make it?

It is a close race. He takes the one and only chance, and throws himself headlong upon the ground for the last slide.

For a moment, all is confusion. Suddenly the dust clears away and the great umpire of the universe is heard to say: "Safe at home."[29]

When the first elections to the Baseball Hall of Fame were held in 1936, plans called for selecting 15 inductees, ten from the twentieth century, to be selected by a committee from the Baseball Writers' Association of America, and five from the nineteenth century, selected by a special body called the Centennial Commission. Seventy-five ballots were cast from a list of 57 candidates, but due to confusion regarding the voting regulations, no candidate received sufficient votes for election. Buck Ewing and Cap Anson tied for first place in the balloting.

A month before the Hall of Fame's opening in June 1939, no nineteenth-century candidate known primarily for his record as a player had yet been selected. In May, a new committee called the Old-Timers Committee, consisting of Baseball Commissioner Kenesaw Mountain Landis, National League President Ford Frick and American League President William Harridge, selected six nineteenth century players for induction: the two candidates who had tied for first place in the 1936 voting, Buck Ewing and Cap Anson, and four others, first baseman-manager Charlie Comiskey, pitcher Hoss Radbourn,

Candy Cummings, the putative inventor of the curve ball, and pitcher and team owner Al Spalding.

The style and substance of *The Sporting News*' report on the inductees selected by the Committee on Old-timers, which was presented in a clipped fashion that simulated a telegraph report, revealed that details of these great players' careers had either been forgotten or were incorrectly recalled. Ewing's section, similar in content, length, and presentation to the others — and full of inaccuracies — read:

> EWING — Celebrated catcher. Born Cincinnati, O., October 27, 1859 ... Mohawk Browns, Cincinnati, 1878 ... Troy, N.L., 1881, 1882 ... New York Nationals, 1883 through 1889; New York Brotherhood, 1890 ... New York Nationals, 1892, Cleveland Nationals, 1893, 1894. Cincinnati, manager, 1895 through 1899; manager New York, part of 1900 ... Lifetime major batting average .311. Died November 20, 1906.[30]

The Sporting News' inaccuracies here include its reference to Ewing's birthplace, the month of his death, his lifetime batting average (.303), and omission of the fact that he played two full seasons in Cincinnati before bench-managing for the team. Ewing's Cooperstown plaque declares him the greatest nineteenth- century catcher, recalls his captaincy of the 1888 and 1889 championship New York teams, and notes his "genius" as a field leader, his unsurpassed ability throwing to bases, and his power hitting.[31]

While modern research tools and techniques have helped provide a clearer picture of Ewing's status as a player, attempts to arrive at a complete understanding of Ewing the man — the mercurial, seemingly self-interested, sly, at times brilliant trickster — will probably always remain incomplete, echoing the previously mentioned observation from his own era that his disposition was "as varied as the colors of the chameleon."[32] Nevertheless, his actions in the last difficult years of his life provide a clue to how he may have wished to be remembered.

During the 1905 and 1906 baseball seasons, Ewing served as a coach for a high school baseball team at the Miami Military Institute in Germantown, Ohio. Founded in 1885, the school was located 40 miles north of Cincinnati and a dozen miles southwest of Dayton. It was a small enterprise, with enrollment never reaching more than 100, and it ceased operations in the 1930s. Here for a final time, the old veteran joined young players on the diamond.

> Even up to a few weeks of his death, "Buck" Ewing took an active interest in baseball, and refusing to give up the command he once had upon the various teams of the big leagues, he assumed the coaching of the MMI team at Germantown, O. "Buck" often visited Germantown on fresh-air jaunts, and the youngsters took an interest in him, and he in them, with the result that hardly a Saturday passed during the last two summers that Ewing was not on hand to

An emaciated Buck Ewing, in greatcoat and bowler hat, stands to the right of the Miami Military Institute's 1906 high school baseball team, in Germantown, Ohio, early spring, 1906. Ewing served as honorary coach for the team in the last two years of his life, after being stricken with Bright's Disease. This is Buck Ewing's last known baseball photograph (courtesy Wright State University Library).

see his youthful favorites perform on the diamond, and to coach them in the finer points of the game.[33]

Ewing's status as "coach" for the school's team must have been largely ceremonial, since by this time he was a shockingly emaciated shadow of his formerly robust self, and the weekly 80-mile round-trip to Germantown would have been a grueling challenge for someone in his physical condition. The school's team photo reveals the extent to which Bright's disease had ravaged Ewing's body. On a cold, late-winter day, he stands to the right of the team, a gaunt stick figure encased in a black greatcoat and wearing a bowler hat.

At the height of his career in 1889, Ewing penned his only baseball narrative — a short essay published in the *Ladies' Home Journal*, which was directed to young boys who wished to start a ball team. In 1902, the year after his retirement, he planned, but never published, a book on the same subject, which was to be entitled *Buck Ewing's Advice to Young Players*. In the two springs and summers before his death, he journeyed north from his Cincinnati home each week to the Miami Military Institute in Germantown, Ohio, to

Present-day photograph of Buck Ewing's East End, Cincinnati, home, at 261 Worth St. Ewing died here on October 20, 1906 (author's collection).

put into practice what he discussed in his essay and planned to discuss in his proposed book: teaching baseball's fine points to a team of young players. Ewing's photograph with the Miami Military nine — his last appearance in baseball — is an image by which he may most wish us to remember him — as a wise old veteran ballplayer passing down pointers on the game to the next generation.

In Ewing's time, Mount Washington, an independent township on the Little Miami River, ten miles southeast of Cincinnati, was a bucolic area of rolling hills dotted with farm houses. Annexed by Cincinnati in 1911, it retained its rural flavor until the 1980s, when apartment complexes built for city commuters began to compete with the single-story clapboard houses of long-time residents. As the area changed, conditions at Mount Washington cemetery, Ewing's final resting place, declined. Today the narrow circular path through

Ewing family grave marker, Mount Washington Cemetery, Cincinnati, Ohio (author's collection).

the memorial garden is unpaved and impassable in bad weather, and vandalism and lack of funding have forced a reduction in visiting hours, which are irregular. Weeds, scrub brush, and secondary-growth trees clutter the landscape, and overcrowding forces the visitor to tread over graves in order to reach the resting places of loved ones. A large, recently erected granite monument bearing the single word "Ewing" presides over the great catcher's gravesite. Ewing's small individual grave marker, which lies on the ground between those of his wife Annie and son Arthur, is blackened by dirt and mold. His name, and his birth and death dates are barely discernible due to neglect. No monument or plaque at the site mentions his famous nickname, by which he was known across the country, or recognizes his storied career and election to the baseball Hall of Fame.

Five miles to the northwest, Buck Ewing's longtime residence, the house in which he died, teeters on the verge of collapse on tiny, three-block-long Worth Street. Many areas

Buck Ewing's gravestone, Mt. Washington Cemetery, Cincinnati, Ohio. There are no markers at Ewing's grave that mention his famous nickname, his illustrious career, or the fact that he was elected to the Baseball Hall of Fame in 1939 (author's collection).

Current-day Sunday co-ed softball game at Schmidt Park, East End, Cincinnati. This site is the location of East End Park, 1891 home of Kelly's Killers, an American Association team managed by Mike Kelly. In the 1870s, the same location was named Pendleton Park. Here, three blocks from his home, Buck Ewing practiced baseball as a teenager. Late in his career, a sports writer familiar with his upbringing, dubbed the great catcher the "Duke of Pendleton" (author's collection).

of the East End that are located closer to downtown Cincinnati have been redeveloped, and luxury town homes have replaced the original wood-frame cottages. Ewing's house and the few others that still surround it are rickety reminders of the East End's humble blue-collar roots. They will soon disappear.

Ewing's name and exploits have been forgotten in the East End, and the few remaining physical remnants associated with his life are vanishing. But in his old neighborhood, the game, in one form or other, goes on.

Three blocks from Ewing's crumbling home, Sunday afternoon co-ed softball games are still played at Schmidt Park, which, 120 years ago, was known briefly as East End Park, the home of "Kelly's Killers," an American Association major league baseball team managed by Mike Kelly. Its original name, however, was Pendleton Park, where young Billy Ewing first honed his baseball skills. The softball teams playing here are unaware that on the same site in the mid–1870s, a young lad who would later became the captain of the New York Giants and the toast of New York, and who one day would be referred to in the national press as "the Duke of Pendleton," was diligently preparing for a future major league career.

Chapter 8

Epilogue: Buck Ewing's Place in Baseball History

"The greatest baseball player who ever lived is dead."—Roger Connor, on learning of Buck Ewing's death, *Cincinnati Enquirer,* October 22, 1906

It is an ironic fact that Buck Ewing's greatest strength as a player—his versatility—significantly complicates the task of assessing his place in baseball history. While he played more games behind the plate than at any other position, his total games as catcher (636) represent fewer than half of his total played (1315). Peter Morris notes that just "Four men in baseball history [Buck Ewing, Mike Kelly, Charley Dexter and Jack Doyle] have played at least twenty-five major league games at catcher, first base, second base, shortstop, third base and outfield."[1] Of these four, only Ewing and Kelly also pitched (Ewing in nine games and Kelly in 12), and Ewing led the league in fielding at two different positions: as a third baseman in 1882, and a catcher in 1890.

Today's most well-known player ranking system was created by Bill James, who developed a list of the top 100 players at each position by combining data gleaned from a complicated statistical analysis [James's "Win Shares" system] and a series of subjective variables.[2] In early editions of his work, he ranked Buck Ewing fifth all-time among catchers, but in subsequent editions, Ewing was dropped to 17th place. The rationale for the drop in ranking was two-fold: the limited number of games Ewing played at the position (all other catchers except one on the list had caught at least 1,000 games), and the suspicion that the New York press had inflated Ewing's accomplishments in its reports. James's first point has merit, although it essentially penalizes Ewing for being either too versatile or too valuable. Regarding the

178

restricted use of both Ewing and Mike Kelly behind the plate, Peter Morris observes that "these two greats often played other positions not because they were injured but in order to prevent them from getting injured. In effect they were considered *too valuable* to be catchers."[3] James's second point, that "when you're dealing with a New York player, you do have to let some of the air out of the [local] press notices,"[4] has been shown in this volume not to be applicable with regard to Ewing, since copious documentation verifies that both the New York and the national press regularly were as vicious and caustic in their criticism of his playing as they were liberal in their praise of it.

The most significant factors not taken into consideration in James's analysis of Ewing's career pertain to the disadvantages that he faced with regard to equipment and rule changes. No other catcher in James's top 30 had the disadvantage, as Ewing did, of playing the position for three years without a chest protector, and for eight years without a catcher's mitt. In the last three of the latter eight seasons, Ewing was catching pitchers who were throwing overhand from a distance of 50 feet. Every other catcher in James's top 30 had the advantage of playing with shin guards and a padded face mask for their entire careers. Ewing never did.

All of James's top 30 catchers except Ewing hit from a distance of 60' 6" from the pitcher for their entire careers. Ewing had to adapt four times to pitcher-to-home plate distances during his career. The number of balls required for a walk was always four for all of James's top 30 catchers except Ewing. For over half of his career, it took from eight to five balls to get a free pass to first base. Ewing's stolen bases were not officially recorded for the first six years of his career. His sacrifices were not officially recorded until 1889, and from that year until 1893, each sacrifice counted as an official at-bat for him. Steals and sacrifices for James's other top 30 catchers were counted as they are today over the entire course of their careers.

There is no objective way to factor such variables into James's (or any other) rating system. The great disparity in rules, equipment, and playing and travel conditions between early-era and modern baseball suggests that the performance of nineteenth-century players can only be appropriately evaluated by the standards of their era. The best interpreters of those standards are the players, managers, and sports writers of the period. While such evaluations cannot alone be used to make comparisons between early and modern players, in Ewing's case they provide a clear sense of how he was rated by his peers as a catcher and all-around player relative to his nineteenth-century counterparts.

In the mid–1920s, two well-known former nineteenth-century players who subsequently managed for over two decades, John McGraw and Connie Mack, announced their personal choices for all-time greats at each position.

McGraw's picks appeared in his 1923 memoir, *My Thirty Years in Baseball*, and represent a balance of players from several eras — those who played exclusively in the nineteenth century, others whose careers began around the turn of the century, and some who played exclusively in the twentieth century. He chose Buck Ewing as the catcher of his "All American Team." In selecting him, McGraw emphasized Ewing's leadership qualities, intelligence, and his running, throwing, and hitting skills:

> Buck Ewing for general all around excellence as a backstop never had an equal. He was smart and aggressive. He came as near to being a catcher without a single weakness as the game has ever known. In fact, Buck Ewing was a Ty Cobb behind the bat. He had a mental capacity equal to his playing ability. Ewing could handle a team perfectly.... While Ewing was not a speed marvel on the bases, he was one of the most successful base stealers of his time. He had an uncanny knack of getting the jump on the pitchers. No player ever studied a rival pitcher's delivery closer and was so quick to take advantage of the slightest false move. As a thrower Ewing excelled. He got the throw away from him with a quick round arm snap, no time being wasted.... He was a hard hitter as well as a scientific place hitter.[5]

Three years later, Connie Mack released his rankings of the best all-time players. Like McGraw's choices, his selections spanned the nineteenth and early twentieth centuries. Ewing was Mack's all-time best catcher. He declared him "the perfect receiver," who "could handle the speediest pitcher,"[6] but said little about his hitting. It took Mack another quarter-century to change his mind about Ewing's top status as a receiver. In his *My 66 Years in the Big Leagues* (1950), he ceded the top spot to Philadelphia Athletics great Mickey Cochrane.[7]

A decade before Mack and McGraw developed their ranking systems, another nineteenth-century player turned twentieth-century manager had also chosen Ewing as the game's best receiver. In his 1914 essay, "Twenty-Five Years in Big League Baseball," former pitcher and then Washington Senators manager Clark Griffith cited Ewing's throwing ability and his craftiness behind the plate as the reasons for his selection.

> I have never seen a catcher the equal of "Buck" Ewing. I call him the best ball player in the world.... He was a great thrower ... marvelously accurate. He was the man who invented most of the tricks that modern catchers use. He was what ball players know as a "foxy guy." In one game I saw him cut loose a new trick on Fogarty, a Cincinnati player.... Ewing was catching and Fogarty was on first base. Ewing dropped the pitcher's throw and Fogarty, trying to steal, was easily thrown out. After the game I learned that Ewing had dropped the ball purposely.... Confident in his wonderful throwing arm, he had muffed deliberately so as to entice the speedy Fogarty into a dash for second base.[8]

A fourth nineteenth-century player-turned-manager agreed with McGraw, Mack, and Griffith. Connecticut-born Ned Hanlon played center field for four National League teams before retiring to the bench, where he managed Baltimore and Brooklyn to a combined five pennants. For Hanlon, "No man ever had anything on Buck Ewing as a catcher. He had a wonderful arm, a great head, and was, in my opinion, the greatest all-around player that ever lived."[9]

Frank Bancroft, who managed six National League teams in the 1880s, added to Ewing's accolades after his death by affirming that "I have been actively interested in baseball for more than 20 years ... and have known personally all the famous players of the national game, besides seeing them work in game after game. I believe that Buck Ewing was the greatest catcher and also the most versatile all-round player that ever appeared on the field."[10] Jim Mutrie, Ewing's own manager while he was with the Giants, agreed with Bancroft, describing his former backstop as "the best man who ever stood in spikes behind the bat."[11]

Despite his on-field rivalries with Ewing, John Ward called him "the greatest catcher I have ever seen,"[12] and fellow catcher Jim O'Rourke described his backstopping as "peerless."[13] For Tim Keefe, Ewing's long-time battery mate, he was "the greatest catcher of ancient and modern times."[14] Chicago outfielder-turned-evangelist Billy Sunday, who played against Ewing for seven years, agreed: "If you want to know the greatest catcher of all time — he was Buck Ewing.... Every catcher who came along afterward patterned his style after him."[15]

Besides managers, teammates and on-field opponents, sportswriters of the period expressed similar sentiments with regard to Ewing's catching abilities. Tim Murnane, the former first baseman who wrote for the *Boston Globe*, declared Ewing "a baseball classic," and echoed Jim Mutrie's praises by calling him "the greatest catcher that ever wore spiked shoes."[16] Ted Sullivan, a County Clare, Ireland, native who was a player, manager, and later a writer for *The Sporting News*, described Ewing as "without an equal ... the best of all catchers."[17] In 1892, O. P. Caylor, who managed Cincinnati's American Association club and served as editor of *The Sporting News* and the *New York Herald*, cited Ewing as the game's premier receiver.

> I have seen every prominent catcher since professional baseball was first played, and am prepared to say without hesitation that Ewing in his prime never had an equal as a catcher. Morgan Murphy, Charles Zimmer, Charles Bennett of today, and Snyder, Clapp, Flint and Deasly of the past are and were simply pigmies in comparison. That is why Ewing's popularity was national. It could not be confined to the city where he gave his services.[18]

After Ewing's death, *Sporting Life* editor Francis Richter provided a succinct summary of many of his attributes as a receiver:

As a catcher he outclassed all we have ever seen, not omitting even the wonderful Charley Bennett. He was a sure catcher, quick on his feet, alert in mind, a splendid coach for the pitcher, a keen reader of batsmen, and his swift, accurate throwing was simply perfect. In addition, he was a grand batsman, always ranking with the leaders, and as a base runner he ranked always with the best. To top all, he was game to the core, genial in manner, good in deportment and abstemious in his habits.[19]

Ballplayers, managers and the press were of a similar mind when discussing Ewing's value and versatility as an all-around player. Three of his former battery mates, all of whom were subsequently elected to the Hall of Fame, recognized these qualities in addition to Ewing's skills as their receiver. Amos Rusie identified him as "The greatest ballplayer I ever knew.... He was good at everything.... He could catch, run or throw."[20] For Mickey Welch, "The greatest all around ball player of all time was Buck Ewing. He could hit, run and throw. I worked with him eleven years and I know what he could do."[21] Tim Keefe was unequivocal in his assessment of Ewing's versatility: "I say unhesitatingly that I never knew an equal as an all-round ballplayer."[22]

Two other former Giants and future Hall of Famers who teamed with Ewing for over a decade ranked him at the top as an all-around player. Jim O'Rourke observed that "When you recall all his playing qualities, it must be conceded that no player who ever lived matched him."[23] Roger Connor simply stated that "he had no peer as a ballplayer."[24]

Jim "Deacon" White was in his 20th major league season in 1890 when he was asked to name the game's greatest all-time star. *Sporting Life* reported that the veteran catcher and third baseman, who had played against Ewing for four different teams in the 1880s, gave the honor to the Giants catcher: "Deacon White says that Buck Ewing is the greatest player on earth, bar nobody, and that in batting, base-running, fielding — everything that pertains to the national game — Ewing stands head and shoulders above anybody in the business."[25]

In like fashion, sportswriters of the period recognized Ewing as the greatest all-around player of his age. Sam Crane, journeyman second baseman for eight teams in the 1880s, and later sports editor for the *New York Press*, described him as "the most brilliant player of his time."[26] The *Boston Globe's* Tim Murnane declared that "No man ever surpassed Ewing in all-round ability on the ball field."[27] Writing in 1895, O. P. Caylor found Ewing to be "the best general baseball player who ever lived."[28] The glowing tribute of Ewing's all-around prowess offered by *Sporting Life's* editor-in-chief, Francis Richter, on the occasion of the Giants star's death, may well be the most laudatory assessment of a player ever issued by a sports writer: 'The death of 'Buck' Ewing removes from the scene of earthly activity the only ABSOLUTELY

PERFECT ball player the writer has ever seen in action in a period of thirty years. He was, in his prime, in all respects the greatest ball player that ever wore a spiked shoe. He was perfect in all departments and had not a weakness."[29]

William "Buck" Ewing was an avowed hit-and-run specialist who cautioned young players not to swing hard, yet he led the National League in home runs, and hit some of the longest four-baggers of his era. He is the only catcher ever to lead his team in steals for a season, and he stole more bases in a game than any receiver in history. Besides performing in splendid fashion behind the plate, he could play third, first, or the outfield, and play them well. In a pinch he could even take over in the pitcher's box and do a credible job. He was declared a "back number" three times by the press: once as a catcher, once as a first baseman, and once as a right fielder. On each occasion he put up banner-year numbers the following season. He could even talk an umpire into changing his decision.

Ewing the player, like Ewing the man, defied categorization. Years after his death, his former teammate and on-field rival, John Ward, best described his impact on the game when he declared simply, "There will never be another Buck Ewing."[30]

Appendix A

"Ins and Outs of Baseball"
By William Ewing

Captain of the New York League Base-Ball Club —
Familiarly Known to the Boys as "Buck" Ewing

I have often been asked to write about base-ball, but I have never done so for the reason that I know where my forte lies. However, I have undertaken this article at the persuasion of the Editor of the *Ladies' Home Journal*, who assures me that his boy-readers will be interested in what I say. If I don't succeed, it will be his fault, not mine.

Base-Ball to me is a great game, a distinctively American game as is cricket and foot-ball in England, and I think there is no doubt that it will easily always be first among our sports.

WHY BASEBALL IS GOOD FOR BOYS

There isn't a doubt in my mind as to the answer a boy would give me if I were to ask him, "What is your favorite game?" Before I could fairly get the words out of my mouth he would say, "Base-Ball." There is no outdoor game that is so fascinating to young America. During the season one may see it played in almost every vacant lot, and oftentimes in the street, in the built-up portions of our cities. Every game has its enthusiastic devotees, or "cranks," but there are more baseball cranks than all the rest put together. I don't altogether blame them. For my part, I consider baseball to be the best and healthiest form of recreation man or boy can indulge in. No other game is more healthful, more conducive to a good physical condition, and less harmful than

[Originally published in Volume VIII, Number 7 (June 1891) of *Ladies' Home Journal*]

the game of base-ball. But the game is not only advantageous as a means of physical training: besides strengthening the muscles, brightening the eyes, and knitting the whole frame of the body into a firmer soul, it produces a corresponding higher plane of morals. When the blood flows in coursing streams of health through the veins, there is a like healthfulness of the moral nature that alone would suffices to put base-ball in the front rank of outdoor games for boys and men.

How the Game First Started

Here is a little history that boys would like to know. The first regular base-ball club or society was the old Knickerbocker Club, founded in New York in the autumn of 1845. Fifteen years afterwards, the Excelsior Club of Brooklyn came into existence. During the period of the Civil War, base-ball was left pretty much to itself, along with many other kinds of sports and games. The men couldn't play, for they were "off to the war," and the boys didn't feel like playing when their fathers were carrying guns and facing the hot fire of their opponents. It was not until about the year 1865 that the attention of boys and men was given to it with any kind of enthusiasm. Then it spread throughout the Union with a hurrah, and came to be recognized as a profession, not a few devoting their whole time to it and receiving compensation for their service. About twenty years ago the Boston Base-Ball club and the Athletics, from Philadelphia, crossed the Atlantic and played a series of exhibition games in England and Ireland, but as anticipated, the pastime didn't find favor. But of late years it has been taken up quite generally in England and Australia. In this country, hundreds of games are played now for every one ten years ago.

To Be a Good Ball Player

If a boy would be a good base-ball player let him fit himself for it by taking regular exercise, such as running, throwing, and catching the ball, and hitting with the bat. It is best to become accomplished in the mechanical part of the game first. Then, when you can throw, catch and bat well, turn to the scientific part of the game. There is a good deal of head-work to be done in base-ball. You must learn in which direction to strike the ball, how far to run. You should be able to estimate whether a hit will give you time to reach first or second base. Don't waste a moment watching the ball. A second counts for much in base-ball, when the ball travels so swiftly and the fielder sends it in like a streak of greased lighting. I would advise boys not to smoke or drink. There's not a particle of good in either practice, and oftentimes there is lots of harm. They have an injurious effect upon the nervous system. Avoid cigarettes, especially.

How to Form a Nine

If you want to form a nine and play the game according to the rules, pick your men and try them at various positions until each is placed in the one best suited to him. Special training is necessary before a boy can become a good pitcher. The other positions are more or less difficult and constant practice only will make a good player. Base-ball requires good catching, throwing and running powers, combined with courage, nerve, good judgment, and quick perception of what to do in the field. Remember that, boys, and when you possess these requirements you will be fit to play with the New Yorks. One reason why baseball is so popular is that it is suited to the national temperament. It is a difficult game, and every lad likes to indulge in and excel at such a game. Then again, it is withal so simple. A child of six can play it. It is also within reach of all. A bat and a ball are all that are required to set up two nines, and furnish a royal game. The whole business could be obtained [for] under two dollars. If you want to play exactly according to the rules, you should get a ball that weighs not less than five ounces, or more than five and a quarter avoirdupois, and which is not less than nine inches nor more than nine and a quarter inches in circumference. The bat should be circular in shape, not exceeding two and a quarter inches in diameter at any part or forty-two inches in length. The bases should be one foot square and ninety feet from each other. Five innings should be played, or it is no game.

A game of base-ball can be played in two hours. A game of cricket often extends over three days. This is another reason why baseball is so popular. It can be played without serious loss of time. Still another reason is that catching and throwing, which are part of the practice of base-ball, may be played almost any time and any place. Clerks and messenger boys carry a ball in their pocket, and at noon-time, after lunch, they throw and catch and catch and throw, while bank presidents, lawyers, and business men pass by on the streets.

The Hardest Positions in the Game

The two hardest positions in the game are those of pitcher and catcher. The catcher must be a man of quick judgment, a hard thrower, and a good backstop. To be an accurate thrower is the principal thing, and to know where to throw. If there is a man on second base and the player at the bat starts for first base, don't try to put him out by flinging the ball to first base, but try to head off the fellow that is trying for third base. The catcher should keep an eye on the position of the players, and know just where to throw the ball at all times. Some people think he must be a horny-handed man. Not so. Gloves are worn, and if the ball be caught in the right manner, the hands will not get hard.

The pitcher also must possess quick and unfailing judgment. He should deliver the ball with speed and cultivate the art of sending a curve ball. Keefe, of New York, is one of our best pitchers. His is a cool as a cucumber, and thoroughly collected at all times. He can send in a ball with the speed of a Minie [*sic*] bullet which will seem to be making straight for your bat when, hey, presto! just before it reaches you it describes a curve and meanders around into the catcher's hand. Keefe is a great pitcher for striking men out. Rusie and Welch are also first-class pitchers. Kelly, of Cincinnati, is one of the country's best catchers. He is a splendid thrower, being accurate and quick. His judgment is always to be relied upon, and he is a cool as anybody could be when the small boy in the bleachers is quaking with suppressed excitement and anticipation.

OTHER POSITIONS ON THE DIAMOND

Second base is the next hardest position. The player who has to watch this point must be very quick-witted and nimble. He must be a good level-headed man. He has to receive most of the throws from the battery and the outfield and he has to meet some long and hard throws. Richardson, of New York, Pfeffer of Chicago, Bierbauer, of Pittsburg [*sic*], and McPhee, of Cincinnati, are our best second-basemen.

As to the rest of the positions, well, they are all about as hard as each other. Every player needs to be quick, a swift and accurate thrower, and to possess good judgment. Shortstops might take pattern of Ward, of Brooklyn, of Brodie, of Glasscock, of New York. There are both [*sic*] splendid players, unequaled as shortstops. Ward especially is a heady player. He is nimble and accurate. He takes great chances, and no player in the country can beat him at stealing bases. He is a good winning man.

THE VALUE OF GOOD COACHING

Anson, Captain and Manager of the Chicago Base-Ball club, is a good example of a coach. He plays first base. He has the reputation of being the most pronounced "kicker" in the country, but no one disputes his ability to coach his men well. The coach should take up a position about half-way between third and home, and fifteen feet from the diamond. Here he should watch his man, and his judgment must be speedy and sure. Suppose the player at the bat were to make a long hit which he himself thought would only allow him to reach second-base; if the coach were not present he might stay at second-base and then turn to see what the chances were for reaching third. The coach's presence renders this unnecessary. All the batter needs to do is tuck his elbows to his side and run for his life. The coach will watch the ball and weigh the chances. His mind should be made up before the batsman reaches second base, so that he may motion to him to come to third, if practicable. In short, the coach must relieve his men from all responsibility of judgment. They must simply bat and run, and watch the coach for instructions.

John M. Ward tells a good story about coaching, though he says he does not vouch for its truth. When the Committee waited upon Abraham Lincoln to notify him of his nomination for the Presidency [*sic*]. They found him in company with others on a vacant lot, with coat off and sleeves rolled up, busily engaged in coaching his men in a very exciting game of base-ball. When the chairman finally succeeded in gaining Mr. Lincoln's attention for a moment, long enough to communicate the object of their visit, his only reply was, "The Presidency be durned — run there, you skinflint!" and he rushed down toward third base to coach one of his runners home.

CHANGES IN THE GAME

There has been some talk of adding one man to each team, and making the number ten, instead of nine. But this does not find favor among those who know the game best and who play it most. A right-short-stop (the player whom it was proposed to add) is not necessary and never will be.

One change will be made, however. Indeed, it has already been made. The pitcher's box is usually fifty-five feet from the plate. It is now proposed to put it back one and a quarter feet more, and make the distance fifty-six and a quarter. This change will make it more difficult for the pitcher, to whom the distance of a foot, or even a fraction of a foot, is a matter of much importance. But it will be easier for the man at the bat, and it will probably raise the batting average for the present year.

But for the ordinary game, as played in every town and village of our broad land, nothing is more necessary than a bat and a ball and eighteen boys, each eager to win the game for his side. If indulged in within the bounds of reason, there is no better employment for a boy. "Satan finds some mischief still for idle hands to do," and a boy is better at the bat than loafing around the streets. Base-ball will harden his muscles, quicken the course of his blood, increase his appetite, and help make a good physical foundation which will be found of inestimable benefit in after days when the cares of business crowd upon him. Practical success in life depends more than you think on physical health, and a man who played base-ball in his youth will meet reverses more calmly and take life more easily than the man who didn't.

Appendix B

Buck Ewing's Major League Offensive Statistics

YR	TM	LG	G	PA	AB	R	H	2B	3B	HR	RBI	SB	BB	BA	SLG
1880	Troy	NL	13	46	45	1	8	1	0	0	5		1	.178	.200
1881	Troy	NL	67	279	272	4	68	14	7	0	25		7	.250	.353
1882	Troy	NL	74	338	328	67	89	16	11	2	29		10	.271	.405
1883	NYG	NL	88	396	376	90	114	11	13	*10*	41		20	.303	.481
1884	NYG	NL	94	410	382	90	106	15	*20*	3	41		28	.277	.445
1885	NYG	NL	81	355	342	81	104	15	12	6	63		13	.304	.471
1886	NYG	NL	73	291	275	59	85	11	7	4	31	18	16	.309	.444
1887	NYG	NL	77	351	318	83	97	17	13	6	44	26	30	.305	.497
1888	NYG	NL	103	442	415	83	127	18	15	6	58	53	24	.306	.465
1889	NYG	NL	99	444	407	91	133	23	13	4	87	34	37	.327	.477
1890	NYP	PL	83	392	352	98	119	19	15	8	72	36	39	.338	.545
1891	NYG	NL	14	54	49	8	17	2	1	0	18	5	5	.347	.429
1892	NYG	NL	105	431	393	58	122	10	15	8	76	42	38	.310	.473
1893	CLV	NL	116	541	500	117	172	28	15	6	122	47	41	.344	.496
1894	CLV	NL	53	237	211	32	53	12	4	2	39	18	24	.251	.374
1895	CIN	NL	105	467	434	90	138	24	13	5	94	34	30	.318	.468
1896	CIN	NL	69	296	263	41	73	14	4	1	38	41	29	.278	.373
1897	CIN	NL	1	2	1	0	0	0	0	0	0	0	0	0	0
Totals			1315	5772	5363	1129	1625	250	178	71	883	354	392	.303	.456

Source: www.baseball-reference.com   *Italics = Team Leader*   ***Bold Italics = League Leader***

Chapter Notes

Chapter 1

1. Knepper, *Ohio and Its People*, 117.
2. U.S. Census, 1850.
3. U.S. Census, 1860.
4. Paul Herbert letter to the National Baseball Hall of Fame, July 8, 1987, Buck Ewing player file, National Baseball Hall of Fame Library.
5. Originally published in the *New York Evening Sun*, this letter was reproduced in the Philadelphia Inquirer on October 11, 1889. All further references to the correspondence are to the *Philadelphia Inquirer*'s edition.
6. I express my sincere thanks to Jean Wallis of the Hillsboro County Historical Society for her assistance in discovering Buck Ewing's origins.
7. Knepper, 133–34.
8. Ibid., 180.
9. Allen, *The Cincinnati Reds*, 4.
10. *Philadelphia Inquirer*, October, 11, 1889.
11. Ibid.
12. *New Castle News* (Pennsylvania), March 22, 1902.
13. *Philadelphia Inquirer*, October 11, 1889.
14. *New Haven Register*, June 27, 1889.
15. Ibid.
16. Ibid.
17. Ibid.
18. *Cincinnati Enquirer*, June 23, 1879.
19. *Cincinnati Enquirer*, May 5, 1879.
20. *Cincinnati Enquirer*, May 12, 1879.
21. *Sporting Life*, December 11, 1915.
22. Ibid.
23. Ibid.
24. *Cincinnati Enquirer*, July 7, 1879.
25. *Cincinnati Enquirer*, April 24, 1880.

26. *Philadelphia Inquirer*, October 11, 1889.
27. *New Haven Register*, June 27, 1889.
28. Ibid.
29. Ibid.
30. McKenna, "Rochester Hop Bitters, 1879–1880," http://baseballblog.com/1368/rochester-hop-bitters-1879-1880/.
31. Ibid.
32. *New York Times*, August 2, 1889.
33. *New York Clipper*, July 3, 1880.
34. Ibid.
35. Ibid.
36. *New Haven Register*, June 27, 1889.
37. *Brooklyn Eagle*, August 9, 1880.
38. *Brooklyn Eagle*, August 12, 1880.
39. *Brooklyn Eagle*, August 13, 1880.
40. Ibid.
41. *Brooklyn Eagle*, August 14, 1880.
42. Jenkinson, "Lipman Pike: Baseball's First Great Power Hitter," http://billjenkinsonbaseball.webs.com/LipmanPikebaseballsfirs.htm
43. Guscov, *The Red Stockings of Cincinnati*, 105.
44. *Fort Wayne News* (Indiana), August 20, 1899.
45. *Brooklyn Eagle*, August 17, 1880.
46. *Philadelphia Inquirer*, October 11, 1889.
47. *New Haven Register*, June 27, 1889.
48. *New York Clipper*, August 28, 1880.

Chapter 2

1. McKenna, "Bob Ferguson," by Brian McKenna, http://bioproj.sabr.org.
2. Ibid.
3. Ibid.
4. Ibid.

191

5. *Sporting Life*, May 12, 1894.
6. *The North American* (Philadelphia), February 12, 1891.
7. McKenna, "Bob Ferguson," http://bioproj.sabr.org.
8. Morris, *A Game of Inches*, 162.
9. Ibid.
10. *Troy Daily Times*, May 26, 1880.
11. *Cincinnati Enquirer*, October 22, 1906.
12. *Troy Daily Times*, September 10, 1880.
13. *New York Clipper*, October 28, 1880.
14. *New York Times*, September 30, 1880.
15. *Troy Daily Times*, July 21, 1881.
16. Ibid.
17. *Troy Daily Times*, August 20, 1881.
18. *Troy Daily Times*, August 3, 1881.
19. *Troy Daily Times*, May 24, 1882.
20. *Troy Daily Times*, June 15, 1882.
21. *Troy Daily Times*, June 16, 1882.
22. *Troy Daily Times*, June 26, 1882.
23. *Troy Daily Times*, July 4, 1882.
24. *Troy Daily Times*, July 26, 1882.
25. *Troy Daily Times*, September 11, 1882
26. Seymour, *Baseball: The Early Years*, 143.
27. *Troy Daily Times*, August 14, 1882.
28. *Troy Daily Times*, September 14, 1882.
29. *Troy Daily Times*, September 27, 1882.
30. Seymour, *Baseball: The Early Years*, 147.
31. *Saint Louis Globe Democrat*, February 19, 1883.
32. Dunbar, "Baseball Salaries Thirty Years Ago."
33. *Waterloo Evening Courier* (Iowa), December 8, 1911.
34. Ibid.
35. Ibid.
36. Di Salvatore, *A Clever Base-Ballist: The Life and Times of John Montgomery Ward*, 181.
37. Thornley, *Land of the Giants*, 18.
38. *New York Times*, July 2, 1883.
39. *New York Times*, July 7, 1883.
40. *Sporting Life*, September 2, 1883.
41. *New York Times*, June 2, 1883.
42. *Sporting Life*, June 10, 1883.
43. *New York Times*, June 16, 1883.
44. Ibid.
45. *New York Times*, July 16, 1883.
46. *New York Times*, June 2, 1883.
47. *New York Times*, June 7, 1883.
48. *New York Times*, October 28, 1883.
49. *New York Times*, May 8, 1884.
50. *New York Times*, May 30, 1884.
51. *New York Times*, July 15, 1884.
52. *Sporting Life*, September 9, 1883.
53. *Cleveland Herald*, February 11, 1884.
54. *Sporting Life*, May 23, 1884.
55. *New York Times*, September 7, 1884.
56. *New York Times*, May 2, 1884.
57. *New York Times*, August 22, 1884.
58. *Sporting Life*, July 2, 1884.
59. *Sporting Life*, August 1, 1884.

Chapter 3

1. *Sporting News*, April 18, 1896.
2. *Sporting News*, June 21, 1891.
3. *Atchison Daily Globe* (Kansas), November 11, 1888.
4. *Los Angeles Times*, November 5, 1906.
5. Ibid.
6. Ibid.
7. Ibid.
8. *Sporting News*, November 10, 1888.
9. *Atchison Daily Globe*, March 12, 1889.
10. *Cincinnati Enquirer*, April 2, 1897.
11. *Atchison Daily Globe*, July 6, 1889.
12. *Fort Wayne News* (Indiana), July 20, 1899.
13. Morris, *A Game of Inches*, 410.
14. *Cincinnati Enquirer*, April 11, 1895.
15. *Sporting News*, February 6, 1892.
16. *Sporting News*, May 9, 1895.
17. *Boston Daily Globe*, August 5, 1888.
18. *Sporting Life*, December 17, 1898.
19. *Cincinnati Enquirer*, May 8, 1896.
20. Ibid.
21. *Cleveland Plain Dealer*, May 25, 1893.
22. *Sporting Life*, April 28, 1892.
23. *New York Times*, May 16, 1885.
24. *New York Times*, June 10, 1886.
25. *Sporting Life*, May 28, 1892.
26. Curran, *Mitts: A Celebration of the Art of Fielding*, 103.
27. *El Paso Herald Post*, January 15, 1934.
28. *New York Times*, July 26, 1884.
29. *Sporting Life*, October 16, 1889.
30. *Loganport Pharos* (Indiana), April 20, 1898.
31. *Salt Lake City Tribune*, November 29, 1930.
32. *Grand Rapids Tribune* (Wisconsin), February 19, 1920.
33. *Sporting News*, October 23, 1897.
34. *Evening Post* (Frederick, Maryland), September 12, 1912.
35. *New York Times*, August 1, 1888.
36. *New York Times*, August 15, 1888.
37. *New York Times*, October 19, 1888.
38. *New York Times*, July 26, 1887.
39. *Brooklyn Eagle*, June 23, 1896.
40. McGraw, *My Thirty Years in Baseball*, 214.

41. *Boston Daily Globe,* October 15, 1888.

42. *New York Sun,* April 27, 1890. Quoted in Morris, *A Game of Inches,* 425.

43. Morris, *Catcher,* 146.

44. *Seattle Daily Times,* September 12, 1923.

45. *San Antonio Express,* October 15, 1930.

46. Ibid.

47. *New York Times,* August 18, 1889.

48. Morris, *Catcher,* 295.

49. *Sporting Life,* December 12, 1886. Quoted in Morris, *Catcher,* 294.

50. *Boston Daily Globe,* July 21, 1889.

51. Morris, *Catcher,* 291.

52. *New York Times,* May 10, 1889.

53. *Sporting Life,* August 26, 1885.

54. *Sporting News,* December 25, 1897.

55. *Encyclopedia of Baseball Catchers,* http://bb_catchers.tripod.com/catchers/stolen.htm.

56. *New York Times,* May 30, 1888; *New York Tribune,* May 30, 1888; *New York Herald,* May 30, 1888; *New York World,* May 30, 1888. I express my deep gratitude to baseball historian Bill Jenkinson for helping me confirm this previously unknown record.

57. *Cleveland Plain Dealer,* April 28, 1893.

58. *Sporting Life,* November 19, 1898.

59. *Boston Daily Globe,* August 4, 1886.

60. *New York World,* June 22, 1889.

61. Sullivan, "Human Mascots: Exploring the Extreme Side of Baseball's Superstition," www.sbnation.com.

62. *New York Times,* August 2, 1885.

63. *New York Times,* June 19, 1886.

64. *New York Times,* September 18, 1886.

65. Hardy, *The New York Giants Base Ball Club: 1870 to 1900,* 80.

66. *Sporting News,* July 28, 1888.

67. *Sporting Life,* August 22, 1888.

68. *Sporting Life,* August 31, 1887.

69. *Sporting Life,* August 6, 1884.

70. *Boston Daily Globe,* October 19, 1888.

71. *Sporting Life,* May 26, 1886.

72. *Cleveland Plain Dealer,* June 24, 1893.

73. *Sporting Life,* October 3, 1891.

74. *New York Times,* May 27, 1891.

75. *New York Times,* August 19, 1886.

76. *New York Times,* August 25, 1886.

77. *New York Times,* August 28, 1886.

78. *New York Times,* September 7, 1886.

79. *Cincinnati Enquirer,* July 13, 1896.

80. *Cincinnati Enquirer,* July 14, 1896.

81. Ibid.

82. *Cincinnati Enquirer,* July 17, 1896.

83. *Cincinnati Enquirer,* May 3, 1897.

84. *Cincinnati Enquirer,* May 7, 1897.

85. *Cincinnati Enquirer,* May 10, 1897.

86. *Cincinnati Enquirer,* May 15, 1897.

87. *Cincinnati Enquirer,* May 27, 1897.

88. *Cincinnati Enquirer,* May 28, 1897.

89. Ibid.

90. *New York Times,* April 1, 1900.

91. *New York Times,* April 10, 1900.

92. *New York Times,* April 12, 1900.

93. I am indebted to Peter Morris for this concept, which he introduced in his keynote speech at the 2010 SABR Nineteenth-Century Baseball Conference, April 2010, Baseball Hall of Fame, Cooperstown, NY.

94. *Boston Daily Globe,* May 11, 1889.

95. *Brooklyn Eagle,* September 3, 1892.

96. *Boston Daily Globe,* June 22, 1888.

97. *Boston Daily Globe,* August 8, 1890.

98. *Arizona Daily Republic,* April 13, 1939.

99. *Sporting Life,* August 14, 1889.

100. Ibid.

101. *Bridgeport Telegram,* March 15, 1922.

102. *Sporting Life,* January 10, 1891.

103. *Brooklyn Eagle,* July 31, 1889.

104. Ibid.

105. *Sporting Life,* September 12, 1888.

106. *Sporting News,* October 5, 1889.

107. *Boston Daily Globe,* September 16, 1889.

108. *Milwaukee Sentinel,* August 15, 1889.

109. *Boston Daily Globe,* September 16, 1889.

110. *Boston Daily Globe,* July 26, 1888.

111. *New York Times,* September 28, 1884.

112. Ibid.

113. Di Salvatore, *A Clever Base-Ballist,* 170.

114. *Boston Daily Globe,* July 29, 1891.

115. *Atchison Daily Globe,* March 27, 1889.

Chapter 4

1. Thornley, *Land of the Giants: New York's Polo Grounds,* 23.

2. Ibid.

3. *New York Times,* May 30, 1885.

4. Peter Mancuso, "Jim Mutrie," www.sabrbioproj.org

5. *New York Times,* July 31, 1884.

6. *New York Times,* July 17, 1885.

7. *New York Times,* July 23, 1885.

8. *New York Times,* May 3, 1885.

9. *Sporting Life,* October 14, 15.

10. *New York Times,* July 12, 1885.

11. *New York Times,* August 7, 1885.

12. Ibid.

13. Ibid.
14. *Sporting Life*, September 9, 1885.
15. *New York Times*, July 5, 1885.
16. *Sporting Life*, December 9, 1885.
17. *Sporting Life*, October 4, 1885.
18. *Milwaukee Sentinel*, January 31, 1886.
19. *New York Times*, May 16, 1886.
20. *New York Times*, July 22, 1885.
21. *New York Times*, September 21, 1886.
22. *Sporting News*, September 20, 1886.
23. *Sporting Life*, July 21, 1886.
24. *Sporting Life*, September 8, 1886.
25. Malloy and Hunsinger, Jr., "George Washington Stovey," 159.
26. *Sporting Life*, February 26, 1887.
27. *Sporting Life*, May 18, 1887.
28. *New York Times*, May 10, 1887.
29. *Sporting Life*, May 18, 1887.
30. *Sporting Life*, May 25, 1887.
31. *New York Times*, May 22, 1887.
32. *Sporting Life*, June 3, 1887.
33. *Boston Daily Globe*, June 13, 1887.
34. *Sporting Life*, July 20, 1887.
35. *Sporting Life*, July 27, 1887.
36. *Sporting Life*, August 31, 1887.
37. *Sporting Life*, August 17, 1887.
38. *Sporting Life*, August 24, 1887.
39. *Boston Daily Globe*, October 16, 1887.
40. Appel, *Slide, Kelly, Slide*, 126.
41. *Cedar Rapids Gazette*, January 13, 1888.
42. *Sporting News*, February 11, 1888.
43. *Sporting Life*, July 18, 1888.
44. *Sporting Life*, July 25, 1888.
45. *New York Times*, October 12, 1887.
46. *Sporting Life*, October 24, 1888.
47. *Sporting Life*, November 10, 1888.
48. *Sporting Life*, November 17, 1888.
49. *Sporting Life*, October 9, 1889.
50. *New York Times*, April 30, 1889.
51. Ibid.
52. *New York Times*, April 18, 1889.
53. *New York Times*, April 4, 1889.
54. *New York Times*, May 17, 1889.
55. *Sporting News*, June 16, 1889.
56. *New York Times*, July 9, 1889.
57. Ibid.
58. *Boston Daily Globe*, August 3, 1889.
59. *New York Times*, June 23, 1889.
60. *Sporting Life*, July 10, 1889.
61. Jenkinson, personal correspondence, June 10, 2011.
62. *New York Times*, July 10, 1889.
63. *New York Times*, August 10, 1889.
64. *Sporting Life*, July 19, 1889.
65. *Sporting Life*, August 23, 1889.
66. *New York Times*, August 28, 1889.
67. *New York Times*, October 6, 1889.

68. *New York Herald*, October 7, 1889.
69. *New York Herald*, October 21, 1889.
70. *New York Times*, December 13, 1889.
71. *Inter Ocean*, December 13, 1889.
72. *Cincinnati Enquirer*, October 22, 1906.

Chapter 5

1. "1889 Cap Anson and Buck Ewing 'Burke Ale' Beer Poster," robertedwardsauctions.com/auctions/2008_preview/1html.
2. Ibid.
3. *Cincinnati Inquirer*, March 18, 1895.
4. *Cincinnati Inquirer*, April 23, 1895.
5. *New Haven Register*, July 2, 1889.
6. Gilbert, *Superstars and Monopoly Wars*, 89.
7. Voigt, *American Baseball*, vol. 1, 165.
8. *Dallas Morning News*, February 23, 1890.
9. *Newark Daily Advocate*, February 18, 1890.
10. *Dallas Morning News*, February 23, 1890.
11. Ibid.
12. *Sporting Life*, May 3, 1890.
13. Ibid.
14. *Sporting Life*, June 28, 1890.
15. *Sporting Life*, July 12, 1890.
16. *Sporting Life*, January 17, 1891.
17. *Sporting Life*, February 14, 1891.
18. *Boston Daily Globe*, August 9, 1890.
19. *Sporting Life*, August 16, 1890.
20. *Philadelphia Inquirer*, August 12, 1890.
21. *Sporting Life*, February 14, 1892.
22. *Sporting News*, October 18, 1890.
23. *Sporting Life*, November 29, 1890.
24. *New York World*, April 22, 1890.
25. *Sporting News*, January 25, 1890.
26. *Sporting News*, February 9, 1890.
27. *New York Times*, May 15, 1890.
28. *New York Times*, June 14, 1890.
29. *New York Times*, July 1, 1890.
30. *New York Times*, July 4, 1890.
31. *Sporting News*, July 26, 1890.
32. *New York Times*, August 21, 1890.
33. *New York Times*, August 24, 1890.
34. *Sporting Life*, June 14, 1890.
35. *Boston Daily Globe*, July 18, 1890.
36. *Sporting Life*, October 28, 1890.
37. Thornley, *Land of the Giants*, 48.
38. *Boston Daily Globe*, April 23, 1891.
39. *New York Times*, October 21, 1891.
40. *Boston Daily Globe*, April 11, 1891.
41. *Boston Daily Globe*, May 3, 1891.
42. *Boston Daily Globe*, May 8, 1891.

43. *New York Times*, May 17, 1891.
44. *New York Times*, May 27, 1891.
45. *New York Times*, June 28, 1891.
46. *Sporting Life*, July 25, 1891.
47. *Sporting Life*, October 3, 1891.
48. *Sporting Life*, August 29, 1891.
49. *Sporting Life*, October 3, 1891.
50. *Philadelphia Inquirer*, October 8, 1891.
51. *Sporting Life*, October 10, 1891.
52. *Philadelphia Inquirer*, October 18, 1891.
53. Ibid.
54. Ibid.
55. *Sporting Life*, October 10, 1891.
56. Ewing, "Ins and Outs of Baseball," *Ladies Home Journal*, June 1891.
57. Ward, *Base Ball: How to Become a Player*, www.gutenberg.org.
58. Ibid.
59. Ibid.
60. Ibid.
61. Ibid.
62. Ibid.
63. Ibid.
64. *The Atchison Champion*, March 24, 1892.
65. Duren, *Boiling Out at the Springs*, 52.
66. *Sporting Life*, March 5, 1892.
67. Ibid.
68. *Sporting News*, January 23, 1892.
69. *Sporting News*, March 25, 1892.
70. *Sporting News*, May 7, 1892.
71. *Sporting Life*, May 14, 1892.
72. *Sporting Life*, June 1, 1892.
73. *New York Times*, June 8, 1892.
74. *Rocky Mountain News*, March 20, 1892.
75. *Sporting Life*, July 9, 1892.
76. *New York Times*, September 24, 1892.
77. *Sporting Life*, July 16, 1892.
78. *Sporting Life*, July 23, 1892.
79. *Sporting Life*, July 20, 1892.
80. *Sporting Life*, August 6, 1892.
81. *Sporting News*, August 13, 1892.
82. *Sporting Life*, May 10, 1890.
83. *New York Times*, August 11, 1892.
84. Ibid.
85. Ibid.
86. *The North American*, August 18, 1892.
87. *Sporting Life*, August 27, 1892.
88. *New York Times*, October 2, 1892.
89. *New York Times*, August 12, 1892.
90. *Sporting News*, August 27, 1892.
91. *Sporting News*, September 10, 1892.
92. *New York Times*, September 14, 1892.
93. *Sporting News*, October 24, 1892.
94. *Sporting News*, September 31, 1892.
95. *Sporting News*, October 15, 1892.
96. *Sporting News*, November 15, 1892.
97. *Sporting News*, February 5, 1893.

Chapter 6

1. Lears, *Rebirth of a Nation*, 169.
2. Seymour, *Baseball: The Early Years*, 269.
3. Ibid., 289.
4. *Sporting Life*, April 15, 1893.
5. *Sporting Life*, September 30, 1893.
6. *Sporting Life*, November 19, 1892.
7. *Sporting Life*, December 10, 1892.
8. *Galveston Daily News*, March 12, 1893.
9. *Sporting News*, March 4, 1893.
10. *Sporting Life*, March 25, 1893.
11. *Sporting Life*, March 11, 1893.
12. *Cleveland Plain Dealer*, March 1, 1893.
13. *Sporting News*, March 11, 1893.
14. McMahon, "Oliver Wendell Tebeau (Patsy)," 124.
15. *Sporting News*, April 1, 1893.
16. *Sporting Life*, April 8, 1893.
17. *Sporting News*, April 15, 1893.
18. *Cleveland Plain Dealer*, April 27, 1893.
19. *Cleveland Plain Dealer*, April 28, 1893.
20. *Cleveland Plain Dealer*, May 10, 1893.
21. *Sporting News*, May 27, 1893.
22. *Philadelphia Inquirer*, December 30, 1904.
23. *Boston Daily Adviser*, August 29, 1893.
24. *Sporting Life*, December 9, 1893.
25. *Cleveland Plain Dealer*, June 6, 1893.
26. *Sporting Life*, June 3, 1893.
27. *Sporting Life*, June 10, 1893.
28. *Cleveland Plain Dealer*, June 23, 1893.
29. *Cleveland Plain Dealer*, June 27, 1893.
30. *Cleveland Plain Dealer*, July 2, 1893.
31. *Sporting News*, August 26, 1893.
32. *Cleveland Plain Dealer*, September 3, 1893.
33. *Cleveland Plain Dealer*, September 19, 1893.
34. *Cleveland Plain Dealer*, September 28, 1893.
35. *Cleveland Plain Dealer*, October 1, 1893.
36. *Cleveland Plain Dealer*, September 19, 1893.
37. *Sporting News*, October 21, 1893.
38. *Sporting News*, November 4, 1893.
39. *Sporting Life*, November 11, 1893.
40. *Brooklyn Eagle*, April 28, 1894.
41. *Cleveland Plain Dealer*, April 27, 1894.
42. *Cleveland Plain Dealer*, April 25, 1894.
43. Browning, *Cy Young: A Baseball Life*, 43.

44. Ibid., 35.
45. *Cleveland Plain Dealer*, May 23, 1894.
46. *Cleveland Plain Dealer*, June 20, 1894.
47. *Cleveland Plain Dealer*, July 3, 1894.
48. *Sporting Life*, July 14, 1894.
49. *Sporting Life*, July 21, 1894.
50. *Atchison Daily Globe*, July 27, 1894.
51. *Sporting Life*, August 4, 1894.
52. Allen, *The Cincinnati Reds*, 55.
53. Ibid., 38.
54. Husman, "Walter Arlington Latham (Arlie)," 76.
55. Suelsdorf, "John Alexander McPhee (Bid)," 91.
56. *Cincinnati Enquirer*, March 25, 1895.
57. *Cincinnati Enquirer*, March 28, 1895.
58. *The North American*, April 17, 1895.
59. *Cincinnati Enquirer*, March 30, 1895.
60. *Cincinnati Enquirer*, April 1, 1895.
61. *Cincinnati Enquirer*, April 8, 1895.
62. *Cincinnati Enquirer*, April 18, 1895.
63. Ibid.
64. *Cincinnati Enquirer*, April 19, 1895.
65. *Cincinnati Enquirer*, April 23, 1895.
66. *Cincinnati Enquirer*, April 22, 1895.
67. *Cincinnati Enquirer*, April 24, 1895.
68. Ibid.
69. *The Massilon Independent*, June 6, 1895.
70. *Cincinnati Enquirer*, August 24, 1895.
71. *Cincinnati Enquirer*, August 6, 1895.
72. *Cincinnati Enquirer*, September 14, 1895.
73. *Cincinnati Enquirer*, September 12, 1895.
74. *Cincinnati Enquirer*, May 12, 1895.
75. *Cincinnati Enquirer*, August 23, 1896.
76. *Cincinnati Enquirer*, April 27, 1896.
77. *Cincinnati Enquirer*, May 4, 1896.
78. *Cincinnati Enquirer*, May 17, 1896.
79. *Cincinnati Enquirer*, May 24, 1896.
80. *Cincinnati Enquirer*, July 2, 1896.
81. *Cincinnati Enquirer*, September 2, 1896.
82. *Cincinnati Enquirer*, March 13, 1897.
83. *Cincinnati Enquirer*, March 19, 1897.
84. *Cincinnati Enquirer*, March 25, 1897.
85. *Cincinnati Enquirer*, March 14, 1897.
86. Ibid.
87. Allen, *The Cincinnati Reds*, 54.
88. *Cincinnati Enquirer*, May 10, 1897.
89. *Cincinnati Enquirer*, May 28, 1897.
90. Carle, "Jacob Peter Beckley (Eagle Eye)," 7.
91. *Cincinnati Enquirer*, June 14, 1897.
92. *Cincinnati Enquirer*, August 20, 1897.
93. *Cincinnati Enquirer*, June 17, 1897.

94. *Cincinnati Enquirer*, August 28, 1897.
95. *Cincinnati Enquirer*, July 20, 1897.
96. *Cincinnati Enquirer*, July 28, 1897.
97. *Cincinnati Enquirer*, August 24, 1897.
98. *Cincinnati Enquirer*, August 15, 1897.
99. *Cincinnati Enquirer*, August 16, 1897.
100. *Cincinnati Enquirer*, August 17, 1897.
101. *Cincinnati Enquirer*, August 18, 1897.
102. *Cincinnati Enquirer*, August 6, 1897.
103. *Cincinnati Enquirer*, August 6, 1898.
104. *Cincinnati Enquirer*, March 25, 1899.
105. *San Antonio Light*, March 13, 1898.
106. Ibid.
107. Ibid.
108. *Cincinnati Enquirer*, July 5, 1896.
109. *San Antonio Light*, March 13, 1898.
110. *Cincinnati Enquirer*, September 29, 1898.
111. Ibid.
112. Ibid.
113. Nemec, The Great Encyclopedia of 19th Century Major League Baseball, 607.
114. Allen, *The Cincinnati Reds*, 63.
115. *Sporting Life*, July 15, 1899.
116. *Sporting Life*, December 2, 1899.
117. *Sporting Life*, December 9, 1899.
118. *Sporting Life*, December 16, 1899.

Chapter 7

1. Di Salvatore, *A Clever Baseballist*, 369.
2. *Sporting Life*, December 16, 1899.
3. Di Salvatore, *A Clever Baseballist*, 363.
4. Hardy, *The New York Giants Base Ball Club*, 159.
5. Ibid., 163.
6. Ibid., 165.
7. *Cincinnati Enquirer*, June 11, 1897.
8. Ibid.
9. Ibid.
10. Nemec, *The Great Encyclopedia of 19th Century Baseball*, 760.
11. *Fort Wayne News*, April 30, 1900.
12. Ibid.
13. *Sporting Life*, July 21, 1900.
14. Ibid.
15. Ibid.
16. *Grand Forks Herald*, August 29, 1901.
17. *Sporting Life*, December 1, 1900.
18. *New Castle News*, March 22, 1902.
19. *Dallas Morning News*, October 31, 1904.
20. *Sporting News*, September 17, 1898.

21. www.entomology.montana.edu.
22. *Sporting Life*, February 10, 1906.
23. *Cincinnati Enquirer*, October 22, 1906.
24. *Cincinnati Enquirer*, October 21, 1906.
25. *Cincinnati Enquirer*, October 22, 1906.
26. *Cincinnati Commercial Tribune*, October 24, 1906.
27. Ibid.
28. *Cincinnati Enquirer*, September 6, 1897.
29. *Wilkes-Barre Times*, October 31, 1906.
30. *Sporting News*, May 11, 1939.
31. baseballhall.org/hof/ewing-buck.
32. *Atkinson Daily Globe*, March 27, 1889.
33. *Cincinnati Commercial Tribune*, October 22, 1906.

Epilogue

1. Morris, *Catcher*, 291.
2. James, *The New Bill James Historical Baseball Abstract*, 331–30.
3. Morris, *Catcher*, 212.
4. James, *The New Bill James Historical Baseball Abstract*, 379.
5. McGraw, *My Thirty Years in Baseball*, 213–14.
6. *Salt Lake City Times*, November 29, 1930.
7. Mack, *My 66 Years in Baseball*, 196.
8. Griffith, "Twenty Five Years of Big League Baseball," 37–38.
9. *Washington Post*, October 28, 1906.
10. *Cincinnati Enquirer*, October 23, 1906.
11. *Waterloo Evening Courier* (Iowa), December 8, 1911.
12. *North Dakota Evening Times*, August 1, 1911.
13. *Cincinnati Enquirer*, October 23, 1906.
14. Ibid.
15. *El Paso Herald*, January 15, 1934.
16. *North Dakota Evening Times*, November 2, 1906.
17. *The Sporting News*, February 24, 1906.
18. *Cedar Rapids Gazette*, August 19, 1892.
19. *Sporting Life*, October 27, 1906.
20. *Tyrone Daily Herald* (Pennsylvania), February 26, 1937.
21. *Arizona Republic*, April 19, 1934.
22. *Cincinnati Enquirer*, October 22, 1906.
23. Ibid.
24. Ibid.
25. *Sporting Life*, March 29, 1890.
26. *The Sporting News*, March 4, 1893.
27. *North Dakota Evening Times*, November 2, 1906.
28. *The North American* (Pennsylvania), June 1, 1895.
29. *Sporting Life*, October 27, 1906.
30. *Moulton Weekly Journal* (Iowa), March 2, 1944.

Bibliography

Articles

Ball, David. "John Reilly." http://bioproj.sabr.org.

Carle, Bill. "Jacob Peter Beckley (Eagle Eye)." *Baseball's First Stars*, Frederic Ivor-Campbell et al., eds. Cleveland: SABR, 1996, 7.

Dunbar, William. "Baseball Salaries Thirty Years Ago." *Baseball Magazine* 1, no. 3, July 1918.

Ewing, Buck [William]. "Ins and Outs of Baseball." *Ladies Home Journal*, June 1891.

Griffith, Clark C. "Twenty-Five Years of Big League Baseball: Stars of Yesterday and Today." *Outing* 64 (1914), 36–42.

Husman, John Richmond. "Walter Arlington Latham (Arlie)." *Nineteenth Century Stars*, Robert L. Tiemann and Mark Rucker, eds. Cleveland: SABR, 1989, 76.

Jenkinson, Bill. "Lipman Pike: Baseball's First Great Power Hitter." http://billjenkinson-baseball.webs.com.

Malloy, Jerry, and Lou Hunsinger, Jr. "George Washington Stovey." *Baseball's First Stars*. Frederick Ivor-Campbell et al., eds. Cleveland: SABR, 1996, 159.

Malloy, Jerry, and Lou Hunsinger, Jr. "George Washington Stovey," *Baseball's First Stars*, Frederick Ivor-Campbell et al., eds. Cleveland: SABR, 1996, 159.

Mancuso, Peter. "Jim Mutrie." http://bioproj.sabr.org.

McKenna, Brian. "Bob Ferguson." http://bioproj.sabr.org.

_____. "Ed Crane." http://bioproj.sabr.org.

_____. "Rochester Hop Bitters, 1879–1880." http://baseballhistory.com.

McMahon, William. "Oliver Wendell Tebeau (Patsy)." *Nineteenth Century Stars*, Robert L. Tiemann and Mark Rucker, eds. Cleveland: SABR, 1989, 124.

Suelsdorf, A.D. "John Alexander McPhee (Bid)." *Nineteenth Century Stars*, Robert L. Tiemann and Mark Rucker, eds. Cleveland: SABR, 1989, 91.

Sullivan, Jeff. "Cap Anson and Buck Ewing 'Burke Ale' Beer Poster." robertedwardsauctions.com/auctions/2008_preview/1html.

_____. "History of Malaria During Wars." malariasite.com/malaria/history_wars.htm.

_____. "Human Mascots: Exploring the Extreme Side of Baseball's Superstition." www.sbnation.com.

Baseball Periodicals

Baseball Magazine   *Sporting Life*   *The Sporting News*

Books

Alexander, Charles C. *Our Game: An American Baseball History*. New York: Henry Holt, 1991.

Allen, Lee. *The Cincinnati Reds*. Kent, OH: Kent State University Press, 2006.

Appell, Marty. *Slide, Kelly Slide: The Wild Life and Times of Mike "King" Kelly, Baseball's First Superstar*. Lanham, MD: Scarecrow Press, 1999.

Browning, Reed. *Cy Young: A Baseball Life*. Amherst: University of Massachusetts Press, 2000.

Curran, William. *Mitts: A Celebration of the Art of Fielding*. New York: William Morrow, 1985.

Di Salvatore, Bryan. *A Clever Baseballist: The Life and Times of John Montgomery Ward*. Baltimore: Johns Hopkins University Press, 1999.

Duren, Don. *Boiling Out at the Springs: 1886–1940*. Dallas: Hodge, 2006.

Gilbert, Thomas. *Superstars and Monopoly Wars: Nineteenth-Century Major League Baseball*. New York: Franklin Watts, 1995.

Guscov, Stephen D. *The Red Stockings of Cincinnati*. Jefferson, NC: McFarland, 1988.

Graham, Frank. *The New York Giants: An Informal History of a Great Baseball Club*. Carbondale: Southern Illinois University Press, 2002. Reprint of the original edition published by G.P. Putnam's Sons, 1952.

Hardy, James D., Jr. *The New York Giants Base Ball Club, 1870 to 1900*. Jefferson, NC: McFarland, 1996.

Ivor-Campbell, Frederick, Robert L. Tiemann, and Mark Rucker, eds. *Baseball's First Stars*. Cleveland: SABR, 1996.

James, Bill. *The New Bill James Historical Baseball Abstract*. New York: The Free Press, 2001.

Kerr, Roy. *Sliding Billy Hamilton: The Life and Times of Baseball's First Great Leadoff Hitter*. Jefferson, NC: McFarland, 2009.

Knepper, George W. *Ohio and Its People*. Kent, OH: Kent State University Press, 1989.

Koszarek, Ed. *The Players' League: History, Clubs, Ballplayers and Statistics*. Jefferson, NC: McFarland, 1996.

Lears, Jackson. *Rebirth of a Nation: The Making of Modern America, 1877–1920*. New York: Harper, 2009.

Lowry, Phillip J. *Green Cathedrals*. Reading, MA: Addison-Wesley, 1992.

Mack, Connie. *My 66 Years in the Big Leagues*. Mineola, NY: Dover, 2009. Reprint of the original edition published by the John C. Winston Company, Philadelphia, 1950.

McGraw, John. *My Thirty Years in Baseball*. Lincoln: University of Nebraska Press, 1995. Reprinted from the 1974 Arno Press edition of the 1923 original edition by Boni and Liveright.

Morris, Peter. *Catcher: How the Man Behind the Plate Became an American Folk Hero*. Chicago: Ivan R. Dee, 2009.

_____. *A Game of Inches: The Stories behind the Innovations That Shaped Baseball*. Chicago: Ivan R. Dee, 2006.

Nemec, David. *The Great Encyclopedia of 19th Century Major League Baseball*. New York: Donald I. Fine, 1997.

Roer, Mike. *Orator O'Rourke: The Life of a Baseball Radical*. Jefferson, NC: McFarland, 2005.

Seymour, Howard. *Baseball: The Early Years*. New York: Oxford University Press, 1960.

Sullivan, Dean A., ed. *Early Innings: A Documentary History of Baseball, 1824–1908*. Lincoln: University of Nebraska Press, 1995.

Thornley, Stew. *Land of the Giants: New York's Polo Grounds*. Philadelphia: Temple University Press, 2000.

Tiemann, Robert L., and Mark Rucker, eds. *Nineteenth Century Stars.* Cleveland: SABR, 1989.
Voigt, David Quentin. *American Baseball.* Vol. I. State College: Pennsylvania State University Press, 1983.
Ward, John. *Base Ball: How to Become a Player.* 1888. Online edition. www.gutenberg.org.

Newspapers

Arizona Daily Republic
The Atchison Champion (Kansas)
Atchison Daily Globe
Boston Daily Adviser
Boston Daily Globe
Bridgeport Telegram
Brooklyn Eagle
Cedar Rapids Gazette
Cincinnati Enquirer
Cincinnati Commercial Tribune
Cleveland Herald
Cleveland Plain Dealer
Dallas Morning News
El Paso Herald
Evening Post (Frederick, Maryland)
Fort Wayne News
Galveston Daily News
Grand Forks Herald
Grand Rapids Tribune
Inter Ocean (Illinois)
Loganport Pharos (Indiana)
Los Angeles Times
The Massilon Independent (Ohio)
Milwaukee Sentinel

Moulton Weekly Journal
Newark Daily Advocate
New Castle News (Pennsylvania)
New Haven Register
New York Clipper
New York Herald
New York Sun
New York Times
New York Tribune
New York World
The North American (Philadelphia)
North Dakota Evening Times
Philadelphia Inquirer
Rocky Mountain News
St. Louis Globe Democrat
Salt Lake City Tribune
San Antonio Express
San Antonio Light
Seattle Daily Times
Troy Daily Times
Tyrone Daily Herald
Washington Post
Waterloo Evening Courier
Wilkes-Barre Times

Online Resources

baseballhalloffame.org
baseballindex.org
baseball-reference.com
bioproj.sabr.org
Encyclopedia of Baseball Catchers: http://bb_catchers.tripod.com/catchers/.
19Cbaseball.com
retrosheet.org

Census and Archives

U.S. Federal Census, 1850, Gallia County, Ohio.
U.S. Federal Census, 1860, Highland County, Ohio.
U.S. Federal Census, 1870, Northumberland County, Pennsylvania.

U.S. Federal Census, 1870, Chatham County, Georgia.
U.S. Federal Census, 1900, Hamilton County, Ohio.
Georgia Archives, Morrow, GA. State of Georgia, Chatham County, Marriage License. William Ewing and Annie L. McCaig, December 12, 1889.

Conference Proceedings

Morris, Peter. Keynote Speech. SABR 19th Century Baseball Conference, National Hall of Fame Library, Cooperstown, NY, April 17, 2010.

Unpublished Sources

Jenkinson, Bill. Player Home Run Logs. Willow Grove, Pennsylvania.
Cincinnati Public Library, Cincinnati, Ohio. Cincinnati Reds clipping file.
National Baseball Hall of Fame Library, Cooperstown, NY. Ewing, William, clipping file.
National Baseball Hall of Fame Library, Cooperstown, NY. Ewing, William, photo file.

Index